ORAL TRADITION IN THE MIDDLE AGES

MEDIEVAL & RENAISSANCE
TEXTS & STUDIES

VOLUME 112

ORAL TRADITION IN THE MIDDLE AGES

edited by

W. F. H. Nicolaisen

medieval & Renaissance texts & studies
Binghamton, New York
1995

Library of Congress Cataloging-in-Publication Data

Oral tradition in the Middle Ages / edited by W.F.H. Nicolaisen.
    p. cm. — (Medieval & Renaissance texts & studies ; v. 112)
    Papers presented at the 22nd Annual Conference of the Center for
Medieval and Early Renaissance Studies, which was held Oct. 21–22, 1988,
State University of New York at Binghamton.
    Includes bibliographical references.
    Contents: Oral composition and "oral residue" in the Middle Ages / Albert
B. Lord — The implication of oral tradition / John Miles Foley — The oral
undertones of late medieval romance / Carl Lindahl — Oral tradition in the
Acallam na Senórach / Joseph Falaky Nagy — Memorization in Anglo-Saxon
England / Gail Ivy Berlin — From theater to ritual : a study of the Revesly
mummers' play / Esha Niyogi De — Or(e)ality : the nature of truth in oral
settings / Jeremy Downes — Wildman in festival, 1300–1550 / Samuel Kinser
— The medieval transformation of the Jews' oral heritage / Saul Levin —
Pættir and oral performance / John Lindow — "A pious legend" : St. Oswald
and the foundation of Worcester Cathedral Priory / Mary Lynn Rampolla —
Speaking in script : the construction of voice, presence, and perspective in
Villon's Testament / Nancy Freeman Regalado.
    ISBN 0–86698–165–9
    1. Literature, Medieval—History and criticism—Congresses. 2. Oral tradi-
tion—Europe—Congresses. 3. Literature and folklore—Europe—Congresses.
I. Nicolaisen, W. F. H. II. State University of New York at Binghamton.
III. Series.
PN663.073 1993
809'.02—dc20   93–14340
                                   CIP

Table of Contents

Acknowledgements

A volume like this cannot be put together without the help of many people, and I am very grateful for their support and encouragement. The process began with the initial planning stages for the conference which ultimately produced the *Acta*; at that time, Paul Szarmach, Marilynn Desmond, and Bernard Levy, all associated with the Center for Medieval and Early Renaissance Studies at SUNY-Binghamton, were of invaluable assistance. At and after the conference itself, comments from conveners of individual sessions helped in the early phases of the sifting process. Later, outside readers who of necessity will have to remain anonymous played an important role in selecting and shaping the content of this volume. Their readiness to read carefully many more articles than could be accommodated is much appreciated, their evaluations and comments pointed us in the right direction, and their sound advice made it possible for us to make what were often difficult and painful decisions. At the editorial and publication stages, the staff of MRTS were unfailingly courteous and capable. If I single out for special praise the Director and General Editor, Mario Di Cesare, and Assistant Editors Katharine Sarah Mascaro and Lori Vandermark, this does not ignore the contributions several others have made to bring about a successful conclusion to this lengthy venture. Finally, I am, of course, only too aware of the patient and constructive involvement of the various authors who have given this volume the substance and quality needed to promise it an existence independent of the 1988 conference.

W. F. H. Nicolaisen
Aberdeen, Scotland

Introduction

Earlier versions of the papers contained in this volume were first read by their authors at the Twenty-Second Annual Conference organized by the Center for Medieval and Early Renaissance Studies at the State University of New York at Binghamton, on October 21–22, 1988. The theme of this conference was "Oral Tradition in the Middle Ages," a topic which suggested itself for two main reasons, as well as some lesser ones: (1) In its distinguished history, the series of CEMERS conferences had never before focused on this subject. (2) The topic was deemed particularly appropriate in October 1988 because the conference coincided with the beginning of the year-long centenary festivities of the American Folklore Society. The meeting was therefore, in part, convened as SUNY-Binghamton's contribution to that learned society's special birthday celebrations.

At the conference, over fifty papers were presented, four in plenary sessions, the others in sectional meetings or in panel discussions. As was to be expected, the largest number of papers was devoted to questions of how oral tradition shaped, influenced, and generally helped to create works of written literature in Old and Middle English. Two of the papers in this category have found their way into this volume whereas one has been published separately in *Mediaevalia*

14.[1] This volume also contains the four plenary lectures and a number of high-quality articles devoted to areas of research other than English. It is the editor's hope that this mixture will be a felicitous one and that this volume will provide a sampling of the vast scope of current studies in oral tradition.

Any focus on oral tradition is bound to imply inter-disciplinary, cross-desciplinary or, at the very least, multi-disciplinary approaches if, that is, the concept of 'discipline' is to have any validity at all. Particularly affected by oral tradition as a medium of creating and transmitting expressive forms of culture are such areas as the study of folklore, history,[2] language, and literature. However, whereas intellectual endeavors in these fields know no geographical or cultural boundaries—they are, in fact, world-wide in nature—the notion of a chronological Middle Age, with its concomitant epithet *medieval*, is, in its hint at a tripartite temporal division, essentially European in origin and application. Any exercise insisting on a double vision in matters concerning *oral* tradition in a *medieval* setting, whether in the form of a conference or a published collection of papers, is consequently, almost by definition, predestined to concentrate on and perhaps even to deal exclusively with, the European scene. Within such a circumscribed world, it might well be fruitful to examine various aspects of oral tradition for their own sake or to investigate the characteristics of pre-literate or non-literate cultural features on the literate culture, i.e., on the manuscript tradition and its contents. It is a generally accepted axiom that the one, oral tradition, precedes the other, written tradition, but a rider might be in order which draws attention to the fact that oral tradition does not cease to function in a literate or partially literate society; nor does it always lead to literate or, more precisely, literary reception and adaptation. In this respect, it is probably true to say that most of the manifestations of oral tradition never enter any literate or literary culture at all while continuing to function effectively in their own cultural register.

---

[1] John F. Vickrey, "*Genesis B* and the Anomalous Gnome," *Mediaevalia* 14 (1991 for 1988): 51–62.

[2] Although projects in oral history have been conducted within the ambience of the unofficial, comparatively recent history of contemporary literate societies, research into oral history has particularly flourished in non- or pre-literate cultures of the Third World. See, for example, Jan Vansina, *Oral Tradition: A Study in Historical Methodology* (London: Routledge & Kegan Paul, 1961), and Ruth Finnegan, *Oral Literature in Africa* (Oxford: Clarendon Press, 1970). Naturally, oral history has had limited impact on medieval studies since most evidence from that period, so heavily reliant on oral tradition, has reached us in written or tangible form.

It is the *folklorists* who have for almost two centuries now not only recognized the existence of such a phenomenon as oral tradition but have also found it to be something worth studying for its own sake in the kaleidoscopic range of its manifestations. In 1846, at the very birth of the English term "folklore," coined as a replacement of the cumbersome and somehow "foreign" sounding "popular antiquities," William Thoms, in proposing this "good Saxon compound," indicated his desire to recover such things as the "recollection of a now neglected custom," "some fading legend, local tradition, or fragmented ballad," from the *memories* of, on the whole, older people.[3] Indeed, oral transmission was for a long time understood to be a *conditio sine qua non* for a definition of folklore and of the role it plays in human cultural behavior. As late as the middle of this century, the famous (or infamous) twenty-one definitions of folklore in *Funk & Wagnall's Standard Dictionary of Folklore, Mythology and Legend*[4] are based on that incontrovertible assumption culminating in the extreme position taken by one of the contributors in his pronouncement: "In a purely oral culture everything is folklore."[5] Admittedly, one can hold the view that all folklore is orally conceived and transmitted, but the opposite is never true insofar as not everything in oral tradition is folklore! The late Richard M. Dorson who, as "a folklorist trained in history,"[6] for many years chaired the Department of Folklore and directed the Folklore Institute at Indiana University in Bloomington, a quarter of a century later, summarizing an earlier article of his own, distinguishes "between properly documented oral folklore collected directly in the field from tellers of the tales and singers of folksong," and what he describes as "the rewritten, saccharine versions of fakelore."[7] One of the most scathing and most deeply rooted condemnations of such "fakelore" (a term powerful in its parodic, punning thrust but ultimately confusing rather than helpful in the numerous shades of interpretations which it permits)[8] is that it lacks the neces-

---

[3] William Thoms, in a letter of August 12, 1846, published in *The Athenaeum*, No. 982 (August 22, 1846): 862–63.

[4] Maria Leach, ed., *Funk & Wagnall's Standard Dictionary of Folklore, Mythology and Legend* (New York: Funk & Wagnall, 1949), 398a–403b.

[5] B. A. Botkin, ibid., 398b.

[6] Richard M. Dorson, ed., *Folklore and Traditional History* (The Hague and Paris: Mouton, 1973), 7.

[7] Dorson, *Folklore and Fakelore* (Cambridge, MA: Harvard Univ. Press, 1976), 5.

[8] For instance, Dave Harker's *Fakesong* (Philadelphia: Open Univ. Press, 1985) is written from a stance of class conscious criticism of the bourgeoisie which is accused of "the manufacture of British 'folksong' [from] 1700 to the present day" (subtitle).

sary quality of orality. It is the present writer's hunch that the current generation of folklorists, many of whom no longer work in the world of academe but in the so-called "public sector," is more tolerant and flexible in its assessment of the modes of transmission of folklore, as a result of an increasing awareness of the powerful role the written media play in the dissemination of all folklore genres, especially the verbal ones. Nevertheless, such changing attitudes do not eliminate the central importance of orality in the folk-cultural register; it is not surprising that folklorists were not only the first to acknowledge this importance but have also been in the forefront of those who have found the relationship between oral and written tradition, between non-literacy and literacy, worth investigation.[9]

Another basic assumption which has had to undergo considerable modification in recent years is the essential anonymity of all acts of creation and transmission in oral folklore. This stress on the anonymous nature of folk-cultural phenomena arose from a fundamental misunderstanding that equated anonymity with namelessness, and this despite the fact that field-workers were well aware of the significance of named and nameable individual tradition bearers and their performances in the process of transsmission.[10] The realization that, in contrast to our own times, we do not know the names of those who created, performed, received, modified, adapted, and transmitted items of folklore in the past, does not diminish their personal role in such acts; nor does it argue for communal creation and re-creation of such items. It goes without saying that groups of all kinds are effective brokers in the maintenance of folk culture—as listeners, as users, as consumers, as critics—but within these groups it is the gifted individuals or the appointed or accepted, often hereditary, guardians and curators of tradition who are the preservers and transmitters of the content of the group's, the community's cultural lore in its multi-faceted actualizations of the traditional models.

It is symptomatic that the origins of *oral literature* research are

---

[9] See, for example, Stith Thompson: "Folklore and Literature," *PMLA* 55 (1940): 866–74; "Folklore and Literature: A Symposium," *Journal of American Folklore* 70 (1957): 1–65; Special Issue "Folklore and Literature," *Journal of the Folklore Institute* 13, 3 (1976): 225–329 (esp. Bruce A. Rosenberg, "Folklore Methodology and Medieval Literature," 311–25; Special Issue "Folklore and Literature," *Folklore Forum* 11, 1 (1978); "Folklore and Literary Criticism: A Dialogue," *Journal of the Folklore Institute* 18 (1981): 97–156.

[10] For a brief allusion to this paradox see W. F. H. Nicolaisen, "Names and Narratives," *Journal of American Folklore* 97 (1984): 259–72.

closely linked with this question of individual authorship and personal contribution to the corpus of tradition, in this case with the so-called "Homeric Question." In the late nineteen-twenties and early thirties the American classicist Milman Parry not only "theorized that the *Iliad* and *Odyssey* were the collective creations of many generations of bards working not individually, but within a poetic tradition"[11] but also argued that such poetry would be made in pre-literate oral performance. This was followed by field-trips to various parts of Yugoslavia where both Parry and his assistant Albert Lord worked with individual, non-literate singers of oral traditional epics. Probably the most seminal publication to come of this work was Lord's *The Singer of Tales* (1960)[12] in which the author applies the discovery of the formulaic nature of such compositions to poems in other literatures, an approach which was the beginning of a rich and extensive secondary literature of theory and analysis; some important responses to Parry's and Lord's work were Francis P. Magoun, Jr.'s "The Oral-Formulaic Character of Anglo-Saxon Narrative Poetry," (published seven years *before* Lord's book)[13] and David Buchan's *The Ballad and the Folk*[14] which tests the formulaic theory on the structural characteristics of Scottish balladry. The formulaic theory[15] has had its supporters and detractors; at this time it constitutes one of many lines of investigation of oral and orally derived literature. An early peak in the sophisticated treatment of this new field of study was Walter J. Ong's pioneering and influential *Orality and Literacy* (1982)[16] the first two chapters of which are still the best concise history of the study of the relationship between orality and writing up to that date. Like Parry's work and Lord's book, Ong's approach has had such a

---

[11] John Miles Foley, ed., *Oral Tradition in Literature: Interpretation in Context* (Columbia: Univ. of Missouri Press, 1986), 3. The first nine pages of Foley's Introduction to this book which is significantly also the outcome of a conference, relieve the present writer of having to provide a detailed and extensive account of the current state of the art in oral literature studies. Foley looks at this situation more comprehensively in his book *The Theory of Oral Composition: History and Methodology* (Bloomington: Indiana Univ. Press, 1988).

[12] Albert B. Lord, *The Singer of Tales* (Cambridge, MA: Harvard Univ. Press, 1960).

[13] Francis P. Magoun, Jr., "The Oral-Formulaic Character of Anglo-Saxon Narrative Poetry," *Speculum* 28 (1953): 446–67.

[14] David Buchan, *The Ballad and the Folk* (London: Routledge, 1972).

[15] See, for instance, also Richard M. Dorson, ed., *Folklore and Folklife: An Introduction* (Chicago: Univ. of Chicago Press, 1972), 36–38.

[16] Walter J. Ong, *Orality and Literacy: The Technology of the Word* (London: Methuen, 1982).

dramatic effect that literary scholars now have difficulty in envisaging a time without its existence. Folklorists may well claim that they had been aware of several of the questions Ong raises for many years before the book's publication, but this does not detract from its enormous significance for the student of literature. It has certainly created a common theoretical denominator which allows new and productive dialogues across the disciplines.

It is a matter of much regret to this writer that Professor Ong, an early invitee to the 1988 conference, was for health reasons unable to participate in the meeting and that it is therefore also not possible to include a paper of his in this volume. The other plenary speakers, however, brought their own considerable expertise in, and acute awareness of, oral literature to their contributions, whether resulting from a lifelong interest in Yugoslav (and other) oral epics (Lord),[17] arising from a highly thoughtful and articulate encounter with the nature of oral tradition in general (Foley),[18] extending a folklorist's, more precisely a folk-narrative scholar's, perspective to medieval English literature (Lindahl),[19] or stemming from an impressive mastery of the interaction of oral and literary factors in early Irish literary tradition (Nagy).[20] Their four main contributions, as well as the shorter sectional papers, constitute a remarkable pooling of exciting new thinking in a field of study which reflects much of the modern direction of contemporary academic endeavors because it transcends the limitations and boundaries of conventional, disciplinary modes of thought.

W. F. H. Nicolaisen
SUNY-Binghamton

[17] See n. 12.

[18] See n. 11. Foley is the Director of the Center for Studies in Oral Tradition at the University of Missouri, Columbia, and also the editor of the journal *Oral Tradition*.

[19] As demonstrated in his book *Earnest Games: Folkloric Patterns in the Canterbury Tales* (Bloomington: Indiana Univ. Press, 1987).

[20] His most important publication to date is *The Wisdom of the Outlaw: The Boyhood Deeds of Finn in Gaelic Narrative Tradition* (Berkeley: Univ. of California Press, 1985).

ALBERT B. LORD

Oral Composition and 'Oral Residue' in the Middle Ages[1]

I n a certain sense the Middle Ages in Europe was a time of transition par excellence, by definition and by destination. Most obviously, it was a period of transition from paganism to Christianity,
and from one social order to another. It was also a period during
which oral literature in the several vernaculars was first recorded in
writing and newly written vernacular literatures gradually emerged.
It was a period when the prestigious Latin language and its written
literature and culture were introduced into the non-Romance cultures
that already possessed their own traditional native literatures. In the
course of time this language and its literature played a highly important

---

[1] I have taken the term "oral residue" from the writings of Walter J. Ong, S.J.,
esp. his chapter on "Oral Residue in Tudor Prose Style" in *Rhetoric, Romance, and
Technology* (Ithaca: Cornell Univ. Press, 1971), in which he defines it as follows: "By
oral residue I mean habits of thought and expression tracing back to preliterate situations or practice, or deriving from the dominance of the oral as a medium in a
given culture, or indicating a reluctance or inability to dissociate the written medium from the conscious at all. Habits of thought and expression inseparable from
the older, more familiar medium are simply assumed to belong equally to the new
until this is sufficiently 'interiorized' for its own techniques to emerge from the
chrysalis and for those more distinctive of the older medium to atrophy," (25–26).

role in producing the amalgams which became the new vernacular literatures.

The fundamental assumption with which the following contribution has been written is that the oral traditional vernacular literatures of Europe in the Middle Ages were formed and had attained a level of sophistication before the introduction of writing among the peoples who created and practised them. It is the purpose of this essay to comment on some elements of stylistic continuity in the vernacular literatures of the Middle Ages from the period when literature was purely oral to that of a developed written literary style.[2]

Oral traditional literature is neither a rigidly monolithic nor a static body of story or song. It contains within itself much that is subject to change, though at differing rates, from one period to another. Thus changes from pagan to Christian religious thought may be made within an oral traditional literary style without any intervention of writing. New elements of thought might be expressed in terms of new vocabulary, or with new uses for old words. But such a transition would not be from an oral to a written style but from pagan to Christian thought still within the oral traditional style. No change in basic metric or poetic structure would be required. Dangerous as it may be, the new wine could be put into old wineskins. There would be new formulas, and the older words and formulas might take on a new layer of meaning or signification, but the basic syntactical and a-coustic patterns, word-boundaries, and the structure of the poetic style, would not be affected; these would continue long into the "written period." That is exactly what happened in the Middle Ages, as I shall try to demonstrate.

§

---

[2] Much has been written previously on various aspects of this subject. A good place to start is Adeline Courtney Bartlett's *The Larger Rhetorical Patterns in Anglo-Saxon Poetry*, Columbia University Studies in English and Comparative Literature, no. 122 (New York: Columbia Univ. Press, 1935). One should also mention: Stanley B. Greenfield, *The Interpretation of Old English Poems*, (London and Boston: Routledge & Kegan Paul, 1972); Francis P. Magoun, Jr., "A Note on Old West Germanic Poetic Unity," *Modern Philology* 43 (August 1945): 77–82; Robert L. Kellogg, "The South Germanic Oral Tradition," in *Franciplegius: Medieval and Linguistic Studies in Honor of Francis Peabody Magoun, Jr.*, ed. Jess B. Bessinger, Jr. and Robert P. Creed (New York: New York Univ. Press, 1965), 66–74.

It would be appropriate early on to clarify the term "oral composition," and define the distinguishing marks that orality leaves on it, be it ancient, medieval, or modern.[3] In his study of the Homeric poems, Milman Parry noted formulas and unperiodic enjambement as characteristics of their oral composition, because their role in its creation reflected the necessities of rapid composition in performance without a fixed text. The formulas provided ways of expressing a regularly used essential idea of the poetry under the most common metrical situations in which it would be employed. And, since the singer composes one line after another, a thought tends to be complete at the end of a line, even though a sentence containing several clauses may not be entirely fulfilled at that point; this is what Parry called unperiodic enjambement. Later Parry began to investigate the "themes" of the poetry, which afforded the traditional singer ready-made models for scenes or passages that recurred in a number of songs. These characteristics as outlined by Parry are basically sound, I believe, and have been demonstrated as the basic in the Homeric songs and in the Slavic oral traditional epic, be it South Slavic, Russian, or Ukrainian. They are also present in Old French and, with some adjustments caused by the alliterative technique, I believe, in medieval Germanic narrative poetry as well, including Anglo-Saxon.

Such a method of "composition in performance"—*to be rigorously distinguished from "improvisation"*—was a thoroughly adequate way of expressing what a traditional culture wanted to say through its traditional poets. This is apparent from the very fact that it was kept long after the constraints of composition in oral performance ceased to exist.

The Formula

The definitions of the formula and of the theme need to be interpreted in terms of each individual culture because, even within the Indo-European umbrella, the several cultures, such as Slavic or those of Western Europe, differ from one another in some significant details. Fortunately, Parry's definition of the formula, while made with Homer in mind, is not specifically for Archaic Greek but is general enough to

---

[3] John Miles Foley, *The Theory of Oral Composition: Theory and Methodology* (Bloomington: Indiana, Univ. Press, 1988). For a bibliography of the subject, see John Miles Foley, *Oral Formulaic Theory and Research: An Introduction and Annotated Bibliography* (New York and London: Garland Press: 1985), and the journal *Oral Tradition*.

allow for ready adjustment to most traditions. In *L'épithète traditionelle dans Homère* he described it as: "An expression regularly used, under the same metrical conditions, to express an essential idea."[4]

The term "essential idea" is important for the definition, because without it one would be talking only about repetitions of groups of words rather than of ideas. For example, the essential idea of the first line of the Oxford manuscript of the *Chanson de Roland*, "Carles li reis, nostre emperere magnes," is "Charles the king." The rest of the words in the line make it possible to say "Charles the king" in a full line of the traditional *chansons de geste*. This does not mean, however, that the words "nostre emperere magnes" are meaningless or unimportant. They mean just what they say; they further define "Charles the king," and they have their own semantic as well as poetic history.[5]

The Theme[6]

A theme is a repeated passage with more or less verbal correspondence among its occurrences. In a paper read at the meetings of the International Comparative Literature Association in Belgrade in 1967 I wrote:

> Although the repeated passages will not be word-for-word alike, there will be at least a sufficient degree of similarity of wording to show that the singer is using a unit of story that he holds already more or less formed in his mind ... the kind of

---

[4] Quoted from the translation by Adam Parry in *The Making of Homeric Verse. The Collected Papers of Milman Parry*, ed. Adam Parry (Oxford: Clarendon Press, 1971), 13.

[5] "Beowulf maðelode / beðrn Ecgðeowes" has the essential meaning of "Beowulf spoke." The poet, by using the appositive "the son of Ecgðeow," has made it possible to say "Beowulf spoke" in a full line rather than a half line. As in the case of "nostre emperere magnes," "bearn Ecgðeowes" designates which Beowulf is referred to. The whole-line is clearly a formula with the essential idea of "Beowulf spoke."

[6] *Theme.* See Alexandra Hennessey Olsen, "Oral-Formulaic Research in Old English Studies: I," *Oral Tradition*, vol. 1, no. 3 (October 1986): 548–606, esp. 577–82. She did not know my article, "Perspectives on Recent Work on Oral Literature," in *Oral Literature: Seven Essays*, ed. Joseph J. Duggan (Edinburgh: Scottish Academic Press and New York: Barnes and Noble, 1975), 1–24, in which I clarified my earlier definition of theme in *The Singer of Tales*.

Block of Formulas. Between the formula and the theme one can distinguish a block of lines that the singer treats as a discernable unit in song. It has a beginning and an ending both of which are marked. It could be considered as an expanded formula or as a short theme. These blocks are most readily seen when one compares two texts of the same song from the same singer.

composition reflected in [such passages] could not be described as "free improvisation." On the other hand, they [the
themes] could not be described as memorized passages either.[7]

To me, memorization implies the conscious and careful word-for-word
reproduction of a previously fixed passage.

The form in which the theme exists in the Homeric songs and the
Slavic traditions is also shared by the *chansons de geste*. The battle
scenes in the *Iliad* have been described from this point of view by
Bernard Fenik.[8] Those in the *Chanson de Roland* are similar in type.
Note the following examples from the *Chanson de Roland*:[9]

> Sun cheval brochet, si li laschet la resne,
> Si vait ferir Escremiz de Valterne.
> L'escut del col li freint e escantelet,
> De sun osberc li rumpit la ventaille,
> Sil fiert el piz entre les dous furceles,
> Pleine sa hanste l'abat mort de la sele.

> He spurs his horse and gives him free rein
> And goes to strike Escremis of Valterne,
> He smashes and breaks in pieces the shield hanging from his
>   neck,
> He tears the mail coif from his hauberk,
> He strikes him full in the chest, on the sternum,
> Running him through, he throws him dead from the saddle.
> > [1290–95]

> Siet el cheval qu'il cleimet Gramimund,
> Plus est isnels que nen est uns falcuns.
> Brochet le bien des aguz esperuns,
> Si vait ferir li riche duc Sansun.
> L'escut li freint e l'osberc li derumpt,
> El cors li met les pans del gunfanun,
> Pleine sa hanste l'abat mort des arcuns.

> He sits astride the horse he calls Gramimont,
> It is swifter than a falcon.

---

[7] See Duggan, 20.

[8] Bernard Fenik, *Typical Battle Scenes in the Iliad. Studies in the narrative techniques of Homeric battle description* (Wiesbaden: F. Steiner, 1968).

[9] *La chanson de Roland*, trans. Joseph Bédier (Paris: H. Piazza, 1931).

He urges it on hard with his sharp spurs,
He goes to strike mighty Duke Samson.
He smashes his shield and rips open his hauberk,
He forces the tails of his ensign into his body,
Running him through, he throws him dead from his saddle.

[1571–77]

The case of the theme in Anglo-Saxon and other Germanic poetries is somewhat different. The reason for this seems to lie in part in
the constraints of alliteration. The situation is too complex for me to
discuss in this paper.

Unperiodic Enjambement

The formula and the theme are elements of poetic language used in
composing lines and songs and are in a different category from unperiodic enjambement, which is a result of the ways in which that language
is distributed over more than one line of verse. Parry noted this type of
enjambement as a characteristic of Homeric style, and it is also strong in
Serbo-Croatian decasyllabic epic; the most frequent exceptions involve preceding subordinate clauses. Here is an example from Avdo
Medjedović's "Osmanbeg Delibegović i Pavičević Luka":[10]

Jedno jutro begler poranijo,
Beg Osmanbeg Delibegoviću,
Na bijele u Osjeku dvore,
Prije zore dva sahata ravna.
A beg zove svoju vernu ljubu:
"Ljubo moja, Ismihan hanumo!
A vidiš li gospodara svoga,
Kako su me sani ostavili?
No, hanumo, Osmanbegovice,
Skoči do kahve odžaka,
I nalozi vatru na odžaku!
Tur' mi, hanko, kahve nekolike!
Nešto su me derti zauzeli.
Sana mene na očima nema."

---

[10] *Serbo-Croatian Heroic Songs*, collected by Milman Parry, vol. 6, *Ženidba Vlahin-
jić Alije, Osmanbeg Delibegović i Pavicević Luka*, kazivao i pjevao Avdo Međedović,
ed. with prolegomena and notes by David E. Bynum (Cambridge, MA: Harvard
Univ. Press, 1980), ll. 31–44.

One morning the bey rose early,
Bey Osmanbey Delibegović,
In his white court in Osjek,
Two full hours before dawn.
The bey called his true love:
"My true love, Lady Ismihan!
See you your lord,
How sleep has left me?
My lady, Osmanbegovica,
Go quickly to the hearth room
And light a fire on the hearth!
Make me several coffees!
A sadness has come upon me.
Sleep has left my eyes."

In medieval epic, the *Nibelungenlied* begins with excellent examples of unperiodic enjambement:[11]

I

Uns ist in alten maeren wunders vil geseit
von helden lobebaeren, von grôzer arebeit,
von fröuden, hôchjgezîten, von weinen und von klagen,
von kueener recken strîten muget ir nu wunder hoeren sagen.

II

Ez wuohs in Búrgónden ein vil édel magedîn,
daz in allen landen niht schoeners mohte sîn,
Kriemhilt geheizen: si wart ein scoene wîp.
dar umbe muosen degene vil verlíesén den lîp.

I

In stories of our fathers high marvels we are told
Of champions well approved in perils manifold.
Of feasts and merry meetings, of weeping and of wail,
And deeds of gallant daring I'll tell you in my tale.

II

In Burgundy there flourish'd a maid so fair to see,
That in all the world together a fairer could not be.
This maiden's name was Kriemhild; through her in dismal strife
Full many a prowest warrior thereafter lost his life.

---

[11] *Das Nibelungenlied, nach der,* Ausgabe von Karl Bartsch, ed. Helmut De Boor (Wiesbaden: F. A. Brockhaus, 1979).

The first *laisse* of the *Chanson de Roland* also illustrates the prevalence of unperiodic enjambement in that epic:

> Carles li reis, nostre empere magnes,
> Set anz tuz pleins ad estet en Espaigne:
> Tresqu'en la mer cunquist la tere altaigne.
> N'i ad castel ki devant lui remaigne;
> Mur ne citet n'i est remes a fraindre,
> Fors Sarraguce, ki est en une muntaigne.
> Li reis Marsilie la tient, ki Deu nen aimet.
> Mahumet sert e Apollin recleimet;
> Nes poet guarder que mals ne l'i ateignet.

> Carlon the King, our Emperor Charlemayn,
> Full seven years long has been abroad in Spain,
> He's won the highlands as far as to the main;
> No castle more can stand before his face,
> City nor wall is left for him to break,
> Save Saragossa in its high mountain place;
> Marsilion holds it, the king who hates God's name,
> Mahound he serves, and Apollyon prays:
> He'll not escape the ruin that awaits.

Necessary enjambement occurs only between lines one and two. The remaining lines present examples of either unperiodic enjambement or of none at all.

§

There are other characteristics of oral traditional stylistics in narrative verse, but these three, i.e., formulas, themes, and unperiodic enjambement, have been most talked of and written about. To Parry, a preponderance of the criteria set forth above indicated that a given text belonged in the category of oral traditional narrative song. The statistical method used in the past to determine orality, however, has been much criticized because, as repetitions, formulas are also found, sometimes in approximately equal amounts, in some epic poetry that we know to have been written. We have now come to realize, I believe, that the statistics are actually an indication, not of whether the text involved was dictated to a scribe by an oral traditional poet, but rather of the degree to which the given text participated in the oral traditional style. In some cases the traits were residual.

It is clear that in order to properly understand "oral residue," one

must know what the traditional element is in oral traditional narrative
sung verse.

§

The carriers of an oral literary tradition in any culture include *all*
those who have composed in it since the beginning of the practise of
singing or telling literature in that culture. Among them are to be
found the most talented as well as the least skillful, and all degrees in
between. Moreover, there is no contradiction in saying that a fully
traditional singer has many individual traits of style. Within a tradition, it seems to me, there is no opposition or incompatibility between
the individual and his tradition. No matter how individual, he is part
of his tradition. The tradition includes Homer and, if I may be so
bold, the poet of *Beowulf.*

Viewed from the perspective of content, be it large or small, an
oral narrative tradition in any geographic area might be thought of as
the body of formulas, themes, and songs that all the traditional singers have ever used or sung in all their "performances" since the beginning of the tradition.

§

Some of the recent work in Ancient Greek epic studies may be
useful in our thinking about tradition and the individual. In his paper
on "Orality in the 'Hymn to Demeter' " in a volume of papers and
discussion devoted to *I poemi epici i rapsodici non omerici e la tradizione
orale,* Charles Segal wrote the following wise words:

> Identifying "creativity" or individual artistry in a formulaic
> tradition is undoubtedly the most controversial and difficult
> problem of current oral poetics. While the poet of our Hymn
> still depends closely upon a system of formulaic patterns of
> rhythm, diction, and theme, these inherited patterns have not
> ossified into mechanically evoked echoes characteristic of an
> imitative poetry like that of Apollonius of Rhodes or Quintus
> of Smyrna or indeed some of the later "Homeric" Hymns
> themselves. His formulas are not literary "tags," but still form
> a living language which he can alter within limits—limits
> which have probably become freer for him than they were for
> his predecessors.[12]

---

[12] C. Brillante, M. Cantilena, and C. O. Pavese, eds. (Padua: Antenore, 1981), 110–11.

This is an especially helpful quotation because Segal tries to differentiate between "tradition" and individual characteristics *within* the tradition rather than *between* oral and written.

§

The more we learn about oral-traditional style and about oral tradition itself, the more we are aware that traditional singers can and do have a great deal of freedom and sometimes bend the parameters of the verse and even create new words. Oral traditional literature is dynamic. While it preserves older stories, it also engenders new ones from older materials or by analogy with the traditional narrative elements. Tradition is always changing *within the parameters of the traditional society and its traditional media*. Changed thoughts and concepts that are not readily assimilable into oral traditional literature, or changed poetic structures from "foreign" influence, move traditional style in the direction of written non-traditional literature. New ideas that cannot fit into the traditional patterns, yet which must be expressed, may lead to the creation of new, non-traditional methods of expression. Or it may be that new poetic techniques from outside the tradition may penetrate its bastion. There seems to come a time in some cultures when outside influences are brought to bear on the traditional singer or poet.

§

The introduction of writing into an "oral culture" does not *per se* change the manner of composition of narrative poetry that has been in use for generations and has been the only way known for composing poetry in the vernacular. In the Middle Ages, literacy outside of the clerical ranks in the monasteries was limited. M. B. Parkes in "The Literacy of the Laity" wrote:

> Throughout the greater part of the Middle Ages the professional reader [i.e., the scholar or professional man of letters] was usually in holy orders.... From the 6th to the 12th century the ability to read and write was more or less confined to the professional reader, or at least to the professed.... Books were written, copied, preserved, and read mainly in monasteries. A few literate laymen were to be found among the reigning families and in their courts.... Apart from the ecclesiastical prose produced in England in the 10th or at the beginning of the 11th century, the written literature of this early period was in Latin: the learned

literature of a closed circle of scholars and savants. The cultivated laity turned to the minstrel or the scop for their recreation, and the vernacular literature (apart from sermons) was transmitted orally by professional singers who were probably illiterate. When in this period vernacular texts were committed to writing, they were set down by monks who had acquired an interest in them, and extant manuscripts, such as the Exeter Book of Old English poetry, survived in monastic libraries.[13]

It is not surprising, therefore, that vernacular poems continued for a long time to be written in the oral traditional formulaic style; writing was at first only a surface phenomenon. Nothing had changed except the mode of "performance," as it were. The singer had moved from a "purely oral" to a special kind of written performance, but the traditional techniques of composition and the traditional poetics remained for long untouched. The transition was from one kind of *performance* to another rather than from one kind of *composition* to another. This phenomenon has been observed in such living traditions as the South Slavic, where purely traditional singers have learned the rudiments of writing and have written their own songs. At first they simply continued in writing what they were doing without it. The Milman Parry Collection at Harvard has many such texts.

M. T. Clanchy notes:

> As the number of documents increased and habits of silent visual reading became more common, levels of literacy (in the modern sense) presumably increased also; but there was no evidence of a crisis suddenly demanding numerous literates. Because the preliterate emphasis on the spoken word persisted, the change from oral to literate modes could occur slowly and almost imperceptibly over many generations.[14]

Later, speaking of the "lawyers' Year Books and handbooks," Clanchy wrote:

> It would be tempting to see (them) as having something in

---

[13] In *The Mediaeval World*, ed. David Daiches and Anthony Thorlby (London, 1973), 555–77. In the article, Parkes "distinguished between three kinds of literacy: that of the professional reader, which is the literacy of the scholar or the professional man of letters; that of the cultivated reader, which is the literacy of recreation; and that of the pragmatic reader, which is the literacy of one who has to read or write in the course of transacting any kind of business."

[14] *From Memory to Written Record: England 1066–1307* (Cambridge, MA: Harvard Univ. Press, 1979), 219.

common with the jongleurs' "stage scripts", in which the vernacular romances are thought to have been first recorded in writing. Scripts, whether for jongleurs or lawyers, enabled "a young man to see [*veer/vere*] how he ought to speak with subtlety" and "see the manner distinctly" (in the words of *The Court Baron*). A student now learned the rudiments of public speaking by reading, by seeing the "shapes indicating voices" (in John Salisbury's phrase) in a book, instead of hearing the words of his master. Yet we should not exaggerate the speed of this development; as long as writing depended on manuscripts alone, the change from oral to literate modes was gradual. Dependence on symbolic gestures and the spoken word persisted in law and literature, and throughout medieval culture, despite the growth of literacy.[15]

There were texts in the Middle Ages, as well as in other periods, that were literally, *physically* written, but were oral in their style of composition. Sometimes the written text was dictated to a scribe by an oral traditional singer or poet. Sometimes the oral traditional singer or poet may have been asked to write down his own words for someone else. There are cases of both of these processes in the Parry Collection. In spite of the writing, both kinds of text were oral traditional compositions if they were formulaic and had the other marks of the oral-formulaic style, and if they came from a truly traditional singer.

§

One of the crucial problems in the comparison of oral traditional composition with written non-traditional composition is the role of the subconscious sense of form, structure, and aesthetics in oral traditional poetry, in contrast to the conscious manipulation of words and groups of words in accordance with an overtly known body of rules and "strategies" that all writers conscientiously strive to follow, or purposely attempt to disregard or even flout. In short, the traditional poetry is composed in a poetic language that is learned just as any language is learned—intuitively and by association—and that the poet uses subconsciously, as naturally as everyday speech.

John D. Niles has pointed out that "there existed a set of Native

---

[15] Ibid., 225–26. See also, *The Court Baron*, ed. F. W. Maitlad and W. P. Bailden, Selden Society IV (1890).

Germanic poetic strategies that deserve the name of *rhetoric* just as much as do the strategies of Latin authors, even though the Germanic tropes were never codified in written treatises."[16]

A culture's basic oral traditional poetic language includes the structure of language itself, the formulas, the various acoustical patterns, such as rhyme, assonance and alliteration, and such rhetorical devices as anaphora and epiphora.[17] In this account of elements in oral traditional style, one should also include similes and antitheses because a sense of the balancing of likes and unlikes, whether it be words, or people, or settings, or concepts (such as brave and cowardly), is present from early times in any poetic scheme. Chiastic arrangements, common in Slavic as well as in other Indo-European poetics, are also manifestations of that impulse to recognize and to put in various spatial relationships things that are like or unlike one another. They too are part of the "oral residue."

One can see, then, that the entire formulaic system was not only a system for verse-making, but also one for the expression and imparting of meaning, and more importantly for us at the moment—a system of oral traditional poetics, a poetics built into it from its very inception— developed and polished by generations of poets. It is not a simple, but a complex poetics, one so complex indeed, that it could not have been invented by one man or even in a single generation. No single vernacular poet of the Middle Ages, or earlier, created the traditional poetics of the cultures of that period any more than Homer created the complex poetics of archaic Greek poetry. Parry himself wrote something similar in 1923 in his Master's thesis at Berkeley:

> We realize that the traditional, the formulaic quality of the diction was not a device for mere convenience, but the highest possible development of the hexameter medium to tell a race's heroic tales.... It was a poetry which for centuries had accumulated all such possibilities—all the turns of language, all the words, phrases, and effects of position, which had pleased the race.... And while it was a technique which might be learned

---

[16] John D. Niles, *Beowulf: The Poem and its Tradition* (Cambridge, MA: Harvard Univ. Press, 1983), 79. David Rubin of the Psychology Department of Duke University has said that learning a poetic language is like learning a second language, perhaps, one might add, a second language that is a close cognate of the first.

[17] While some of these devices make lines and groups of lines easy to remember, they were not, I believe, originally intended to be mnemonic, but were repetitions of sound or structure that conferred some special power to support and reinforce ideas, or were simply aesthetically pleasing.

parrot-like by men of little genius who added nothing to their inheritance, it was also a technique which furnished inexhaustible material for genius: the work of bringing to perfection is never finished.[18]

All this forms part of the "oral residue" that continued to operate after writing was introduced. It could be argued that the poet who wrote naturally in his inherited traditional style about traditional subjects for a traditional audience was still an oral traditional poet. He was still an "insider."

But the traditional singer can be influenced by outsiders, by people outside of his tradition, by the literary "modes" of people in a written literary tradition. I am reminded of some Serbo-Croatian texts in the Parry Collection that were dictated (or sung) by a traditionally trained singer who had tried to memorize a fixed, published text. When his memory failed, he composed in the traditional way to which he was accustomed; he had not forgotten that technique. The published text that our singer had memorized had been collected from a traditional singer. The text that we have, therefore, consists partly of a singer's memorization of someone else's traditional text and partly of his own traditional composition. The resulting text could be thought of as transitional between oral-formulaic composition and memorization. It employs a mixture of two techniques. I suspect that something similar may well have taken place in the Middle Ages also, especially in the later period when "minstrel books" were available, providing that the art of composition itself was still alive at the time.

Is there such a thing as a "transitional text?" On the simplest level both an oral-dictated and an autograph oral text are "transitional." The transition from oral to written is literally going on in the very process of transferring the text from sound to writing. Is the style affected by this process, which essentially slows the tempo of composition and eliminates the melody and the musical instrument? I discussed this to some extent in *The Singer of Tales*. Some singers have difficulty making proper lines without the musical accompaniment, but most eventually become accustomed to this way of doing things. Although we have abundant material for the study of the differences between sung and dictated versions of the same song by the same singer, no really thorough investigation of the question has been made, to the best of my knowledge. As in the sung version, the form

---

[18] Cited in *The Making of Homeric Verse: The Collected Papers of Milman Parry*, ed. Adam Parry (Oxford: Clarendon Press, 1971), 425.

that the lines take in the dictated version depends on the rhythmic circumstances of the moment of composition. In this respect the dictated version may not differ any more from a sung version than the sung versions differ from each other. Also dependent on the circumstances of the moment is the degree of expansion of any theme within a song or of the song itself. Dictated versions may be longer or shorter just as sung versions may be longer or shorter.

§

At some point in the transitional period between oral and written style, where there is one, be it that of the individual singer or of the poetic style itself, one can begin to note differences, changes in the traditional matter. For the poetic style itself, let me cite as an example the case of the generalizing of end-rhyme in some South Slavic poetry. The oral tradition makes occasional use of both internal- and end-rhyme. Early in this century, however (indeed probably even long before that), some "traditional" poems began to be written in what seemed to be the traditional manner, using some of the familiar formulas, but in rhymed couplets. We might call this style "transitional" because of the persistence of the formulaic diction to which emphasis of one element, rhymed couplets, an emphasis that came from outside influence, had been added. The style had in it both the old and the new, the formulaic language and the non-traditional use of the oral-traditional literary device of end-rhyme.

One such song, a poem that became standard for some Montenegrin singers in the thirties, was entitled *Prva varnica svjetskog požara, spomen na 10-godišnjicu atentata 1914 g.*, "The First Spark of the World Conflagration," written by Aleksa Guzina, Volunteer from Nevesinje (dobrovoljac iz Nevesinja), Sarajevo, 1926, Nikšić, 1928 and 1931. This was by chance the first song that Parry heard in the field! It was from the singer who was to become his closest assistant in the collecting of songs. Parry wrote of the incident in his field notes, which he called *Ćor Huso*:

> The singer in question was Nikola Vujnović, a stone mason by trade, from Stolac in Hercegovina, who was drinking wine and putting the *gusle* (one stringed bowed musical instrument, ABL) in order when Kutuzov and myself arrived. He sang quite willingly for us the first evening. The first song he sang and so the first of the songs which I heard was the beginning of the poem, *Prva varnica svjetskog požara*.... The poem is typical of a large number of poems which have made the poor attempt to adapt the old heroic songs to modern events. The poem, which

first tells of the assassination of Franz Ferdinand, begins with
the traditional enough themes of the two crows who fly with
the tidings to the castle of the Austrian Emperor, and the
telephoning (instead of letter-writing) by the Emperor to his
allies. However, the poem is written as most of the new poems
are, in rhyme, and while the themes and phrases of the poetry
show on the one hand a habitude of the old poetry, other
verses clearly indicate the influence of the newspapers....
Poetically this poem is negligible, whatever its value may be as
a document of the popular thought. A popular poetry rises to
greatness only in the measure that it shows a full understanding of the life which is portrayed or symbolized in its verses
(and then, of course, only as that life itself is admirable), and
it is the very possibility of an oral poetry by its very nature of
doing this which explains the high quality of so much of it. But
when the civilized world, with complexities which can only be
grasped by the educated mind as we understand it, encroaches
upon the earlier life, the result is naivety of different degrees....
When I asked him (Nikola) to recite the poem from the beginning he was able to do so only for twelve verses, and then lost
himself in making the rhymes.... His explanation which, in its
way, is doubtless true, was that it is very easy to forget poems
that are rhymed. With this should be compared the statement
which he made a week ago at Novi Pazar when Đemail Zogić
remarked that no two singers ever sing the same song alike.
He then stated that the one exception was with rhymed poems.
All this means that the song without rhyme heard in the
manner habitual to the traditional poetry is recreated by each
singer in his own verses more or less as an improvisation each
time. The poem in rhyme, however, must be learned by heart,
and when forgotten it cannot be reimprovised on the instant,
since the rhymes present too great an obstacle to such improvisation. Corroborating this is Milovan's statement of last year
that one could not improvise in rhyme to the *gusle* but must
have the time provided by writing materials if he would
compose a rhymed poem.[19]

I have reservations about Parry's use of the word "improvisation"
for the process involved in composition in performance in this tradi-

---

[19] Quoted from the original typescript. Sections of this passage were published
by Adam Parry in his volume of his father's collected papers, 441–42. See note 18.

tion—and I am sure that he too would have had similar reservations, had he seen the misunderstandings that have arisen from its use. But the indication that poems with rhymes in this tradition are hard to remember exactly, and must be memorized, is significant. We are often told that rhyme is a mnemonic device! Evidently the singers in this tradition do not believe that to be true.

§

Very occasionally we can find a series of texts that show a singer moving from the oral-traditional style, in which he was brought up, to a written-literary style. Elsewhere I have written of the case of the prince-bishop of Montenegro in the first half of the nineteenth century, Petar Petrović II Njegoš,[20] who was an oral poet, but through travel in Russia and elsewhere and through knowledge of written literature in Russian and French, became a thoroughly written author, developing his own style. (Yet he could still compose in the traditional manner.) We can trace this development in his style in detail from his earliest traditional verses, through transitional texts, to his highly advanced literary masterpieces such as *Luča mikrokosma*, "The Ray of the Microcosm," a philosophical poem reminding one of Milton, whose poetry he knew in translation, and his crowning work *Gorski vijenac*, "The Mountain Wreath," a heroic drama.[21] He began to in-

---

[20] See my "The merging of Two Worlds: Oral and Written Poetry as Carriers of Ancient Values," in *Oral Tradition in Literature*, ed. John Miles Foley (Columbia: Univ. of Missouri Press, 1986), esp. 30 ff.

[21] Ibid., 19–64. In *Comparative Literature* 32 (1980): 390–401, Edward R. Haymes published an article on "Formulaic Density and Bishop Njegoš," in which he compared the formulaic density of one of the oral epics in vol. 2 of *Serbo-Croatian Heroic Songs*, collected by Milman Parry, ed. Albert B. Lord (Cambridge, MA: Harvard Univ. Press, 1958) with that of one of Njegoš's poems written in the style of the oral traditional epic. The percentage of formulas, i.e. repeated lines, in the former was 34.8 and in the latter 29.6; the difference is insignificant. His concluding comments are worth noting:

> the difference in repetition density between a real oral text and an imitation of the same tradition is not great enough for us to make a clear distinction on that basis alone. . . . Imitations of the kind we find in Njegoš's poem do not come into being in a vacuum; they are totally dependent on a living oral tradition for their form, their language, and their themes. Recognizing oral form in a medieval poem does not mean that the poem was the product of a dictating session in which the dictating poet was a real oral singer of tales. It does, however, mean that there were such singers and that they sang essentially similar songs with practically the same language and the same narrative devices (400–401).

troduce non-traditional structures into poems that were otherwise written in the traditional manner. For example, he wrote a song in the traditional style entitled "Pjesna za Vida i Mirčetu, kako su skupili četu i uzeli top s Spuža" (a song of how Vido and Mirčeta gathered a raiding band and seized the canon from Spuž).[22] The style is traditional, yet there are small indications, if one looks closely with a trained eye, that it is not quite a fully traditional song. A careful analysis of such songs uncovers traits that show the influence of non-traditional style on the author.

In other poems, however, such as "Cestitanje novoga ljeta gospodinu Gagića," Njegoš wrote in a clearly written-literary, non-traditional style:[23]

Gledaj Feba ka' je uhitao
na krilatim svojim konj'ma
i plamenosipnoj kolesnici
da nam Novo ljeto dopoteže.
Zevs je njemu starcu otsudio
(a za kakvo ne znam prestupljenje
il' nagradu—to je od nas skrito)
da kurirski trči po Uranu.

See Phoebus as he hastens
with his winged horses
in his flaming chariot
to bring us the New Year.
Zeus decreed the old one
(for what misdemeanor I know not
or reward—that is hidden from us)
to run as courier in Uranus.   [1–8]

There is nothing very traditional about these lines either in content or style.[24]

---

[22] Petar Petrović Njegoš, *Songs, The Sunbeam of the Microcosm, Prose, Translations,* Collected works of Petar Petrović Njegoš, no. 20:93–98.

[23] Ibid. no. 41:146–47.

[24] One notes that the second line is octosyllabic and that the third fails to observe a caesura after the fourth syllable. The song continues:

On je valjda za njegove trude
i obdaren najsjajnijom krunom
il' za kazan može biti kakvu
valjda su mu duge i sijede
iz zavisti zapalili vlase.
Ta otsuda tko zna dokad mu je—

One can, then, distinguish Njegoš's oral traditional style from his written non-traditional style. In his case one can even observe a kind of transitional text.

§

It is likely that at least some of the Old French or Anglo-Saxon oral traditional epics were composed by traditional singers, some of whom became monks or clerics and learned to write. It is reasonable to assume that, in addition to continuing to sing their usual repertory, they may have also composed new songs that expressed the concepts of a new religion. Cædmon appears to have been a case in point.[25]

§

I have earlier discussed "objective" ways of determining whether a given text is "oral" or "written" by statistical means. One should

---

> il' je vjecna ili vremenita,
> el' dovoze ovo Novo ljeto.

> Possibly for his labors he was
> granted a resplendent crown
> or as punishment perhaps
> his long gray
> locks they kindled out of envy.
> Who knows how long this judgement will last—
> whether it's eternal or temporary
> as he brings this New Year. [9–15]

The structure of the lines 9–13 above belongs decidedly to Njegoš's written-literary style. The necessary enjambement at the end of line 9 binds lines 9 and 10 together. The same can be said for lines 11 through 13; line 11 has no verb (except for the parenthetical "može biti," which does not count), line 12 has the auxiliary "su," but only in line 13 is the verb completed with the past participle "zapalili." Moreover, the adjectives "duge i sijede" at the end of line 12 modify "vlase" at the end of line 13. Finally, there are no formulas in the passage, although such a line as number 15 follows a familiar traditional pattern.

[25] A number of scholars have noted that it seems most likely that Cædmon had a repertory of songs that he had heard and had a good passive knowledge of before he produced his hymn. The hymn is considered the earliest oral-traditional poem in Anglo-Saxon of which we have a record. It is certainly not transitional in its content between pagan and Christian, and its style seems completely traditional. It appears to have been the first poem in traditional style that was written down. (See Dobbie edition in *Anglo-Saxon Poetic Records*, 1942, and his book, *The Manuscripts of Cædmon's Hymn and Bede's Death Song, with a critical text of the Epistola Cuthberti de obitu Bedae*, by Elliot Van Kirk Dobbie [New York: Columbia Univ. Press, 1937], and the work of Donald K. Fry. For further references, see Olsen [reference in note 6 above]).

address head-on also the question of whether or not the two styles can be detected by the type of aesthetic analysis represented by the recent work of Fred C. Robinson.[26] Does his study of the appositive style in *Beowulf* prove that poem to be a written literary text, or are at least some of the phenomena that he has discussed to be found also in oral-traditional style? This is a crucial question. Are such phenomena part of the "oral residue" or do they belong to the new?

Speaking of some of the implications in the boar image on Beowulf's helmet, Robinson cites the description beginning in line 1451:[27]

> befongen freawrasnum, swa hine fyrndagum
> worhte wæpna smið, wundrum teode,
> besette swinlicum, þæt hine syðþan no
> brond ne beadomecas bitan ne meahton.

He translates: "encompassed with lordly bands, as the smith fashioned it in ancient days, provided with supernatural powers, set about with boar images," that afterwards no brand nor battle sword might dent it, and continues:

> Since *wundrum* specifies supernatural powers, and since the boar was the animal associated with Freyr in Scandinavian mythology, it is tempting to see in the unique compound *freawrasnum* an allusion to an Anglo-Saxon god Frea (cognate with Freyja, the Old Icelandic deity). But such an explicit naming of the pagan god seems unlikely; it is more probable that the word meant 'lord,' and there is present here that carefully maintained double sense seen elsewhere in *Beowulf* where a word which had in earlier times been applied to pagan gods and was in Christian times transferred to the Christian deity is used with calculated ambiguity in the context of the world of *Beowulf.*[28]

The one word that bothers me in the above is "calculated." I am ready to accept "carefully maintained," if one means "carefully maintained by the traditional singers," but I have a problem with the concept of the *Beowulf* poet calculating in a highly conscious way the use of "freawrasnum" because it had possible "allusion to an Anglo-Saxon god Frea." I doubt if there was intended ambiguity, a purposeful pointing in two directions.

---

[26] Fred C. Robinson, *Beowulf and the Appositive Style,* The Hodges Lectures Series (Knoxville: The Univ. of Tennessee Press, 1985).

[27] I am following Dobbie's text in vol. 4 of *Anglo-Saxon Poetic Records.*

[28] Robinson, 69.

Let me give a brief illustration of what I think may be a similar phenomenon in South Slavic oral traditional epic. In a well-known song belonging to the Kosovo cycle, "Smrt majke Jugovića" (The Death of the Mother of the Jugovići),[29] the mother of the nine Jugovići prays that she may have the eyes of a falcon and the wings of a swan so that she may fly to the battlefield of Kosovo to see the fate of her husband and their nine sons. The imagery is traditional. Birds play a large role in the poetry. The heroes themselves are often addressed as "falcons" (sokolovi). Two black crows (dva vrana gavrana) are frequently found as messengers. One may admire the imagery on its own terms, that is as strong images, but there is more than that involved. Such figures call up the shamanic cultures in which I believe they originated, where human beings with special abilities could for a time become more than human and travel and see as birds or animals. To call heroes "falcons" is not only to emphasize and praise their speed and bravery, but also to endow them with supernatural powers. The two black crows that serve as messengers are the souls of dead heroes reporting from a scene of carnage.[30] Beneath the plea of the mother of the Jugovici to have the eyes of a falcon and the wings of a swan is the implication that anxious lady wishes to acquire the powers of a shamaness to fly to the battlefield at Kosovo. The ambiguity is there even though it is no longer consciously felt by either singer or audience. These are the multiple references given to the poetry by tradition. The contemporary singer is not aware of the source of the imagery, but he uses it aptly because the tradition has maintained it in appropriate contexts.

The following quotation from the closing pages of Robinson's challenging and brilliant book deserves our serious attention:

---

[29] The classic text is that in Vuk Stefanović Karadžić, *Serbian Folksongs*, vol. 2 (Belgrad, 1958), no. 47 (from Croatia), 296–99.

[30] Compare the training of the hero in the *bylina* of Volx Vseslavevic:

> And when Volx was already ten years old,
> Volx was instructed in high wisdoms.
> And the first wisdom Volx studied—
> To turn into a bright falcon;
> And the second wisdom Volx studied—
> To turn into a gray-haired wolf;
> And the third widsdom Volx studied—
> To turn into a bay aurochs,
> A bay aurochs with horns of gold.

From "The Vseslav Epos," Roman Jakobson and Marc Szeftel, *Russian Epic Studies*, ed. Roman Jakobson and Ernest J. Simmons, (Philadelphia: The American Folklore Society, 1949), 28.

Words referring to vows occur next to words referring to drink; terms for boar images appear in apposition with words like *wundor* denoting supernatural power; and references to nature seem to cluster more around descriptions of monsters than of men, while the latter are loosely associated with artifacts. Like many of the most important meanings in the poem, these must be inferred from juxtapositions and loose associations, and throughout *Beowulf*, readers' minds are conditioned to make just such inferences. For constantly at work in the poem's style, exercising the readers' imagination in drawing conclusions from verbal collocations and juxtapositions, are the appositional devices. . . . Whether seen in the narrow context of grammatical apposition, or in the larger context of appositive style in general, this literary device or habit of mind is subtly yet powerfully present in *Beowulf* at every level, serving the expressive needs of a theme which by its very nature must emerge more through suggestion than through assertion. Of the two terms just used, "habit of mind" is perhaps preferable to "literary device," for apposition works at a more elemental level of expression than does a "device." It occupies a middle ground between grammar and style, between syntax and narrative method. Appositions and appositive style are the automatic means by which an Old English poet proceeds from thought to thought. They can be simultaneously transitional, nominalizing and emphasizing as they bring out by suggestion the complex meanings of events, motifs, and words. Their most important function, perhaps, is their role in focusing attention on the homonymic character of Old English poetic diction, for this serves most pervasively the expression of pagan-Christian tensions which concern the poet so deeply. It is the combining of this concern and the appositional style that enables the poet to release the power of his inherited diction in a way unmatched in any other Anglo-Saxon poem.[31]

There is much here I can agree with. Yet, when Robinson speaks of "the reader," I wonder if we should think rather of the traditional audience, and the singers who formed part of it, by whom and for whom the poetics was created. The term "habit of mind" is an excellent one and an inspired suggestion, because "device" implies a conscious crafting on the part of the last teller. Traditional poetics is

---

[31] Robinson, 79–80.

the result of the usage of generations of story-tellers in song. Its internal references emerge from these many tellings. Only when one has experienced a large section of the traditional poetry, noting the multiple contexts of words and groups of words, can one begin to understand the traditional poetics itself, the intricate relationships among the various expressions.

I would like respectfully to suggest that a part of what Robinson has described so well in his book on the appositive style in *Beowulf* is the oral-traditional poetics of the Anglo-Saxon bards. I wonder whether any poet of the ninth or tenth centuries, let us say, could know consciously all that Robinson attributes to the poet of *Beowulf*; but the tradition could have known it and could have imbued the poetry with it. The traditional *Beowulf* poet sang or wrote in the Anglo-Saxon tradition with its traditional poetics, which he used intuitively and subconsciously. The gifted singer/poet expresses the concepts of the traditional society to which he belongs, with all its inherited depths and many facets, but that traditional society still has room for the individual. His is the perfect expression of the best in the tradition.

Finally, it seems to me that we have still before us the task of determining, if we can, the points at which the medieval epic narratives in the vernacular separted from the traditional style, and why and how they did so. We must look most probably to Latin language and literature and to the clerical schools of the Middle Ages for at least some of the answer. In the meantime, it appears that we have been learning more about the traditional vernacular roots of the poetry.

JOHN MILES FOLEY

The Implications of Oral Tradition

A s a preface, I turn to Albert Lord's sage words near the conclusion of *The Singer of Tales*:

> Yet after all that has been said about *oral* composition as a
> technique of line and song construction, it seems that the term
> of greater significance is *traditional*. Oral tells us "how," but
> traditional tells us "what," and even more, "of what kind" and
> "of what force."[1]

Because the early stages of the study of oral tradition and ancient and
medieval texts were so concerned with the novelty of a new method of
composition, and with whether that method necessarily meant that the
manuscript in hand was a recording of a performance by an illiterate
bard, the emphasis remained almost exclusively on the *oral* term in the
equation. Studies of the tectonics—really the "philology"—of oral traditions will and should always be with us; without their fundamental
contribution any interpretive edifice we may wish to design is doomed

---

[1] Albert B. Lord, *The Singer of Tales* (Cambridge, Mass.: Harvard Univ. Press,
1960), 220.

to fall. But perhaps now is the time to place increased stress on the *traditional*, on the analysis not only of how a work was composed, but also of *how it means*; not only of the nature of its idiom, but also of the expressive quality of that idiom. What I propose to sketch out in this essay is a brief aesthetics for oral and oral-derived texts, including those from the ancient and medieval periods, an aesthetics that respects the tectonic singularity of these works and yet illuminates their *(il-)*literary art.[2]

To begin, let me state my assumptions. I assume first that enough scholarship has been done to certify, as far as possible in the absence of fieldwork evidence, that an oral tradition lies in the background of, for instance, the Homeric epics and many Old English poems. Studies of formula, theme, and other aspects of these works, as well as historical and comparative investigations, are much too numerous and too familiar even to mention at this point, but their consensus is clear enough.[3] I also assume that literacy, or better, textuality, also played some role in the composition and/or transmission of most of the ancient and medieval works before us, so that we claim a "primary orality" for any of them only at our peril. Preferring a more judicious position, one that sacrifices neither oral tradition nor textuality to the creation of a simplified model, I would describe these works as *oral-derived*, or, as Burton Raffel has put it with deserved rhetorical emphasis, *oral-connected*.[4] By either of these terms I mean a text that has reached us in written form but which has roots in oral tradition. Obviously, there must have been a spectrum of such works, according to the different contributions of oral tradition and textuality in each case, to say nothing of differences in language and genre. But let us be clear about what the *oral-derived* model does for us: it disenfranchises neither oral tradition nor textuality, allowing us to take full account of the complexity of the work of art. It avoids, in short, "throwing the baby out with the bathwater."

---

[2] This discussion is excerpted from my *Immanent Art: From Structure to Meaning in Traditional Oral Epic* (Bloomington: Indiana Univ. Press, 1991). Both the essay and the larger work are dependent for their philological foundation on John Miles Foley, *Traditional Oral Epic: The Odyssey, Beowulf, and the Serbo-Croatian Return Song* (Berkeley: Univ. of California Press, 1990).

[3] For bibliography, see Foley, *Oral-Formulaic Theory and Research: An Introduction and Annotated Bibliography* (New York: Garland, 1985), with updates in *Oral Tradition*; for a historical survey, see Foley, *The Theory of Oral Composition: History and Methodology* (Bloomington: Indiana Univ. Press, 1988).

[4] See Burton Raffel, "The Manner of Boyan: Translating Oral Literature," *Oral Tradition* 1 (1986): 11–29.

As we begin our inquiry, then, it will be well to keep in mind the role of *tradition* in the aesthetic interpretation of medieval and other works, and to remember that oral traditional texts comprise not a diametrically opposed alternative to literary works (themselves wonderfully various) but a heterogeneous collection that shares a pre-literary heritage. In order to speak to as many of these different but related situations as possible, I shall be dealing with oral tradition and aesthetics primarily from a general theoretical viewpoint, leaving specialists to make more exact applications to their own fields of expertise. A few illustrations will be drawn from ancient Greek epic, with occasional references to other areas.

§

First, then, to the question of meaning. If traditional phraseology and narrative pattern are conventional in structure, then they must also be conventional in their modes of generating meaning. That is, at least part of the answer to the question of "how" these elements function is "in the same way each time." There will of course be room for the individual poet to contribute to the negotiation of meaning even in primary oral works, the relative importance of that contribution depending on factors such as the idiosyncrasies of different traditions, genres, and texts. But by and large, the referential function of traditional units will remain consistent, everything else being equal.[5]

But does a consistently demarcated referentiality damn the poetic content to cliché, imprisoning the poet in a hackneyed, flat language and all-too-predictable scenic repertoire? Many have translated the recurrency of the traditional idiom to this kind of unresponsive, predetermined medium, but such an interpretation reflects the reasoning of the scholar trained in literary criticism and is an inappropriate conclusion for oral traditional works. The key difference lies in the nature of tradition itself: structural elements are not simply compositionally useful, nor are they doomed to a "limited" area of designation; rather they command fields of reference much larger than the single line, passage, or even text in which they occur. Traditional elements reach out of the immediate instance in which they appear to the fecund totality of the entire tradition, defined synchronically and diachronically, and they bear meanings as wide and deep as the tradition they encode. The "how" of the traditional idiom, while overlapping at

---

[5] This is really no more than saying that these units are traditional.

some points with the "how" of the literary text, also—and crucially—
includes an extratextual dimension uniquely the property of oral traditional art. This idiom is liberating rather than imprisoning, centrifugal
rather than centripetal, explosively connotative rather than claustropho-
bically clichéd.

Traditional referentiality, then, entails the invoking of a context
that is enormously larger and more echoic than the text or work itself, that brings the lifeblood of generations of poems and performances to the individual performance or text. Each element in the phraseology or narrative thematics stands not simply for that singular
instance but for the plurality and multiformity that are beyond the
reach of textualization. From the perspective of traditional context, these
elements are foci for signification, still points in the exchange of meaning between an always impinging tradition and the momentary fossilization of a text or version. Even when the process becomes one of making oral-derived texts, traditional phraseology and narrative patterns
continue to provide unique ways for the poet to convey meaning, to
tap the traditional reservoir. Poets do not persist in employing traditional structures after the advent of literacy and texts out of a mis-
placed antiquarianism or by default, but because, even in an increasingly textual environment, the "how" developed over the ages still
holds the key to worlds of meaning that are otherwise inaccessible.[6]

Such a process of generating meaning I call *metonymy*, designating
a mode of signification wherein the part stands for the whole. It is this
aspect of traditional art that may be understood as "conventional," as
long as one realizes that in this case the convention allows for much
more than a pre-set, one-to-one allusiveness; in this case we are speaking about a situation in which a text or version is enriched by an un-
spoken context that dwarfs the textual artifact, in which the experience
is filled out—and made traditional—by what the conventionality attracts
to itself from that context. The phrase, or scene, or tale as a whole commands its meaning by synecdoche.

Another way of highlighting this difference is to speak of the relative balance of *conferred* versus *inherent* meaning. In the modern, literary work of art, we place the highest priority on a writer's personal
manipulation of original or inherited materials, rewarding the work

---

[6] On the issue of persistence of oral traditional structures in early medieval
writings, see the dialogue represented in Jesse Gellrich, "Orality, Literacy, and
Crisis in the Later Middle Ages," *Philological Quarterly* 67 (1989): 461–73; and Foley,
"Toward an Oral Aesthetics," *Philological Quarterly* 67 (1989): 475–79. Of related
interest is Brian Stock, *The Implications of Literacy* (Princeton: Princeton Univ. Press,
1983), 42–59.

that strikes out boldly in a new direction by providing a perspective uniquely its own, memorable because it is new, fresh, or, best of all, inimitable. In such a case the work is praised for the finesse with which an author (not a tradition) *confers* meaning on his creation; if the text also draws meaning from literary tradition, it does so only through the careful intercession of the author, who is largely personally responsible not only for what the text encodes, but also for how that encoding takes place.

In contrast, a traditional work depends primarily on elements and strategies that were in place long before the execution of the present version or text, long before the present nominal author learned the inherited craft. Because the idiom is metonymic, summoning conventional connotations to conventional structures, we may say that the meaning it conveys is principally *inherent*. The "author" uses this idiom most felicitously when he or she orchestrates inherent meaning coherently, so that the performance or text makes sense not only at the superficial (that is, decontextualized) level but, more importantly, with reference to the tradition.[7] While no work of verbal art depends exclusively on the one or the other channel for conveying meaning, the traditional work will lean much more heavily on encoding and expression through inherently meaningful forms. That is to say, its "how" will involve not only the inscribed, textual, and made-to-happen, but much more tellingly, the immanent, extratextual, and metonymically implied.

The balance of conferred and inherent meaning can be affected in two major ways. First, the ability of the poet will have a great deal to do with how effectively he or she orchestrates the traditional idiom, for, romantic theories notwithstanding, not all traditional poets are equally talented.[8] The lesser of them use the traditional inheritance

---

[7] Thus, traditionally generated narrative inconsistencies, for example, are not crucial errors; they may disturb the surface of the text at hand, but may not interrupt its metonymic communication with the traditional context. For an illustration of this phenomenon at the level of story-pattern, see Foley, *Traditional Oral Epic*, chap. 10.

[8] Where one has a well-collected tradition to consult, it is possible to gain a sense of the range of poetic talent. Of those Serbo-Croatian *guslari* ("singers, bards; those who play the single-stringed instrument, the *gusle*") recorded by Parry and Lord whom I have been able to analyze (see Foley, *Traditional Oral Epic*, chaps. 4, 8, 10), for example, by far the greatest number are adequate to mediocre bards; they can perform fluently enough, but have limited or redundant repertoires and employ a relatively small subset of the available traditional idiom in making their poetry. Two of the singers from the region of Stolac—Ibro Bašić and Mujo Kukuruzović—have a certain talent: their repertoires are somewhat longer and more varied, and they use the idiom with greater control of its implications. One of the

with limited success; the more accomplished will both command its inherent possibilities with greater precision and fidelity to the tradition, and make more impact by the individual conferral of meaning.[9] Second, as the general theory is tailored to particular cases involving oral-derived texts, it will be necessary to redistribute the balance, moving to some degree toward the pole of conferred meaning. Quite obviously, the poet who embraces to any extent the world of literary texts also must place his or her personal signature on a work, merely by participating in a different mode of artistic creation. But we must not forget that, to a greater or lesser degree, negotiation of meaning through traditional structures will continue to entail inherent connotation as well; the metonymic contract so long in force and so faithfully observed cannot be suddenly suspended or ignored. Indeed, in oral-derived texts the tie to traditional referentiality remains a cornerstone of what may be seen as aesthetic creativity.

Perhaps it is now evident that metonymy and the necessary connotations implied in inherent meaning point in the same direction: toward a whole summoned by its parts, toward a story or event or idea that lies at least in part outside the scope of literary art, toward a medium that has its own rules for expressibility. The paradox is that the primary oral "work" can by its very nature never be wholly captured by textual fossilization; no matter how long or detailed the exposition, no matter what the medium of recording, any one performance or text will remain only a partial record of the oral traditional work. The lesson for oral-derived works is similar: because texts exist as islands in the vast sea of the traditional idiom, only part of their aesthetic reality can be understood by insisting on the islands as the entire known world. And yet each of these versions or texts boasts the authority given it by the power of traditional referentiality, so that

---

Stolac *guslari*, Halil Bajgorić, surpasses Bašić and Kukuruzović in his ability to tell a tale elaborately yet with simplicity and grace, but he does not usually approach Avdo Medjedović, the best of the Parry-Lord singers (see Milman Parry, Albert Lord, and David Bynum, colls., eds., trans., *Serbo-Croatian Heroic Songs (Srpskohrvatske junačke pjesme)* [Cambridge, Mass.: Harvard University Press and Belgrade: Serbian Academy of Sciences, 1953–], esp. vols. 3–4). This situation is exactly what one would expect of poets, traditional or not, in any culture; most are workaday, a few are talented, fewer still are brilliant. It would be wrong to expect each (or perhaps any) *guslar* to measure up to Homer, primus inter pares in ancient Greece and arguably the major figure in western European literature.

[9] It is nonetheless well to remember that the individual contribution, except in the case of the kind of fossilization textuality can provide, is evanescent. Even that fossilization is, of course, only partial; on the textual libretto as an incomplete record of the performance, see, e.g., Elizabeth Fine, *The Folklore Text: From Performance to Print* (Bloomington: Indiana University Press, 1984).

each, according to its lights, summons the work or event or idea metonymically, causing that which is immanent to become part of the
artistic creation in the present time and experience of the individual
version or text. Since it may thus be said that the traditional metonymic signals do not "repeat" but rather *re-create*, the networks of inherent meaning enrich the momentary with the timeless, the situa-
tional with the all-pervasive, the story-specific with the traditional. In
an essential sense, traditional referentiality means that the ever-in-
complete performance or text is the only medium through which we
can completely experience the oral traditional work of art.

That a traditional work and its parts should encode and express
meaning metonymically is expectable; one definition of "traditional"
in this context must after all be "immanent."[10] With respect to text or
version, to narrative structure, and to phrase, what is traditional is implicit, inherent, present even in its silence. What is more, a variety of in-
vestigators dealing with numerous different traditions have come to
parallel conclusions about the experience of the work of art. The reports
of these scholars reveal a startling consistency in their agreement that
pars pro toto representation—what we have been calling metonymic
referentiality—is a fundamental mode of conveying meaning.

In the arena of Serbo-Croatian or Yugoslav epic, focusing on the
shorter Christian songs, Svetozar Koljević has shown that

> dramatic unity lives on formulas and their historical and imag-
> inative implications, on repetition and variation which mark oral
> epic singing as an art of allusion: many lines and many themes
> seem to echo the whole tradition.[11]

This kind of echo cannot, by definition, exist without reference to the
tradition as a whole; without the extratextual body of myth impinging
on the nominal text or version, there can be no such allusion. Thus it is

---

[10] As Werner Kelber phrases it in relation to the oral and the written gospel
("In the Beginning Were the Words: The Apotheosis and Narrative Displacement
of the Logos," *Journal of the American Academy of Religion* 58 [1990]: 503): "In the
absence of visual signifiers and spatialized verbalization, oral signification is more
adequately understood as a dynamic networking of connotative meanings than as
deferment to absent signifieds. Each oral performance can take on significance
within a collective memory shared by hearers. The objective here is to make
meaning present in the context of tradition...." See further Kelber, *The Oral and the
Written Gospel: The Hermeneutics of Speaking and Writing in the Synoptic Tradition,
Mark, Paul, and Q* (Philadelphia: Fortress Press, 1983).

[11] Svetozar Koljević, "Vuk Karadžić and the Achievement of His Singers," in
Vuk Karadžić and South Slavic Tradition, edited by Michael Branch and Celia
Hawkesworth (London: Macmillan, 1993), forthcoming.

that Albert Lord says of the longer Moslem narratives from other singers:

> We have learned that a tradition is made up not of discrete songs but of songs, or, preferably, stories about a limited number of heroes, tales that overlap and intertwine, in such a way that in the experience of both the singer and his traditional audience any one traditional song can evoke subconsciously a large group of other songs, or stories, in the tradition.[12]

Native American taletelling traditions can function similarly, as we learn from perceptive statements like the following caveat from Dell Hymes on the nature of the teller's audience:

> Those who already know the stories would have them brought to mind by the details that were given. The assumption that a part stands adequately for the whole remains alive, and people who credit one with knowledge of the stories sometimes act surprised that one has to ask about a detail that had not been given. . . .[13]

The referential system supporting a traditional version or text is such that what impinges, as distinguished from what is denoted explicitly, is enormously greater than our literary training would lead us to expect. Indeed, even with oral-derived traditional texts from the medieval period, we would do well to retrain ourselves to recognize traditional metonyms; as Alain Renoir puts it,

> familiarity with oral-formulaic elements will enable us to sense much more through association than is explicitly stated in a text composed within the oral-formulaic tradition.[14]

Submerged beneath the surface of the single tale or element lies a wealth of associations accessible only under the agreement of metonymic representation and interpretation. As Robert Kellogg remarks in relation to African, Finnish, and other epic works:

---

[12] Albert B. Lord, "Vuk's Impact on the Tradition: The Importance for Homer," in *Vuk Karadžić and South Slavic Tradition*, edited by Michael Branch and Celia Hawkesworth (London: Macmillan, 1993), forthcoming.

[13] Dell Hymes, "Discovering Oral Performance and Measured Verse in American Indian Narrative," *New Literary History* 8 (1977): 442.

[14] Alain Renoir, "Repetition, Oral-Formulaic Style, and Affective Impact in Mediaeval Poetry: A Tentative Illustration," in *Comparative Research on Oral Traditions: A Memorial for Milman Parry*, edited by John Miles Foley (Columbus, Ohio: Slavica, 1987), 541.

Clearly the necessity for sequence applies to some elements of single performances, but allusions of every sort to the whole never-performed epic are not only possible but necessary. Every performance of a traditional narrative takes place in a vast context of story, and must be understood so by the critic, to exactly the same extent that the opposite assumption must be made about "high" narrative art.[15]

Among the key concepts addressed by this statement is that of sequence, an analytical concept and literary value often invoked in discussions of textual unity. But linear textual progression must remain a secondary feature of oral traditional works, since their primary loyalty is to an order and unity that lie outside the immediate text or version. In Carol Clover's words, "the question arises whether the consecutive approach to narrative—the idea that one starts at the beginning and proceeds to the end—is not merely a literate habit of mind."[16]

Indeed, the notion that we have the "whole work" at our fingertips—not seldom memorialized in a standard edition—is symptomatic of the assumptions customarily made about how works of verbal art convey meaning. The Bhopa who performs Pabuji epic in rural Rajisthan, however, never makes this assumption, singing and dancing episodes from the "whole story" in front of a *par*, a tapestry on which are depicted scenes from the larger epic. In addition to his musical instrument, often the *jantar*, he uses a pointer made of peacock feathers to indicate the one episode—from among the many visually represented behind him—that he will perform, and his assistant further focuses the audience's attention by holding a lamp nearby the appoint-

---

[15] Robert L. Kellogg, "Varieties of Tradition in Medieval Narrative," in *Medieval Narrative: A Symposium*, edited by Hans Bekker-Nielsen et al. (Odense: Odense Univ. Press, 1979), 124–25.

[16] Carol J. Clover, "The Long Prose Form," *Arkiv för nordisk filologi* 101 (1986): 25. Clover's explanation follows upon her proposal of "immanent epic" in oral tradition: "the idea, that is, that there can exist a 'whole' epic in the minds of performers and audiences alike even though it never be performed as such." Both Clover's and Kellogg's prespectives on sequence harmonize well with Eric Havelock's description of the analytical developments ascribable to the coming of literacy and literary thought in ancient Greece (e.g., *Preface to Plato* [Cambridge, Mass.: Harvard Univ. Press, 1963]; "The Linguistic Task of the Presocratics," in *Language and Thought in Early Greek Philosophy*, edited by Kevin Robb [LaSalle, Ill.: Hegeler Institute, 1983], 7–82).

ed place on the *par.*[17] Similarly, with reference to the African *Mwindo Epic* tradition, Daniel Biebuyck reports:

> The interesting point is that the narrator would never recite the entire story in immediate sequence, but would intermittently perform various select passages of it. Mr. Rureke . . . repeatedly asserted that never before had he performed the whole story within a repeated span of days.[18]

Perhaps from one point of view, that which acknowledges the referentiality of traditional materials, both Mr. Rureke of Zaire and the Rajasthani Bhopa allowed their audiences full access to (if not actually performed) the "whole story."

Pars pro toto logic extends from the macrostructure of the tale as a whole to the microstructure of its smallest component parts. As Bridget Connelly observes of Arabic oral epic, "close listening by the scholarly auditor reveals the poet's art as essentially metonymic and integrative." Moreover, "in the segmental mode of composition that the tradition and its parts use, the part contains the whole, the episode the larger sira, and the most minute level of composition, the rhyme, incorporates the story."[19] In the linguistically and generically very different area of Hispanic balladry, the operative mode of signi-

---

[17] For more information on this mode of performance, see Om Prakash Joshi, *Painted Folklore and Folklore Patterns of India* (Delhi: Concept, 1976); and John D. Smith, *The Epic of Pabuji: A Study, Transcription and Translation* (Cambridge: Cambridge Univ. Press, 1991), 14–70.

[18] Daniel P. Biebuyck, ed. and trans. with Kahombo C. Mateene, *The Mwindo Epic from the Banyanga* (Berkeley: Univ. of California Press, 1969), 14. On the question of episodes and the entirety of the tale, Biebuyck adds elsewhere: "I conclude, . . . from my experience among the Nyanga and Lega that, in practice, there is a complete text in the mind of every knowledgeable individual narrator—a text that has a beginning and an end—which follows a basic structure and constitutes a coherent and well-rounded whole" ("The Epic as a Genre in Congo Oral Literature," in *African Folklore*, edited by Richard M. Dorson [Garden City, New Jersey: Doubleday, 1972], 266).

[19] Bridget Connelly, *Arab Folk Epic and Identity* (Berkeley: Univ. of California Press, 1986), 56. Later on (187), she notes that never before the recent advent of serious collection by the folklorist-entrepreneur have the singers ever been asked to perform the "whole" epic. Biebuyck furnishes another example of metonymic signification in his remarks on the function of personal names in Nyanga tales ("Names in Nyanga Society and in Nyanga Tales," in *Comparative Research on Oral Traditions: A Memorial for Milman Parry,* edited by John Miles Foley [Columbus, Ohio: Slavica, 1987], 61): "The names reveal, overtly or covertly, a quality, a skill, a character trait, a physical feature, or an ambiguity about the actor(s). They dispense with further elaborate description and announce the tone and plot development of the tale, regardless of the setting or activity involved."

fication is strikingly similar. Diego Catalán puts it this way:

> Formulas are tropes; they mean something different from the phrases of which they are made up. Although the literal information that a formulaic expression offers cannot be rejected as not being pertinent, since it generally represents a realistic visualization of the plot, what matters for the development of that plot is the "lexicalized" meaning of that expression. *The formula is synecdochic in that it designates by means of a restricted concrete representation something of a broader or more abstract reality* (emphasis mine).[20]

Catalán's formula—and here the model could and should be extended to all phraseological and narrative metonyms—conveys its meaning by an institutionalized association, its simple, denotative concreteness standing by prior agreement for a richer, more complex, and more resonant reality.[21]

Such a prior agreement demands both the poet's and the audience's adherence to established rules in what Receptionalist critics would view as their mutual project of creating the traditional work of art. Unless they both proceed in accord with what has been negotiated by those who engaged in the same activity in earlier times, the project will be a failure.[22] Either the text will be unintelligible, the victim of indeterminacy unrelieved by the traditional signals that act as points of reference, or the audience will find themselves at a loss because of a lack of "training," unable to communicate in the unfamiliar language of the text.

§

---

[20] Diego Catalán, "The Artisan Poetry of the *Romancero*," *Oral Tradition* 2 (1987): 410.

[21] Compare Howard Bloch's formulation of the relationship between signifier and signified in the verbal art of the early Middle Ages (*Etymologies and Genealogies: A Literary Anthropology of the French Middle Ages* [Chicago: Univ. of Chicago Press, 1983], 101): ". . . the importance of signification—meaning determined by the fixed relation between words or stock phrases and their extralinguistic attribute—overshadows the contextually defined production of meaning through the surface play of self-signifying terms."

[22] This does not mean that the author and reader must adhere slavishly to the rules of earlier generations, contributing nothing of their own, but it does call for some connection to the "givens" of artistic creation within the history of the art form. What is at risk without such (natural and in most cases undeliberate) adherence is intelligibility.

Since the rules for the communication of verbal art must be only a small and highly specialized subset of the rules for linguistic communication in general, and since, further, the rules for a given genre, for example, must comprise an even smaller and more limited set, we should recognize that the creation of fictional "reality" in any given medium is founded on a text-reader agreement of a particular kind. To borrow a phrase from the art historian Ernst Gombrich, it is an agreement that the representation of reality will be "a transposition, not a copy."[23] In fact, the various styles of pictorial representation studied in his appropriately named *Art and Illusion* offer a suggestive analogy for our present discussion.

As Gombrich convincingly illustrates, a style of painting can be said to convey reality only because it embodies that reality by illusion. Making reference to myriad forms of visual representation, he shows time and again that most artists make no attempt either to "photograph" or to "truthfully re-create" a scene or person, but rather transpose the subject of their work into a limited, agreed-upon code—from which metonymic intermediary the perceiver once again registers a reality. The impression received by the admirer of a Constable landscape painting, for example, depends not upon true-to-life colors or architecturally perfect lines, but rather on the internal logic of the artist's idiom and its intelligibility to whoever views his or her work.[24]

In a traditional art, one which depends primarily on inherent over conferred meaning, the code for pictorial representation becomes more metonymic and the relationships among its parts become more institutionalized within the artistic idiom. Thus, as Gombrich observes, visual stereotypes take on acquired meanings that speak volumes, and the "repetitive" pictorial language is rife with implication. If indeed "the mind of the beholder also has its share in the imitation,"[25] and if that mind is filled with information on and strategies for translating structure to image according to traditional criteria, then stereotypes must be the order of the day for all of the generations that employ them.

What is more, perhaps we can now appreciate that these stereotypes comprise not simply a convenient method of representation but a *set of cognitive categories*. If the interpretive compact "signed" by

---

[23] Ernst Gombrich, *Art and Illusion: A Study in the Psychology of Pictorial Representation*, 4th ed. (London: Phaidon Press, 1972), 41.

[24] For a fine discussion of Constable's artistic idiom, see Gombrich, *Art and Illusion*, 29ff.; near the end of this discussion he observes that "a style, like a culture or climate of opinion, sets up a horizon of expectation, a mental set, which registers deviations and modifications with exaggerated sensitivity" (53).

[25] Gombrich, *Art and Illusion*, 155.

painter and viewer alike is adhered to, both participants are perceiving according to these categories; to put it even more strongly, they cannot share perception without them. Gombrich recognizes this fundamental point when he notes that the artistic idiom of a traditional culture determines the perceptual process at both ends, that is, in encoding as well as decoding: "the relatively rigid vocabulary of the Chinese tradition acts as a selective screen which admits only the features for which schemata exist."[26] This is the double edge of stereotypes deployed as cognitive patterns; by virtue of their inherent meaning they can convey enormously more than structures invented for the uniqueness of the present moment, but the connotative burden they bear "restricts" the artist who uses them to the referentiality they command.[27] From the modern viewpoint, detached as it is from metonymic representation, this seems a high price to pay; the modern wants to find a place for the new, the original, the heretofore unportrayed. But tradition sees it otherwise: to leave behind the stereotypes is to cancel out the immanent complexity subsumed in the simple form.

What the simple forms amount to, then, is an artificial code for portrayer and perceiver. Like the Homeric epic language, which was comprised of a dialectal mélange never spoken by anyone except as the special language of epic poetry, this code cannot be viewed as "realistic" or denotatively correspondent to the image it presents. Artifice creates illusion, as, in Gombrich's words, "we tend to project life and expression onto the arrested image and supplement from our experience what is not actually present."[28] Of course, in the case of oral traditional works the question of whether the supplementary material is really present is a phenomenological one: it may not be physically present in the text or performance before us, but, being ever-immanent, it is so necessarily implied that one would have difficulty denying its "presence." But however the case is construed, the fact remains that Gombrich has shown how simple forms conjure complex artistic illusions in partnership with the perceiver, and that these forms amount to cognitive categories that serve as the communicative idiom for the aesthetic experience.

Likewise, in the audience's or reader's act of co-creating the oral

---

[26] Gombrich, *Art and Illusion*, 73.

[27] This "restriction" exists only in the mind of the post-traditional artist or perceiver, who, having fragmented the metonymic system of representation, must struggle to represent its parts without the advantage of traditional referentiality.

[28] Gombrich, "The Mask and the Face: The Perception of Physiognomic Likeness in Life and Art," in *Art, Perception, and Reality*, edited by Maurice Mandelbaum (Baltimore, Md.: Johns Hopkins Univ. Press, 1972), 17.

traditional work, the perceiver may be said to resort to the making of
illusions based on the text and prior experience. The simple forms at
the mutual command of the poet and audience are the traditional
structures of the text, to be imbued with extratextual meaning, in a
manner not unlike that which Gombrich describes for ancient Chinese
and Egyptian art.[29] The crucial point of the analogy, however, is that
these traditional structures—far from being mere phraseological and
narrative counters that allow the poet to compose easily and without
interruption—are *the very cognitive categories that underlie the artistic
act.*[30] These forms, in other words, provide nothing less than the
foundation on which the aesthetic experience takes shape and the
perceptual grid through which it is transmitted. It is no exaggeration
to say that the traditional structures enable the aesthetic experience.
The converse is also true: without these cognitive categories, traditional art is disabled; in fact, unless the artist and perceiver know
how to interpret the simple forms as the complex reality they stand
for, the illusion will collapse and the song will be silenced.

Transposing into a specialized idiom presupposes an implied audience able to "speak" the idiom. Because the translation to metonymic language shifts the bulk of the burden of signification from the
textual and denotative to the traditional and connotative, the simple
forms of phraseology and narrative structure are not as important in
and of themselves as those of us trained in literary criticism might assume. The relationship between a traditional structure and its metonymic implication is at its core a *nominal* one, precisely because the
phrase or narrative element stands for a reality it cannot denotatively
embody. This is not to say that there can be no superficial, external
logic to the deployment of traditional structures; indeed, as Catalán
recognized in respect to Hispanic balladry, we cannot do without an
ordered surface. But the special magic of traditional metonymy works
because there is a fixed relation between structure and meaning, a relation that is, as we have seen, more than literary.

---

[29] E.g., Gombrich, *Art and Illusion*, 73–75.

[30] That traditional structures—rather than such literary items as paragraphs,
chapters, or even (conventionally defined) words—should comprise the basic
cognitive categories in oral tradition is confirmed in an instructive way by some of
the Serbo-Croatian *guslari* interviewed and recorded by Parry and Lord. Three
different singers from the Stolac region, for example, when asked what a "word"
(*reč*) was in a song, replied by reciting one or more whole lines; during discussion
it became apparent that they thought of a "word" as a unified utterance rather
than a dictionary entry, and that for them it designated a unit between one line and
an entire song in length. For a fuller description and a comparison with the ancient
Greek *epos* and Old English *word*, see Foley, *Traditional Oral Epic*, 44–50, 157, 219.

Given this relation, we would seem to need a new perspective on the idea and implications of "repetition" in oral traditional works. For centuries critics have lambasted Homer, to take perhaps the most prominent example, for his apparent inclination to repeat himself, to use the same phrase or scene where a cultured literary sensibility tells us he should have introduced a pleasingly original variation. Translators, for instance, have not seldom balked at rendering formulaic expressions with the same English phrase each time,[31] and those oralists content with a merely metrical logic underlying such consistency of naming and portraying have produced no satisfactory artistic explanation of repetition.

Taking into account what we have learned about the referential process in oral traditional works, perhaps we can now understand that "repetition" is in fact a misnomer. If the anaphoric fields associated with phrases and scenes were simply contiguous lines or passages in the unique work, then one could speak with some authority of the poet's having "repeated" these elements, having used them once again. The primary relationship between or among the items in question would be a linear one confined to a single, invariable text; there would be a "first" instance followed by one or more "repetitions," and one could describe the lines or text in question as coextensive with the referential field.

But for the oral traditional element, whether employed in the oral performance or in an oral-derived text, the referential field is, as we have seen, coextensive not with any single line, passage, or text, but rather with the tradition as a whole. Under these conditions there is no "first" occurrence of a traditional structure nor any "subsequent" usage; each instance of the phrase or scene is both ubiquitous and unique in that it commands a fixed referent, an inherent meaning, every time it appears, but without necessary recourse to an earlier or later partner. The linear aspect of the text has only limited importance here, since whatever has a beginning, middle, and end in itself also has a larger identity vis-à-vis the poetic tradition. Traditional elements can no more "repeat themselves" than a much-told traditional tale can be frozen into a uniquely authoritative form.[32] Each element

---

[31] Robert Fitzgerald often translates a formulaic phrase differently from one occurrence to the next in his *Homer, The Odyssey* (New York: Doubleday, 1961); for Fitzgerald's views on phraseology and Parry's theories, see pp. 490ff.

[32] In order to "repeat themselves," traditional elements would have to be severed from their primary allegiance to extratextual meanings and confined to the carefully circumscribed arena of the unique and therefore authoritative text.

in the idiom, comprising as it does a cognitive category whose meaning lies chiefly in what it connotes, can occur—bringing with it all of the referentiality accorded it by tradition—and then, later on, it may occur again. But the primary relationship of these occurrences will be to the metonymic meaning each summons, and not to each other. Instead of "repetition," the oral traditional text implies *re-creation*, and it is this mode of signification its audience is asked to share.

Thus we once again confront a phenomenological difference between the literary and the oral traditional work. Re-creation of the oral traditional work—either its parts or the whole—is an activity very much unlike what we call repetition, for it demands as response that we put aside the analytical tools designed for literary dissection and learn to find meaning in the institutionalized relationship between the simple form and its complex referent.[33] To focus on the phrases and scenes at the expense of their metonymic meaning is to reduce re-creation to repetition, and thus to denature the traditional idiom. Even when in oral-derived, transitional texts we are presented with mixed signals for the decoding of textual structures—with some oral traditional and some quite literary responses called for—it will be a mistake to level this hybrid character to the smooth surface of denotative, post-traditional, purely textual signification. Their surface morphology notwithstanding, oral traditional structures have enormous and consistently realized referentiality, all aspects of which are available to the poet and the audience who together create the work of art. And they do so in imitation of generations gone before them, without repeating a single word.

§

In the space that remains, let me offer a few brief but I hope indic-

---

[33] Of the simple forms of phraseology and narrative pattern, Franz H. Bäuml ("The Theory of Oral-Formulaic Composition and the Written Medieval Text," in *Comparative Research on Oral Traditions: A Memorial for Milman Parry*, edited by John Miles Foley [Columbus, Ohio: Slavica, 1987], 34) writes: "By increasing semantic redundancy, they [the formulas and themes] decrease the indeterminacy of a text, its possibilities for interpretation. The decrease in indeterminacy, which is brought about by the 'thrifty' use of traditional stereotypes, aids the conservation of tradition in the production of the 'message' of the text as well as in its reception. Along with this reduced indeterminacy, the 'thrift' of formulas and themes also determines the participation of the audience in the production of the text in performance." I would add that these and other traditional structures not only ensure conservation and affect audience participation; because they are metonyms, they also make present the extratextual world of the tradition, enriching the aesthetic experience.

ative illustrations of how traditional referentiality comes into play when we consider the aesthetic content of actual oral and oral-derived works. The first example is a formulaic phrase employed by the Parry-Lord *guslari* from the region of Stolac, whose songs I have been editing, and by other Serbo-Croatian singers as well:

A od tala na noge skočijo

And he jumped up from the ground to his feet.

This rather homely line seems simply to describe a person getting to his or her feet from a sitting or prone position and is ubiquitous in the Stolac singers' repertoires. In addition to its raw frequency of occurrence, however, the *od tala* phrase also offers us the opportunity to test the explanatory power of traditional referentiality, for there are not a few cases in which its content appears to be highly unusual and even jarringly out of place. These problematic instances must lead us to ask whether the *guslar* is either inattentively nodding or resorting to ready-made, generic phraseology that fails to fit certain situations in every detail—a familiar dilemma.

Two typical examples of the deployment of this phrase will furnish a rough idea of its contribution to context. Near the middle of Mujo Kukuruzović's *The Captivity of Ograšćić Alija*, a minor hero, Gojenović Ibro, is called upon to risk his life in order to deliver a message. Fulfilling this command means penetrating enemy lines, and Ibro is not likely to survive the attempt. Nonetheless, "he jumped up from the ground to his feet" ("A od tala na noge skočijo"),[34] and went courageously off to an almost certain death. In an instance in Halil Bajgorić's *Halil Rescues Bojičić Alija*, the Turkish hero of the given title braves the Christian stronghold of Kotar in order to complete his mission. With the help of the innkeeper Mara, the female intermediary figure heavy with traditional associations, he secures Bojičić Alija's release. As a reward for this heroic action, Alija offers Halil the honor of immediately claiming his betrothed, Alija's sister Zlata, without assembling the usual wedding party. In response "Halil jumped to his feet from the ground" ("Halil skoči na noge od tala"[35]).

---

[34] Text *6617*, line 1034. Here and below I quote unpublished texts and recordings from the Milman Parry Collection at Harvard University, with the permission of the Curator, using the notation devised by Milman Parry and Albert Lord. Italic numerals indicate sung or recited texts preserved in acoustic form, Roman numerals designate texts taken down in writing from dictation. Editions and translations are my own.

[35] It will be noted that this line, 6703.627, is Bajgorić's idiolectal variant of the

In neither of these two examples does the denotative meaning of the line—that the hero quickly assumes a standing position—seem to mesh particularly well with the narrative context, so we may want to consider what other kind of meaning they might convey. In both cases, the character performing the action is responding honorably and heroically to a chain of events that has led to the present crux; the burden now passes to him and he must react, for to do otherwise would be cowardly or demeaning. Whether the driving force behind his reaction be fidelity to the heroic code (far the more common motivation) or adherence to social custom, the illocutionary force of this phrase emphasizes his alacrity in responding to a difficult or unusual situation. Instead of merely describing a physical movement, then, the phrase seems to connote a heroic or honorable response to an unexpected or threatening turn of events that demands the principal's immediate attention.

Within another song, Ibro Bašić's *Alagić Alija and Velagić Selim*, this traditional and metonymic implication, as clearly distinct from the nominal denotative meaning of the phrase, harmonizes well with the inherent meaning of its surroundings. At line 536, for example, Velagić Selim, returning home from prison according to the agreement for temporary release he struck with his captor, the ban, spies his tower overgrown with ivy and a large encampment of troops in the nearby plain. This sight prompts him to "jump up from the ground to his feet,"[36] and he then continues down into the marketplace and the town until he reaches his home, where, still disguised, he will challenge and defeat the rival suitors in athletic competition, causing them eventually to flee. Velagić Selim's response is certainly *heroic* and *honorable*, for he is thinking as he should of his wife, mother, and home, and the situation he is forced to confront is without doubt both *unexpected* and *threatening*; although AA had previously warned him of the dilapidated dwelling and the existence of a rival, he must now face the reality of the armed force gathered for the purpose of assuming control over all that he holds dear.

Less obvious, and in its way correspondingly more illuminating, is the instance of the same phrase later in the song (line 837). By this point the tale has shifted focus to the prisoner Alagić Alija, who, despairing of life, has written a last will and testament releasing his be-

---

phrase under consideration, formed under the same traditional rules that govern related phrases. For discussion of idiolectal phraseology and traditional rules in the *deseterac* (decasyllable) epic poetry, see Foley, *Traditional Oral Epic*, chap. 5.

[36] 6597.536: A od tala na noge skočijo.

trothed Fata from her nuptial promise and instructing his mother to divide or sell his possessions. The messenger bearing this unhappy missive knocks at the gate of the hero's tower, and his old mother, head of the household in Alagić Alija's absence, orders Fata to go down to the courtyard and ascertain who has arrived. Out of duty to her prospective mother-in-law, a duty that derives from and bespeaks her fidelity to Alagić Alija, Fata "jumped up from the ground to her feet"—"A od tala na noge skočila." As the italicized feminine ending to the past participle indicates, the action is without doubt the young woman's, even though the "ground" she "jumps up from" is the upper chamber in her future mother-in-law's *kula*. In other words, neither the action, much too rough and ready for the young woman at this juncture, nor the description of the place she occupies suits the immediate narrative situation. What has happened is obvious: the *guslar* has not erred, nor has he yielded mindlessly to the pressures of a generic, ready-made idiom; rather he has harnessed a phrase of nominal denotative significance but of institutionalized inherent meaning to describe "an honorable response to an unexpected or threatening turn of events that demands the principal's immediate attention."

If such a phrase can be used of a young woman in her in-laws' chamber without violation of narrative logic, indeed employed fluently and idiomatically with full traditional resonance, then we may not be surprised to encounter other superficially "inappropriate" usages. One of the most striking in the *Alagić Alija and Velagić Selim* involves Muminaga, Fata's father to whom the girl writes for help as she prepares to journey to Zadar in an attempt to rescue her imprisoned fiancé. Along with the letter requesting aid in the form of an army, she cautions the servant and messenger Huso to observe a detailed protocol in his approach to Muminaga; should her father accept her request, she says, Huso may expect hospitality and fair treatment, but should the old man react negatively to the message, its bearer had better absent himself quickly. The underlying cultural dilemma here is how an aged hero of great prominence will deal with the cancellation of his daughter's wedding plans, especially when it is the bridegroom who has cancelled them. There is a question of honor and reputation involved that goes far beyond the betrothal per se,[37] and it

---

[37] A wedding in Moslem epic is no small undertaking, especially for the parents of the bride and the groom, and customarily involves the sending of numerous invitations and the assembling of an enormous wedding party. In facing a rupture of his daughter's marriage contract, Muminaga thus stood to be severely dishonored among his peers.

is this question that worries Fata and, as we shall see, quite predictably exercises her father.

When Huso delivers the letter, Muminaga stares at its contents for
a moment and then reacts as Fata feared (and as the metonymic structure and content of her prior warning actually implied):

> Od tala je na noge skočijo;
> Kako lako dedo pa skočijo!—
> A bi rek'o, a bi se zakleo
> Nema dedi vet' dvadeset ljeta.
>
> He jumped up from the ground to his feet;
> How easily the old man jumped up!—
> One would say, and one would swear
> That the old man hadn't more than twenty summers.[38]

In his rage over the insult done him and his family, Muminaga may
nominally, at the most superficial narrative level, be visualized as
leaping to his feet, but metonymically he is "responding heroically
and honorably to an unexpected or threatening turn of events that
demands his immediate attention." The extent to which this phrase
acts as a cognitive category, as a metonym with extra-situational import, may be glimpsed in the three lines that follow it. Here the poet
adds to the inherent force of the phrase by emphasizing how unusual
it is for an elderly man like Muminaga to carry on in this way. At
one level he speaks of the patriarch's surprising athleticism, of course,
but more fundamentally the brief passage stresses Muminaga's incan-
descent rage and the nature of the response such a hero must make,
in spite of his age.

This brief phrase thus offers an example of how much distance
may exist between the concrete denotative meaning of a phrase and
its institutionalized referentiality.[39] Although the two levels of signification may be complementary, the superficial meaning, nominal as

---

[38] 6597.995–98.

[39] Other lines from the Stolac songs which we might see as related, verses such
as "A Huso je na noge skočijo" (6597.1073) and "A cura je na noge skočila" ("And
the young girl [Fata] jumped to her feet," 6597.1185), embody virtually the same
inherent meaning. On the relationship between and among phrases in this traditional diction, see Foley, *Traditional Oral Epic*, chap. 5. It is only prudent to acknowledge the possibility that the *od tala* phraseology may have other implications
in the songs of singers from other regions; it would be rash to assume an archetypal unity of meaning without evidence. For the purpose of demonstrating the
principle of traditional referentiality, however, it is sufficient that the Stolac
community uses this phrase with a consistent metonymic implication.

it must be in this poetics of immanence, does not itself contain the inherent association. Once textualized and cut off from its traditional context, "A od tala na noge skočijo" and its morphological kin will appear to indicate only that the named character jumps to his or her feet—nothing more, nothing less—and the audience or readership will be at a complete loss to justify what will in many cases seem to be an inappropriate or irrelevant description. The key to a faithful interpretation, that is, to bridging the gap left at this point in the concrete surface of the performance libretto, is to recognize the metonymic signal for what it is, and to use the map of traditional referentiality to make the immanent signification part and parcel of the (co-)created work.

Turning now to the Homeric oral-derived and traditional epics, we might first mention the most obvious case of the much-studied noun-epithet formulas. On the basis of what has been said, we would expect the noun-epithet phrases to serve as metonymic pathways to the poetic conjuring of personalities. Like similar phrases in other traditions, the Homeric naming formulas should neither respond primarily to context nor reduce simply to generic "fillers"; rather they should reach outside of individual instances to larger-than-textual realities, and stand pars pro toto for complexes of ideas too evanescent for commitment to the single occurrence.

If the Homeric idiom is understood in this fashion, if it is reinvested with even a portion of its traditional metonymic resonance, then many of the problems that have beset scholars wrangling over conflicts between mechanism and aesthetics fall away. Anne Amory Parry's jousts with oralists, most memorably in her monograph on "blameless Aegisthos,"[40] Paolo Vivante's excellent study of the art of the epithets,[41] and numerous other works of philology and aesthetic criticism can be in part assimilated to studies of the traditional structures of phrase and scene, if we are truly ready to consider both sides of the question. Vivante, for example, for all of his insight into the poetic meaning of the epithetic phrases, criticizes the "Parryists, [who] ascribe this style to traditional phraseology, to traditional themes, and to the need of oral composition, thus leaving us in the dark as to any fundamentally poetic reason" and, speaking of the "rosy-fingered dawn" and "winged words" formulas, claims that

---

[40] Anne Amory Parry, *Blameless Aegisthus: A Study of AMΥΜΩΝ and Other Homeric Epithets* (Leiden: E.J. Brill, 1973).

[41] Paolo Vivante, *The Epithets in Homer: A Study in Poetic Values* (New Haven: Yale Univ. Press, 1982).

"from an aesthetic point of view, it does not make the slightest difference whether they are traditional or not."[42]

But it does make a difference, a crucial one, for the traditional
provenance of Homer's phraseology is the very source of its expressive-
ness, of its extratextual connotation, of its referentiality. Indeed, Vivante
speaks eloquently of precisely the kind of meaning we have been calling
metonymic when he explains that "the very way a thing is named fills
us with a satisfying sense of what it is. The feeling of beauty is not
directly expressed, but it is always implicit."[43] It is implicit not because a literary, post-traditional Homer has done the categorically
impossible—built up an extra-situational, extratextual network of
necessary associations in the close confines of a single text, but rather
because a poet steeped in the traditional idiom *and its necessary
implications* has harnessed them brilliantly, achieving an individual
realization of traditional potentials and through the single text or performance providing his audience entry into the world of mythos.[44]
A major part of Homer's eloquence is that he is the grand conveyor
of inherent meaning, the master rhetorician whose figures of anaphora have larger-than-textual fields of reference.

The metonymic content of such an idiom may be glimpsed as well
in phrases outside the noun-epithet system, but still very much within the arena of traditional referentiality. At one end of the spectrum,
simple congruency with traditional rules for generating phraseology
amounts to the "speech-act" signature that invokes the authority of
the epic tradition. What follows, the mere form certifies, will take place
in the special and familiar arena of heroic epic song.[45] This most general level of metonymic implication thus allows the audience and poet
to place themselves in the proper frame of reference, in a world of
story resonant with prior associations and open to further exploration

---

[42] Vivante, 56, 169.

[43] Vivante, 118. At 147 he adds this on the dynamics of the epithets: "When
they occur, they help contain a single act or state in its sudden *immanence*" (emphasis mine).

[44] Compare the findings of Michael Nagler on the traditional and the "spontaneous" (*Spontaneity and Tradition: A Study in the Oral Art of Homer* [Berkeley:
Univ. of California Press, 1974], esp. chaps. 1–2).

[45] This adherence to traditional rules is not equivalent to the literate artist's
adherence to form. Traditional rules prescribe not a "recipe" for an external form
but criteria for admissibility to an idiom; the apparent structures that result—for
instance formulas and formulaic systems—are second-level products that may
eventually gain lives of their own (see Foley, *Traditional Oral Epic*, chap. 4) but
which are at root only the hypostatized issue of rules that remain dynamic and
open-ended.

according to a map of metonymic meaning already shared by all involved.

Regions defined by this referential map include, for example, the combinations of formulaic "answering" and related expressions studied comparatively by Parry himself as early as 1933. Far from having situation-specific relevance, these expressions introduce a type of Homeric event, sounding the knell, as it were, for a character's action or reply. Other relatively large elements include the whole-line rhetorical marker "ἀλλ' ἄγε, μοί τόδε εἰπὲ, καὶ ἀτρεκέως κατάλεξον" ("But come, speak it to me, and tell me truthfully"), common to both the *Iliad* and the *Odyssey* as an indication that the focus of the conversation is about to change to an important, often hidden or secret subject that will require sharing a confidence with the interrogator.[46] As another level of metonymic referentiality, we may point to what James Holoka has shown about the implicit content of the phrase *hypodra idôn* ("looking darkly"), which "conveys anger on the part of a speaker who takes umbrage at what he judges to be rude or inconsiderate words spoken by the addressee."[47]

All of these elements, and of course countless others, reveal the structural complexity and metonymic richness of a phraseology made up of simple forms. It can neither be reduced to lock-step mechanism nor diluted to metrically appropriate "essential ideas." Moreover, and most importantly, Homeric diction is not "literary" in its power of inherent signification; imbedded in the idiomatic fabric are metonymic meanings derivable only from the extratextual context. In this complexity, so apparent on both structural and aesthetic levels, lies the proof that Homer, far from being an artist held in thrall by his diction, depends on its referentiality, the depth of its resonance, as the wellspring of his poetic art.

In considering the diction of *Beowulf*, we move still further away from the tradition-dependent model of Serbo-Croatian epic, not only to oral-derived texts but also a phraseology structurally rather remote

---

[46] In the *Odyssey* this line most often serves as a rhetorical marker to shift the conversation toward ascertaining a guest's lineage and mode of transportation (e.g., 1.169, 8.572); but it can also introduce questions as painful as Odysseus' asking his mother how she died (11.170) and his father whose land he is tending (24.256). The metonym appears with similar force in the *Iliad* where, for example, Odysseus demands that Dolon divulge information about Hektor and the Trojan army (10.405), and Achilles asks Priam how many days will be needed for Hektor's funeral (24.656).

[47] James P. Holoka, "'Looking Darkly' (ΥΠΟΔΡΑ ΙΔΩΝ): Reflections on Status and Decorum in Homer," *Transactions of the American Philological Association* 113 (1983): 1–16.

from its ancient Greek and Serbo-Croatian counterparts. Because the
Old English symbiosis of meter and traditional idiom was established
under the aegis of a prosody primarily dependent not on syllable-
count and caesurae but on syllabic stress and half-line alliteration, the
encapsulated units so typical of Serbo-Croatian and Homeric phraseology are almost totally absent. What occurs instead is a regularity of
stress sequence and alliteration that contribute to a set of tradition-dependent compositional rules.[48] These rules prescribe word-type placement and other parameters and create a background for recurrent diction, with the recurrency manifesting itself principally as single roots of
words with a much more malleable immediate environment than is true
of either of the other two phraseologies.

Against this background, the noun-epithet phrases constitute the
most focused elements in the spectrum of phraseology, both structurally and metonymically. But far the more common—really the typical—kind of phraseology one encounters in Old English poetry
consists, as we might predict, of a spectrum of much more loosely organized diction formed under the aegis of traditional rules. As noted
above, since these rules are based on the tradition-dependent features
of stress and alliteration, metonyms tend to be not the encapsulated
phraseology of ancient Greek and Serbo-Croatian epic but the root
syllables of stressed and alliterating words. And because Old English
prosody actually encourages enjambement and actively discourages
economy through the compositional figure of variation,[49] roots can
also be bound into a *cluster* of items, the whole rather than the individual parts achieving a traditional identity. Or, if the alliterative
pattern is more prominent than stressed syllables, the multi-element
pattern may take shape as a *succession of half-lines*. In fact, we find in
Beowulf evidence of half-line phrases, whole- and multi-line patterns,
alliterative collocations, and clusters, and we should be aware that
each of these traditional structures bears some degree of metonymic
meaning.

---

[48] Indeed, when such units do appear, and they do so only very rarely, it is not
because they are in any direct way the product of traditional rules for Old English
phraseology, but rather because circumstances conspire to fossilize a particularly
useful phrase. For a full explanation of the tradition-dependent character of Old
English diction, see Foley, *Traditional Oral Epic*, chap. 6.

[49] Fred C. Robinson ("Two Aspects of Variation in Old English Poetry," in *Old
English Poetry: Essays on Style*, edited by Daniel G. Calder [Berkeley: Univ. of
California Press, 1979], 129) defines *variation* as "syntactically parallel words or
word-groups which share a common referent and which occur within a single
clause." See further Robinson, *Beowulf and the Appositive Style* (Knoxville: Univ. of
Tennessee Press, 1985).

For an example of meaning conveyed through traditional narrative patterns in Old English verse, meaning that could not be made available except through the referential resources of the metonymic idiom, we may consider the "Joy in the Hall" theme found in numerous Anglo-Saxon poems.[50] Here, in the tradition-dependent shape taken by some Old English multiforms, the core of the theme consists of a cluster of key words, among them *gomen* ("joy"), *song* or *singan* ("song" or "to sing"), and *sweg* ("sound"). That is, the pattern of "Joy in the Hall" depends primarily not on any prescribed sequence of actions, but rather on the concatenation of these and other words, the group comprising a metonymic element that calls up a certain traditional context.[51] When these words co-occur, they jointly refer to celebration—feasting and traditional singing—in the hall, the Anglo-Saxon analog of the ancient Greek "Feast" theme in metonymic implication.

As Jeff Opland has shown, there are some seven occurrences of this small theme in *Beowulf*,[52] each juxtaposing the inherent meaning of "Joy in the Hall" against the specific action at various points in the poem. In order to fill out the picture and to give a further example of traditional referentiality, we may adduce another instance of the same theme from another poem. In *The Seafarer*, an oral-derived text probably further removed from oral tradition than *Beowulf*, we hear that the exiled protagonist has lost all attachment to human community and is forced to suffer alone on the sea:

> Hwilum ylfete *song*
> dyde ic me to *gomene*, ganetes hleoþor
> ond huilpan *sweg* fore hleahtor wera,
> mæw *singende* fore medodrince.

> At times the swan's *song*
> I took as my *joy*, the gannet's cry
> and the curlew's *sound* in place of men's laughter,
> the seagull *singing* in place of mead-drinking.[53]

---

[50] For detailed structural analyses, see Jeff Opland, "*Beowulf* on the Poet," *Mediaeval Studies* 38 (1976): 442–67, and Foley, "Genre(s) in the Making: Diction, Audience, and Text in the Old English *Seafarer*," *Poetics Today*, 4 (1983): 683–706.

[51] Old English themes may also be primarily sequences of actions, with no specific phraseology uniting the instances; see further Foley, *Traditional Oral Epic*, chap. 9. Compare Donald K. Fry's distinction between "theme" and "type-scene" ("Old English Formulaic Themes and Type-Scenes," *Neophilologus* 52 [1968]: 48–54).

[52] Opland, 449.

[53] *The Seafarer*, edited by I.L. Gordon (New York: Appleton-Century-Crofts, 1966), lines 19b–22.

Clearly enough, the simple juxtaposition of the two situations—the exiled speaker's deprivation versus the archetypal rite of community—creates a memorable tension, driving home just what it means to be without the cultural shelter of the *comitatus*. But what charges this scene with a more than literary electricity is the metonymic force of the "Joy in the Hall" theme as summoned by the key words. The traditional idiom reinforces the literary progress of the narrative by contrasting the immediate situation with that which is immanent, by playing off the abject loneliness of the Seafarer against the ideal condition of order and happiness among one's fellows. Whatever we decide about the actual provenance of the *Seafarer* text in relation to oral tradition and literary artistry—and this is open to some debate—to silence the traditional resonance of "Joy in the Hall" in these lines is to miss the richness and complexity inherent in the simple form, and thus to miss an important aspect of the poem's aesthetic excellence.

§

The usual charge levelled against oral traditional works is that they are repetitive, monotonous, somehow inferior to the stately *literature* extolled as the precious possession of "high culture." We sometimes hear this bias in accounts from the field by collectors and ethnographers who ought to know better, and we hear it more often from medievalists and classicists who also ought to know better. Indeed, as Albert Lord, Walter Ong, and others have shown either explicitly or implicitly, the literate and literary prejudice runs deep; it is hard for us to credit a perceptual and expressive mode so utterly different from the one we use to describe that difference. It is difficult even for the unbiased to maintain a clear focus on the dynamics, the phenomenology of oral tradition, and to keep on explaining—to ourselves as well as to others—what is for us a vestigial medium.

As for *repetition*, as explained earlier it seems to me an irrelevant concept, a non-category in respect to oral tradition. And as for *monotony*, I agree wholeheartedly with Rita Lejeune's brilliant *riposte* more than thirty-five years ago on the traditional qualities of the Old French epic:

> Les chansons de geste aux formes immuables sont 'monotones'
> comme sont 'monotones' les sculptures romanes—et même
> gothiques—de nos cathédrales, avec leurs thèmes identiques:
> 'Jugement dernier' ou 'Anonciation' à leur portail. . . .

The *chansons de geste* set in their immutable forms are "monotonous" in the same way as the Romanesque—and even Gothic—sculptures of our cathedrals are "monotonous," with their identical themes: "Last Judgment" or "The Annunciation" on their portals. . . .[54]

Like those great cathedrals, whose uniquely managed iconographic programs drew their vitality as much from what was implied as from what was physically depicted, oral traditional art will speak most eloquently to us only when we learn its metonymic mother tongue. Then we will understand how, in a world of verbal art enormously larger than even the most expansive text, the very richest and most complex meanings are natural partners to the very simplest of forms.

---

[54] Rita Lejeune, "Technique formulaire et chansons de geste," *Le Moyen âge* 60 (1954): 331.

CARL LINDAHL

The Oral Undertones of
Late Medieval Romance

M any of the Middle Ages' most dramatic oppositions are centered in romance. As a linguistic term, "romance" signifies both
the "vulgar" and the courteous extremes of twelfth-century speech. As
a genre, romance intertwines the scenes and themes of the aristocratic
epic and the lowly folktale—and shows unmistakable genetic relationships to both forms. As a cultural mirror and cultural battleground, romance seems to blend voices from all ranges of society: secular and
sacred, rural and urban, rich and poor. Although the last of these
three statements may be the most easily challenged, few, I hope, reject the major point: because romance has roots and branches in both
the most popular and the most refined segments of medieval society,
it is a promising medium through which to seek a culturally variega-
ted view of medieval oral artistry—or at least a view more balanced
than those now prevailing.

Past scholars viewed medieval culture as if it were governed by
some social analogue of gravity, always moving downward from the
privileged to the masses.[1] Although the greatest artists of the Middle

---

[1] Among the best succinct critiques of elitist historiography are the statements

Ages clearly reversed this flow, deriving themes and scenes from the oral traditions of the lower classes, we have continued to work from the supposition that such borrowings were merely details, and that the governing structures into which artists worked these details were always elite. It has been painfully easy to "prove" such suppositions, because we have used only elite frames of reference in which to set our data. Chaucerians have claimed, for example, numerous elite models for the structure of the *Canterbury Tales*: the doctrine of *caritas*, the topos of life as a pilgrimage, philosophical and architectural conceptions of the shape of creation. But until very recently, we failed to take Chaucer at his word—to examine the possibility that what he presented as a festive processional storytelling contest indeed bears the marks of folk entertainment enacted in the fourteenth century.[2]

Elite models have inevitably generated more elite models, elite questions, elite solutions—and little else. Elite culture has so dominated medieval studies that scholars who search for a folk world often feel impelled to seek it where they know nearly nothing can be found: the elite world is one of writing, so the folk world must be exclusively oral; the elite view is mainstream, so surely the folk view is so deviant that even the chroniclers of heresy are incapable of describing it. Witness Carlo Ginzburg's *The Cheese and the Worms*, a resourceful attempt to reclaim a world of folk thought from the heresy trials of one socially marginal man.[3] Because trial transcripts are among the few sources that record peasant speech verbatim, Ginzburg relies heavily upon them. Yet only one accused heretic speaks at length about a religious system decidedly different from the elite system, and his words spoken under duress become the basis of an entire peasant philosophy. Although Ginzburg and his fellow New Historians have made the most important recent contributions to medieval studies, their methodology often leaves us with less than we need and far less than we could have—if we would stop assuming that folk culture is in every respect opposed to elite and is always that which is lost in the translation from speech to writing.

---

of three of the greatest New Historians: Carlo Ginzburg, *The Cheese and the Worms: The Cosmos of a Sixteenth-Century Miller*, trans. John and Anne Tedeschi (New York: Penguin, 1982), xiii–xxvi; Jacques Le Goff, "The Historian and the Ordinary Man," in *Time, Work, and Culture in the Middle Ages*, trans. Arthur Goldhammer (Chicago: Univ. of Chicago Press, 1980), 225–36; Emmanuel Le Roy Ladurie, "History That Stands Still," in *The Mind and Method of the Historian*, trans. Siân and Ben Reynolds (Chicago: Univ. of Chicago Press, 1981), 1–27.

[2] This argument was first advanced in Carl Lindahl, "The Festive Form of the Canterbury Tales," *English Literary History* 52 (1985): 530–74.

[3] Though Ginzburg does cite some additional support for his materials, most of his argument is based on heresy trials.

Clearly, the culture and artistry of the lower classes cannot emerge intact simply from the testimony of an accused heretic. To be able to reclaim even part of the folk world, we must supply for it some things that the elite world possesses abundantly: contexts, structures, and value systems of its own, all distinct from those assigned by the dominant culture. Because elite culture crafted most of the records that have survived, we have to retranslate and reinterpret these and read them "upside down" as we begin to build a better model. If, for example, clerical chroniclers condemn celebrants of the Feast of Fools for singing impious songs "both scurrilous and unchaste"[4] and hold up these verses as evidence of the crudeness and degradation of peasant value systems, we must be prepared for the possibility that the revelers themselves would characterize the songs as commentaries on the degradation of the religious and civic leadership. But in either case we cannot throw out the chronicles. No matter how elite the shadings of such sources, they present valuable evidence on which to base tenable propositions on the nature of oral folk culture.

I have studied the festivals Chaucer knew of and probably witnessed: upper-class entertainments, such as the *Cour amoureuse* and courtly May Games, as well as mixed-class feasts, including the Feast of Fools and Boy Bishops celebrations, I found—quite predictably—that the festivals most important to the poor were known almost exclusively through prohibitions in which the churls' celebrations were always given negative values and represented as carnival mirrors of the elite festivities. From such records, it is relatively easy to build a dialectical model in which elite and folk are set up in opposition. The text of the *Canterbury Tales* would certainly support such a reading: Chaucer divides his cast into two classes, the *gentils* and *churls*; and the two groups differ greatly in their festive speech. For example, the gentils are politely obsequious, while the churls are bold and prepossessing in their attempts to secure their festive rights. When asked by Host Herry Bailly to tell their tales, the upper-class pilgrims defer to this less-than-noble leader, although they outrank him in real life. "Biheste is dette," says the Man of Law; "I wole obeye / Unto your wyl," says the Franklin; "I am under youre yerde," says the Clerk.[5] But the lower-class pilgrims break into the storytelling. The Miller,

---

[4] This quotation is from a medieval record translated by E. K. Chambers in *The Medieval Stage* (London: Oxford Univ. Press, 1903), 1:246.

[5] All textual references to *The Canterbury Tales* are from *The Riverside Chaucer*, ed. Larry D. Benson, 3rd ed. (Boston: Houghton Mifflin, 1987). These citations are, respectively, 2.41, 5.703–704, and 4.22.

Reeve, and Cook seize the center of attention, showing no sign of deference, without asking the Host's permission at all. True to their roles
as carnival revelers, they defiantly cross boundaries that would restrain
them at other times. Furthermore, while the gentils tend to compete
individually and politely, noble against noble, the churls compete by
factions, creating tiny wars between master and apprentice, trade and
trade, laity and clergy. Finally, while the play hierarchy of the gentils
duplicates the social order (with the most powerful people assigned
the most exalted play roles), the churls' game plan places the most
lowly in the highest positions.[6]

These two opposed styles of acting and speaking—the gentil and
the churl—are not only apparent throughout the *Canterbury Tales* but
also found everywhere in the records of actual medieval festivals—indicating clearly that, whatever else his designs, Chaucer successfully
imitated the play styles of the major social factions of his day. Furthermore, he set these styles against each other so boldly and clearly
that the tension between them becomes a structuring principle of his
poem. One of the pilgrims, Herry Bailly, condenses all the oppositions.
In him, Chaucer creates a middle man who alternatively plays by gentil
and churl rules—at once obsequious to the gentils and parodically abu-
sive of the churls, fostering the gentils' refined competition while abet-
ting the churls' class warfare. There is sufficient data from actual medieval celebrations to affirm that the Host mediates the festive voices of his
company without greatly distorting them.

Herry Bailly can speak upscale. Addressing the Reeve, he sounds
as "lordly as a kyng" (1.3900). He defers to his social superiors with
such delicate addresses as "Sire Man of Lawe ... so have ye blis"
(2.33) and "My lady Prioresse, by youre leve" (7.47). To lower-class
pilgrims, however, he speaks like the churlish Bishop of Fools. In the
folk celebrations the mock bishop would sing songs elevating the lowly
in order to ridicule the pretensions of leaders. There was a hymn of
praise of the ass that carried Mary and Joseph from Jerusalem:

> Behold the son
> Yoked below his massive ears!
> Extraordinary ass!
> Lord of Asses!
> That strong jaw ...

---

[6] For a more detailed version of this argument, see Lindahl, *Earnest Games:
Folkloric Patterns in* The Canterbury Tales (Bloomington: Indiana Univ. Press, 1987),
54–61.

> Pulverizes the fodder ...
> Wheat from the chaff
> He divides on the threshing-room floor![7]

As the Bishop of Fools intones these words, the congregation brayed in response. Similar mock epic inflation of the mundane marks Herry Bailly's strategy for praising the Physician by exalting the basest tools of the medical trade:

> I pray to God so save thy gentil cors,
> And eek thyne urynals and thy jurdones. . . . (6.304–305).

A little later in the *Tales*, Herry Bailly "playfully" sanctifies the Pardoner's genitals:

> I wolde I hadde thy coillons in myn hond ...
> They shul be shryned in an hogges toord!
> (6.952, 6.955).

This is precisely the sort of imagery at work in the Feast of Fools, when the office and artifacts of the church were ridiculed with low humor—when the imitation bishop wore the real bishop's holy britches on his head—and dung, rather than incense, was burned in church censers. So Herry Bailly commands both gentil and churlish dialects. Through him the many languages of medieval festival speak.

Though everyone recognizes that class differences play a role in the *Tales*, the extent to which these oppositions mirrored actual festive practice is striking. Whatever force refined esthetic, philosophical, and political abstractions exert upon the poem, Chaucer gave it demonstrably concrete foundation in festive custom—and that fact strengthens the possibility that Chaucer's depiction of festive oral artistry is not only amusing and artful, but also ethnographically accurate.

Yet the gentil and churl festivals also strongly resembled each other. Though they differ in verbal style and degree of contentiousness, the classes agree in more particulars then they differ. Both the upper-class and the lower-class games embrace at least six common elements: an autocratic ruler, master of the revels; amateurs who serve both as performers and audience; penalties to enforce participation; rigid frameworks of rules; processions incorporated in the festive structure; and a blending of sacred and profane elements. For all their differences, then, the gentil and churl festive forms were frequently indistinguish-

---

[7] This is my translation of a medieval "missal" for the Feast of Fools; the original Latin appears in Chambers, *The Medieval Stage*, 2:279–82.

able. And since the festivals had so much in common, their origins are usually impossible to establish. What sense does it make to label mumming a noble or folk pastime when both classes observed the festival and molded it to fit their specific social frameworks? If this observation can be extended to other contexts we will experience a breakthrough in our pursuit of medieval oral art. A common pool of churl and gentil data would enlarge significantly the base of information from which to consider both societies in performance.

A social portrait derived at least in part from the common traits of the two cultures would also serve as a corrective to the polar model of medieval culture. To view two subcultures as always and irrevocably in opposition is to neglect the fact that no group exists solely to oppose another.[8] In addition to expressing its antagonism, a culture must ensure its own survival through the promotion of those values and practices that support it from within.

The common ground of the elite and folk cultures seems to expand with each added wave of research. Modern social historians are rediscovering the truth of the claim made by their nineteenth-century predecessor, J. J. Jusserand: "If the distances were great between class and class [in fourteenth-century England], familiarity was still greater."[9] The more penetrating our researches, the more the oppositions disappear. For example, literacy rates in rural communities were significantly higher than once supposed; conversely, no matter how pervasive literacy among the upper classes, the preference for oral entertainment survived.[10] Thus, the development of a written vernacular may have had far smaller influence than once supposed in separating the "sophisticated" court literatures from "crude" peasant entertainments. Similarly, historians have now dismissed the old image of the rustic village so isolated that its inhabitants lived in ignorance of the city.[11] The mutual familiarity of peasants with upper classes and of urban with

---

[8] On this point, note the words of Pierre Bourdieu as quoted and elaborated upon by Jacques Le Goff in "The Learned and Popular Dimension of Journeys in the Otherworld in the Middle Ages," in *Understanding Popular Culture*, ed. Stephen L. Kaplan (The Hague: Mouton, 1984), 20–22.

[9] J. J. Jusserand, *English Wayfaring Life in the Middle Ages*, trans. Lucy Toulmin Smith (London: Ernest Benn, 1889), 204.

[10] On the question of medieval literacy versus preference for oral entertainment, see Franz Bäuml, "Varieties and Consequences of Medieval Literacy and Illiteracy," *Speculum* 55 (1980): 237–65; Brian Stock, *The Implications of Literacy* (Princeton: Princeton Univ. Press, 1983); Sylvia Thrupp, *The Merchant Class of Medieval London* (Ann Arbor: Univ. of Michigan Press, 1948), 158–64.

[11] Alan MacFarlane, *Reconstructing Historical Communities* (Cambridge: Cambridge Univ. Press, 1977), 9.

rural societies, the mutual accessibility of upper and lower class narrative poetry—suggest that a courtier of Chaucer's day knew significantly
more about the daily life of churls (both urban and rural) than most
contemporary college professors know about life in twentieth-century
urban ghettoes.

Chaucer presents a remarkable example of this breadth of artistic
experience and understanding. Not only is he the "great translator"
of Boethius and the *Roman de la Rose*, he is also a man familiar with
alliterative verse patterns. He has the Parson confess his inability to
compose alliterative verse "'rum, ram, ruf,' by lettre" (10.43). And in
"Sir Thopas" he presents such a trenchant parody of popular tail-
rhyme romance that no one doubts he knew the form inside out.
Such parodies can be created only by and for people thoroughly con-
versant with the parent form. The more you look at Chaucer, the better you *hear* him—and the greater grows the sense that the poet's experience of fourteenth-century artistry spanned the entire social
range, from spoken tale to courtly written romance.

What then if we were to use Chaucer as a *common ground* in which
both elite and folk oral styles might be voiced? In my study of festival, I found it most useful to work from the middle out, to test the common ground before defining the differences between elite and oral performances styles. In marking out those many aspects of artistry shared
by elite and folk cultures—and simply labeling that body "neutral" instead of "elite" (as we've previously done), I can begin to construct performance models free of the elite prejudices expressed in prior attempts
to portray medieval culture.

My aim, therefore, is not to erase the real and important distinctions between folk and elite cultures; indeed, the interaction between
the two domains cannot be thoroughly studied until their differences
are adequately articulated. In order to establish where the two cultures truly diverge it is essential to know where and how they meet.
For example, the many traits shared by elite and folk festivals helped
enunciate the most important differences between the two. In com-
paring the two social forms, I repeatedly invoked the principle, *the
more similar two things, the more significant their differences.*

Elite romance tradition plainly bears out this motto. The changes
that Chaucer imposes on the French Griselde story or the changes the
French text imposed on Petrarch, are minimal but—as Chaucerians
since Kittredge have continually argued—great in impact.[12] The es-

---

[12] The great effects of Chaucer's minimal revisions of the Griselde tale are well
weighed in Alfred David, *The Strumpet Muse: Art and Morals in Chaucer's Poetry*

thetic of minimal change for great effect also guides even the most in-
novative rewriters of romance—such as Thomas Chestre, whose *Sir
Launfal* (by romance standards, a revolutionary departure from such
sources as the *Lanval* of Marie de France) performs almost all its changes through *additions* to the text, and does nearly nothing to change the
lineaments of the older part of the story, which maintained its shape
through two centuries.[13]

In all its social forms, the romance has a certain authority and a
certain stability of plot and diction; version to version, romance changes in glacial fashion, slowly and sometimes subtly, but powerfully.
Romance is, like Herry Bailly, a medieval "middle man" through
which many medieval cultural dialects are voiced. True, like Herry
Bailly and Chaucer the narrator, romance tends to claim an affinity
with the gentils, but (much as John Ganim has suggested) I maintain
that the churls' voices, customs, and ideals are bound up in romance
and cannot be erased completely even from its most elite expressions.[14]

So one principle of both oral and written romance—the principle
of minimal change—functions to communicate and to alter heavy
loads of meanings and values. Both elite and folk culture would seize
upon a basic plot and, with a few strategic, symbolic manipulations,
turn a neutral story into a folk romance—or into an elite one. As long
as the narrator feels free to readjust a story to fit a special context and
audience, something of the oral world remains in the tale.

A second way in which a more or less neutral plot can become either an oral or a folk creation has to do with the way that it is glossed.
According to Eugène Vinaver's theory of the origins of romance, folklore provided the parent forms, but romance—from its very beginnings—marked a revolutionary departure from its oral past. The defining impulse of romance is to mix the story with its signification, to
doctor an old tale with explanatory and internalizing voices—to present simultaneously both the plot and the author's interpretation. Vinaver argues that this juxtaposition of the story with its *sens* was rooted
in the monastic technique of interlineal and marginal glosses. He
shows us manuscript leaves on which narrative is both presented and

---

(Bloomington: Indiana Univ. Press, 1976), 159–69; and James J. Sledd, "The Clerk's
Tale: The Monsters and the Critics," *Modern Philology* 51 (1953): 73–82.

[13] For a discussion of some of the changes Thomas Chestre effected in the
Lanval of Marie de France, see Bernadine McCreesh, "The Use of Conversation in
Medieval Literature: The Case of Marie de France and Her First Redactor," *Revue
de l'Université d'Ottawa* 53 (1983): 189–97.

[14] John Ganim, "History and Consciousness in Middle English Romance,"
Literary Review 23 (1980): 481–96.

decoded—and suggests that the generation of Chrétien de Troyes, reading silently, was inspiried by such models to merge the story with its gloss. This, of course, is a purely literary way to encode a romance plot. Vinaver is explaining the origin of a certain elite style of romance, to the exclusion of certain oral styles.[15]

In oral performance such glosses are rare. The meaning of an utterance is most often clarified in context. The presence of an audience, the gestures of the speaker, and most especially the speaker's voice work to make a meaning more specific, if not precisely articulated. But generally the oral artist leaves much for the audience to interpret.[16]

The lack of interpretation has several important causes, but two of the most important have to do with engaging the audience. First is a matter of consensus. The more listeners involved in an oral performance, the better the chance that the performer will be heard again— but also the greater the chance of variety in interpretation. By letting each member of the audience assign her or his own meaning to an unexplained symbol or action, the teller allows many diverse readings of the performance. Second is the question of engagement: psychological tests tend to support the conclusion that an unglossed verbal image holds the attention of the listener more effectively than almost any other type of communication. The power to be suggested *to*—rather than to be told—enfranchises the oral audience, giving them a greater role in the creative process. Whatever the causes of the symbolic mode so characteristic of folk performance, its greatest effect is freedom of interpretation. While elite glosses limit meaning to support authoritarian dicta, folk communications remain unfinished, openended, and relatively free.[17]

The oral folk romance specializes in one—and only one—type of gloss: the formulaic epithet. Whether employed to help the composer to remember (or to compose) a text or to help the audience find their

---

[15] Eugène Vinaver, *The Rise of Romance* (New York: Barnes and Noble, 1971), 15–32.

[16] The argument of this and the following three paragraphs is presented in greater detail in Carl Lindahl, "The Oral Esthetic and the Bicameral Mind," *Oral Tradition* 6 (1991): 130–36.

[17] The psychological literature on the impact of heard images remains inconclusive. Recent articles on the subject include Ian Begg, Douglas Upfold, and Terrance D. Wilton, "Imagery in Verbal Communication," *Journal of Mental Imagery* 2 (1978): 165–88; Michael J. Dickel and Stefan Slak, "Imagery Vividness and Memory for Verbal Material," *Journal of Mental Imagery* 7 (1983): 121–26; Mary Doll, "Hearing Images," *Journal of Mental Imagery* 7 (1983): 135–42; Joe Khatena, "Analogy Imagery and the Creative Imagination," *Journal of Mental Imagery* 7 (1983): 127–34; and the Lindahl discussion cited in note 16.

way through the cast and plot, formulas fill late medieval popular romance. In England, especially, formulas were far more common than other glosses. There, romance was never to find the same use of the revolutionary literary treatment—the same degree of introspective reading—that Chrétien had given his *Lancelot*. Even the best read English descendants of Chrétien—Chaucer and the *Gawain* poet—never fully duplicated his depth of internalization and interpretation. Rather, English poets let at least part of the story speak for itself, retaining a certain imagistic magic. The English tended to observe one of the fundamental laws of the oral esthetic, which holds that the most concrete images are the most powerful because they are the most suggestive. They repeatedly translate idea and emotion into action and symbol, as surely as Chrétien does the opposite.[18] Chrétien glosses the traditional tale that is his source for *Yvain*, but the anonymous English poet who translates Chrétien often strips the story back to a simpler, symbolic narrative format.

To apply and further explain the points raised here, consider the oral undertones of three specific versions of a famous late medieval plot, which seems to have many social backgrounds. It is best known as the Wife of Bath's Tale. The common elements of the three versions boil down to a simple plot:

> A man is punished with the task of finding what women most desire. If he loses the test, he pays with his life. On his quest he encounters a loathly lady who tells him she will answer his question only if he marries her. Her answer, of course: women desire sovereignty over men. The man is saved and, with great reluctance, he marries the hag. In their wedding bed, she poses another test in asking him, "Would you have me fair by day and foul by night?" or vice versa. (Or "Would you have me faithful and ugly or false and fair?") The man asks the hag to decide, in effect giving her sovereignty, and she instantly becomes young and beautiful—and everything the man wants.

This plot exists in two fourteenth-century texts from court poets, Chaucer and John Gower—and a later romance of less elevated social

---

[18] On the two *Yvains*, see Norman J. Fry, "A Comparative Study of Metaphor in the *Ywain* Legend," *Dissertation Abstracts International* 34 (1973): 3392A, Stanford University; Tony Hunt, "Beginnings, Middles, and Ends: Some Interpretative Problems in Chretien's *Yvain* and Its Medieval Adaptations," in *The Craft of Fiction: Essays in Medieval Poetics*, ed. Leigh A. Arrathoon (Rochester, Michigan: Solaris Press, 1984), 83–117. Both authors point out interesting differences between the French and English poems, though I disagree with the conclusions of both.

origin, *The Wedding of Sir Gawain and Dame Ragnall* (see fig. 1).[19] There is also a much later ballad, dated about 1650, from which the story just outlined varies somewhat. Because the earliest versions are the most refined, critics invoke the old idea of *gesunkenes Kulturgut*: the tale must have started with the writings of elite artists and then devolved and unraveled as retold by inferior folk artists. But—as elite manuscripts of any sort are nearly always the oldest and the most numerous—let us for the moment *neutralize* the plot, assume a common ground, and then seek to determine the implication of the power structures in the three tales, as well as to discover the extent to which each explains itself through glosses and symbolic coding as the product of a specific social discourse.

The most notable thing about the three as a group is their interest in feminine power. Intrinsic to their shared plot is a dramatic social statement on the prime desire of women: sovereignty over men. Because the issue of female sovereignty is a major one in European peasant tales as far back as they can be traced, we cannot be sure of the age or social origins of this story.[20] But it is unlikely that a tale turning on this question could have existed, in elite form, before the twelfth century, when women enter literature in force, as representatives of class conflicts: between the greater and lesser nobility, for example, or between the nobles and the wealthy merchants. In social fact, the female became the agent through which wealthy families with marriageable daughters bought their ways into nobler households, and through which indigent nobles could restore their wealth.[21] By Chaucer's time social

---

[19] All textual references to the non-Chaucerian loathly lady tales are from *Sources and Analogues of Chaucer's Canterbury Tales*, ed. W.F. Bryan and Germaine Dempster (Chicago: University of Chicago Press, 1941). *Florent* is found on pp. 224–35 of that volume, *Gawain and Ragnall* on pp. 242–64.

[20] Among the many medieval tales dealing with battles between the sexes for sovereignty are six listed in Antti Aarne and Stith Thompson, *The Types of the Folktale* (Helsinki: Suomalainen Tiedeakatemia, 1961), Folklore Fellows Communications, no. 184. These are tale types 901 ("The Taming of the Shrew"), 1164 ("The Evil Woman Thrown into the Pit"), 1365 ("The Obstinate Wife"), 1380 ("The Faithless Wife"), 1406 ("The Merry Wives' Wager"), 1408 ("The Man Does the Wife's Work"). See Stith Thompson, *The Folktale* (New York: Dryden Press, 1946), 104, 194–96, 206–210; Lutz Röhrich, *Erzählungen des Späten Mittelalters* (Berne: Francke Verlag, 1967), 2:307–52.

[21] Among the many discussions of medieval woman as medium of exchange for rank and wealth, see Renate Bridenthal and Claudia Koontz, eds., *Becoming Visible: Women in European History* (Boston: Houghton Mifflin, 1977), esp. the essays of Jo Ann McNamara and Suzanne F. Wemple; Ann McMillan, trans., *The Legend of Good Women* (Houston: Rice Univ. Press, 1987), 49–55, 164–73; and Susan Mosher Stuard, ed. *Women in Medieval Society* (Philadelphia: Univ. of Pennsylvania Press, 1976), esp. the contributions of Stuard and David Herlihy. Louise O. Fradenburg poses a

Figure 1

THREE LOATHLY LADY STORIES

Gower's Tale of Florent, from *Confessio Amantis* c. 1390	Chaucer's Wife of Bath's Tale c. 1390	Anonymous *Wedding of Sir Gawain and Dame Ragnall* c. 1450

A KNIGHT

kills another in fair combat, grandmother of dead knight demands he discover	rapes a lady, is condemned to death; merciful female intervention gives him pardon if he can find	[K. Arthur meets giant whose lands Arthur has seized. Giant says Arthur must discover]

WHAT WOMEN MOST DESIRE

IF HE FAILS, THE KNIGHT MUST DIE

Gawain takes on
Arthur's task

KNIGHT MEETS LOATHLY LADY, WHO IS

richly described (lines 1675–92)	undescribed (3.999)	richly described (lines 228–51)

LADY ANSWERS THE QUESTION
ON CONDITION THAT THEY MARRY

WOMEN DESIRE SOVEREIGNTY

In love

IN THE BRIDAL BED, LOATHLY LADY ASKS KNIGHT
WOULD YOU HAVE ME

fair by day, foul by night, or vice versa	fair and untrue or foul and true	fair by day, foul by night, or vice versa

LADY IS TRANSFORMED INTO

princess who had been under enchantment	beautiful woman (no clear class affiliation or explanation for transformation)	lady who had been under enchantment

flux had grown so great that as many as half of England's noble families were either newly arrived from the merchant classes or threatened with extinction by them. At the same time that merchant marriages were breaking and re-making the aristocracy, the upper reaches of the peasantry were encroaching from below upon the domain of the middle class.[22] Depending on one's status, the answer to that magical question—"What do women most desire?"—could be viewed as either a threat or a promise. The plot at the base of the Wife of Bath's tale does not properly belong to either the nobles or the bourgeois or the peasantry; it is rather a direct development of the blurring but tension-ridden boundaries between the classes. This plot has as many potential connections to the popular romance as to the elite form, and a narrator could encode a given version with the value of any class.

As Georges Duby and others have pointed out, the woman's rise in literature coincided with an erosion of her economic sovereignty. Her hefty dowry could ennoble her parents or enrich her husband, but it could not free her. As she became a vehicle of male wealth, her power to determine the disposition of her own assets diminished. In the flux of the late Middle Ages, women who struggled against these growing constraints became extremists—heretics, mystics, or saints— who allied themselves with the underclasses and other socially marginal groups to contest male-dominated elite culture. The figure of the loathly lady could serve as a social magnet to which other disenfranchised groups were drawn.[23]

Viewed in such terms, the riddling question of the loathly lady may appear as an element of the paranoia of the ruling classes. But, just as her demand for sovereignty embodies the fears of the powerful, her transformation to a beautiful lady may represent the wish ful-

---

slightly different but very stimulating view of the historical circumstances underlying the emergence of loathly ladies in "The Wife of Bath's Passing Fancy," *Studies in the Age of Chaucer* 8 (1986): 31–58.

[22] The recent work of social historians has revealed much about the extraordinary social flux of Chaucer's era. Witness the words of Christopher Dyer: "Of the 136 barons who attended the house of lords at the end of the thirteenth century, the direct descendants of only 16 survived in 1500, and only about a fifth of the gentry of 1500 can be traced back to the landed families of their countries in 1300"; *Standards of Living in the Later Middle Ages: Social Change in England. c. 1200–1520* (Cambridge: Cambridge Univ. Press, 1989), 47. Dyer's book also provides excellent descriptions of peasant living standards and mobility.

[23] For the argument that women were magnets for other disenfranchised groups, see Georges Duby, *The Knight, the Lady, and the Priest: The Making of Modern Marriage in Medieval France*, trans. Barbara Bray (New York: Pantheon, 1983), 107–39.

fillment of the powerless. The barest outline of the Wife of Bath's Tale is peculiarly linked to a time when the fears of the titled and the hopes of the untitled overlapped. For all its listeners this plot performs a fundamental function of fantasy: it solves on the level of fiction a problem that is difficult or impossible to solve in real life, granting both the noble but impoverished knight and the economically powerful but unacceptable lady the union of their dreams.[24]

John Gower, the most secure financially of the three authors, and clearly the most conservative politically, presents an elitist version. His hero, Florent, is the most orthodoxly elite of the three leading men. The nephew of an Emperor, Florent falls upon trouble through no fault of his own, but for killing in fair combat a certain knight. The slain knight's grandmother—the real female threat, and really the only threat to his noble life—imposes on him the task of discovering woman's prime desire. She does so because she realizes that Florent is too nobly connected to be killed by any but treacherous means. In neither of the other tales does there appear a female figure who so clearly symbolizes an attack against basic feudal values. Florent quests and finds the loathly lady and her answer, which differs significantly from the answers of the other two tales: women desire not simply sovereignty, but specifically sovereignty *in love*—a qualification inescapable in Gower's tale, for both at its beginning and end, the moralizing narrator intrudes with the message—men must be obedient only in love. This gloss strictly limits the loathly lady's threat to the dominant male and cancels the attack of that other female figure—the conniving grandmother—who desires sovereignty in hate, sovereignty in vengeance. Once the loathly lady has dispelled the ominous figure of the grandmother, she further dispels any hint that she may limit the knight's status. She reveals herself to be a king's daughter, the only *royal* hag found in the three tales. *Florent* is a paean to the nobility that Gower served and by whom he was served so well. In its symbolic structure and its glosses, the poem reaffirms that a modicum of deference is all that is required to maintain male dominance.

Gawain and Ragnall, beyond doubt a romance of more popular idiom, demonstrates how broad the discourse of romance really is, for this tale is implicitly a male vassal's critique of a corrupt male power structure. Though the poem opens with a panegyric describing King Arthur as unequalled in nobility and courtesy, this gloss is cos-

---

[24] This function of fantasy is discussed in some detail by John G. Cawelti in *Adventure, Mystery, and Romance* (Chicago: Univ. of Chicago Press, 1976).

metic. Arthur's actions belie such fawning epithets: he is a weak king, who has distributed his power unwisely by allotting to Gawain lands belonging to the giant Gromer Somer Joure. It is this angry giant who assigns Arthur the penace of finding what women most desire. But Arthur merely compounds his weaknesses, first by breaking his promise to keep the encounter with Gromer a secret, then by failing the test of finding women's greatest wish. Instead, Gawain fulfills the task, and it is Gawain, ironically, who must pay the king's ransom by wedding the loathly lady and saving Arthur's life.

Gawain and Ragnall, unlike *Florent*, can be read two ways in regard to women's sovereignty. First, one can see the lady as a simple reward for one man's loyalty to a more powerful man. But, because the tale is unglossed on this issue, we are also presented with an implicit comparison between the weak Arthur, who rewards service poorly, and the loathly lady, who rewards Gawain's service surpassingly well. Nothing keeps the tale from suggesting the moral superiority of women—as well as their greater power, for Gawain's one service to Ragnall does more to elevate him than his lifetime of loyalty to Arthur.

One thing, however, is clear: this tale does challenge the power structure. And the narrator, who in closing describes himself as one "be-sette withe gaylours many" (844), reinforces the fact that this poem is a plea for liberation as well as a charter for undermining the authoritarian world. With the elevation of Ragnall comes at least the implication that others—including the jailed knight himself—can rise.

Finally, the Wife of Bath's Tale: symbolic content and narrative strategies bring Alison's narrative closer to the wish-poetry of *Gawain and Ragnall* than to the courtly world of *Florent*. The *Canterbury Tales* depicts Alison's story as an oral performance, and Alison follows the oral mode of presenting symbolic, unglossed actions. Hers is a more penetrating critique of power than even *Gawain and Ragnall*, for in the Wife's story women have almost entirely displaced Arthur and his knights at the locus of power. Alison's knight protagonist, unlike the worthies in the two analogues, has no virtue. Neither a warrior nor a faithful servant, he is rather a rapist spared execution by Arthur solely through the intervention of Guenever and her court of ladies. (This is an exact role reversal of the power relations in *Florent*, where the faultless knight is unfairly tried by a criminal woman.) In the Wife's fictional world, men are capable only of violence, but the knight's rape and Arthur's intent to execute the knight are eventually judged and corrected by the more humane rule of Guenever and the court of ladies. The knight's penance is in effect an education in the superior value system of women.

Just as important as the Wife's manipulation of plot—though less obvious—is the way she handles glossing. Chaucer shows his thorough knowledge of both written and oral conventions in his artful reversal of them. Chaucer's male lead is a rapist—the only villain among the three—and the Wife underscores that point brilliantly by refusing to describe him. In conventional romance a knight is loaded down with epithets, especially when he first appears. In *Gawain and Ragnall*, for example, Arthur is described as unmatched by any of his contemporaries, a "lord riche," a "kyng curteys and royalle," "the flowyr of kyngs," "the honor of knyghthood"—all in the first eight lines. In contrast, Alison's rapist knight is first described, appropriately, as a "lusty bacheler" (3.883), and thereafter simply as "this knyght" (3.891, 913, 983, 1030, 1098, 1228) or "the knyght" (3.900, 1000, 1013, 1032, 1047, 1050, 1083, 1250). There is no male lead in any other romance known to me who is so unadorned with epithets; the absence of comment is the most effective insult possible.

Furthermore, in the analogues the loathly lady is described at length in her hideous disguise; and later, when disenchanted, she tells the story of her transformation. By providing striking descriptions and explanations, these glosses work to limit the power of the romance heroine. The Wife of Bath, however, turns the process upside down: she refuses to describe the loathly lady or to explain the reason for her appearance. Of the hag, the Wife says only "A fouler wight ther may no man devyse" (3.999).

Not only is Alison's loathly lady unglossed, but in parody of the orthodox romance pattern, the hag does all the glossing herself. On their bridal night, the monstrous lady asks the rapist why he refuses her. He gives three reasons: she is ugly and old and of low status—to which *she* replies with a lengthy lecture, more than a quarter of the tale's length—in which she cites Dante, Boethius, Juvenal, and Seneca. The mystical female figure that men fear and seek some way to limit is here ironically transformed into a parody of an authoritarian cleric.

But Chaucer works in one more twist, a comment on the value of elite glosses. The knight abhors the hag's age, ugliness, and lowly birth; in response, she devotes 100 lines of her 110-line speech to the issue of status. Only ten lines address the two problems of age and ugliness. But these, we soon find, are the two real problems, because when the hag transforms herself into a young, beautiful woman, the knight no longer rejects her. The lengthy lecture on poverty was a false gloss. Chaucer leads us toward the very *oral* conclusion that a gloss will weigh in inverse proportion to its length. Alison of Bath, so often admired as a great comic individual, is also a great oral technician, working sometimes with and sometimes against the conventions of popular romance to personalize and strengthen the message of her tale.

Thus, the shared plot of these three tales can be made the property of any late medieval class or value system. I am convinced that all three versions were orally performed, probably frequently. The more we learn about daily life in the late Middle Ages, the less we doubt that such poetic works of entertainment were read aloud—but the clearer it becomes that they *were read.* The more important point is that some books are more bookish than others. The prospect that Gower's *Tale of Florent* was read aloud does not stop it from *sounding* like a book. The fact that *Gawain and Ragnall* was written in manuscripts does not stop it from reading like an oral performance. The Wife of Bath's Tale falls somewhere between. Although it employs (even as it parodies) bookish convention, it must have been written for an audience thoroughly familiar with oral romance.

It has been claimed that Chaucer's and Gower's poems differ too much to make it possible to speak of a common source.[25] Such an argument draws on the assumption that authors from elite backgrounds will inevitably write elite, authoritarian romances which vary little, if at all, from their sources. Yet, as Chaucer and Gower almost certainly knew each other's poems, it is entirely possible that the Wife of Bath's Tale was intended as a playful inversion of, and a festive response to the sober clerical cast of Gower's tale. Chaucer's is in many ways a folk perfomance. Writing does not in itself destroy this sort of oral tradition. As long as literary artists reshaped their tales to fit the values and needs of a community of listeners, romance remained a vital oral form.[26]

---

[25] Among those holding this opinion is B. J. Whiting, "The Wife of Bath's Tale," in *Sources and Analogues,* ed. Bryan and Dempster, 224.

[26] I thank Ann McMillan and John McNamara for their careful critiques of earlier drafts of this article and Daniel Barnes for his thoughtful reading of this one.

JOSEPH FALAKY NAGY

Oral Tradition in the
Acallam na Senórach

O ne of the best-known yet least-read works of medieval Irish
literature is the lengthy text known as the *Acallam na Senórach*
"Colloquy of the Ancients." Copies of the *Acallam* have survived in numerous manuscripts down to the nineteenth century. Such ubiquity at-
tests to its long-lived popularity; no manuscript containing the *Acallam*,
however, dates from earlier than the fifteenth century. From the earliest
sources we have for the text (including Bodleian MS. Laud 610 and the
Book of Lismore) it is possible to piece together a recension of the
Acallam, and this is precisely what Whitley Stokes did in his edition of
the work published in the *Irische Texte* series.[1] Stokes's edition superseded that of Standish Hayes O'Grady, which was based solely on
the Book of Lismore version.[2] To be profitably compared with the
earliest extant recension of the *Acallam*, as provided by Stokes, is the
later, much-expanded version of the text edited by Nessa Ní Shéagh-

---

[1] Whitley Stokes, ed., *Acallam na Senórach*, *Irische Texte*, Fourth Series, vol. 2
(Leipzig: S. Hirzel, 1900).
[2] Standish H. O'Grady, ed. and trans., *Silva Gadelica*, 2 vols. (London and
Edinburgh: Williams and Norgate, 1892).

dha,[3] and the recension known as the *Agallamh Bheag*, the "Little *Ac-allam*," a portion of which was edited by Douglas Hyde in the first volume of the Irish journal *Lia Fáil*.[4] The analysis presented in this paper is based upon the Stokes *Acallam*, which numbers over 8000 lines of prose and verse, although much, if not most, of what I will say can be equally applied to the later incarnations of the text.

As Robert Nuner demonstrated in his pioneering study of the verbal system of the earliest extant recension of the *Acallam*,[5] it would be philologically unsafe to date the language of the text as we have it in fifteenth-century sources much earlier than 1200, for what we find in the *Acallam* is very late Middle Irish, indeed the beginning of Early Modern Irish. It is certainly possible that the text had already gone through a considerable period of evolution before the ca. 1200 recension. A reference in the twelfth-century so-called "Recension C" of the poetic *dindshenchas* or place-name lore of Ireland to the *acallam* (dialogue) between Patrick and Caílte as a source for a poem concerning Tonn Clídna, has been taken by some scholars to be a reference to an existing text of the *Acallam na Senórach* and thus proof of the work's existence in the twelfth century.[6] Even though this poem about Tonn Clídna does in fact appear in the *Acallam* as we have it,[7] it is just as likely that the *dindshenchas* reference is to a *tradition* concerning an informative conversation that took place between Patrick and Caílte, rather than to a specific text entitled the *Acallam*.

An initially surprising characteristic of the *Acallam* as it survives in manuscripts is that it is never complete and always lacks at least an end, and oftentimes even a beginning. Our surprise may wear away, however, when we consider the nature of the text: this is essentially a frame tale, which by definition has a rather flexible structure and variable content. The *Acallam* is an account of the adventures of two heroes, Caílte and, to a far lesser extent, Oisín. These are prominent figures from the Fenian story cycle, who, according to the *Acallam*, live on into the post-Fenian era, after the death of their leader Finn mac Cumaill and their heroic companions, all of whom constituted the *fian*, Finn's warring and hunting band. The bulk of the text consists of Caílte's re-

---

[3] Nessa Ní Shéaghdha, ed., *Agallamh na Seanórach*, 3 vols. (Dublin: Oifig an tSoláthair, 1942–45).

[4] Douglas Hyde, ed., "An Agallamh Bheag," *Lia Fáil* 1 (1925): 79–107.

[5] Robert D. Nuner, "The Verbal System of the *Agallamh na Senórach*," *Zeitschrift für celtische Philologie* 27 (1958–59): 230–309.

[6] Ní Shéaghdha, 1:xi–xii; Gerard Murphy, *The Ossianic Lore and Romantic Tales of Medieval Ireland*, rev. Brian Ó Cuív (Cork: Mercier Press, 1971), 24.

[7] Stokes, 109.

sponses, most in narrative form, to questions posed to him by people he
meets of this latter era concerning the significance of various obscure
place-names and/or concerning the lesser-known details of episodes
from the Fenian *epos*. (These two topics are hard to distinguish in the
Acallam, since most of the place-names about which information is
sought from Caílte turn out to have something to do with Fenian adventures, while the heroic tales he recounts almost always include
place-name lore.) In the course of his quite thorough travels throughout the provinces as told in the *Acallam*, Caílte, with some help from
his now-you-see-him-now-you-don't companion Oisín, maps out a
specifically Fenian Ireland, a terrain that stands almost in contrast to
the Ireland of the more catholic body of place-name lore presented in
the metrical or prose *dindshenchas* collections. This revival of topo-
nymical awareness that Caílte fosters, like that of the medieval *dindshenchas* tradition as a whole, entails a keen sensitivity to the passing
of time: Caílte and the author of the *Acallam* frequently remind their
audiences that many of these names that are mentioned, discussed,
and explained are no longer the names used to designate these places
in the now of their narrative.

One of the most pointed of these references to changes of place-
names occurs at the beginning of the *Acallam*, directly before the old
Fenians meet Patrick:

> They went away from that place onto the grassy field, where
> they held council. The decision they made was to leave one an-
> other, but it was like the soul leaving the body. But leave one
> another they did, with Oisín going to Síd Ochta Cleitig (where
> his mother Blái, daughter of Derg Dianscothach, lived), and
> Caílte going to Inber Bic Loingsig a Bregaib (now called Main-
> istir Droichit Átha)—the place where Becc Loingsech fell, the
> son of the king of the Romans who came to conquer Ireland
> but was drowned by a tidal wave there.[8]

The Mainistir Droichit Átha mentioned in the passage is Mellifont,
the first Cistercian monastery founded in Ireland (1142) and, in effect,
a symbol of the reforms in the Irish church that occurred in the

---

[8] Is andsin táncatar rompu assan bhaile imach aran fhaithche bféraigh, 7 gníset
comairle ann sin, 7 as í comhairle dorónad accu ann, scarad re chéile; 7 ba scaradh
cuirp re hanmain a scarad. Ocus dorínset amhlaid sin, uair dochuaidh Oisín co
Sídh Ochta Cleitigh, bhail a raibhe a mháthair .i. Bla inghen Déirc Dhianscothaig,
7 téit Cáilte roime co hIndber mBic Loingsigh a mBregaibh, risi-ráidter Mainistir
Droichit Átha isin tan so .i. Bec Loingsech mac Airist itorchair ann .i. mac ríg
Rómán táinic do ghabháil Eirenn co rus-báidh tonn tuile ann hé (ibid., 2).

twelfth century.[9] It was, to a significant extent, through the impetus of these reforms that the era of monastic patronage of vernacular literature came to an end in Ireland, and the era of scribal families carrying on the literary tradition (as exemplifed by the *Acallam*) began. According to Proinsias Mac Cana, this migration of literary activity from monastic scriptorium to secular school and court occasioned a rearrangement of the traditional Irish hierarchy of verbal performers, both literate and nonliterate, with erstwhile occupants of lower rungs ascending to higher status[10]—a syndrome prominently on display in the *Acallam* itself, as we shall see. Thus, Caílte, a pagan from the oral past, unwittingly advances toward Patrick and the written culture he represents by way of what is to be Mellifont, which represented for the audience of the *Acallam* a much more recent turning point in the history of Irish literary tradition than the coming of Patrick and Christianity. Caílte, as he heads toward the epochal meeting, moves forward in time, but the text, passing from Mellifont to Patrick, moves backward. The itineraries of both character and text, moreover, contrast dramatically with the sojourn of Caílte's dear friend Oisín, who regresses altogether into the comforting past of his mother's otherworldly home, far away from clerics and their new-fangled notions.

Like the once-lost but now recovered lore they disseminate, the Fenian protagonists of the *Acallam* represent a fortuitous glitch in time. They should *not* still be living and well in the era in which the *Acallam* places them, but in some unspecified way they are. Caílte and his companions transcend time and sequence, paralleling the innumerable anachronistic references to place-names they and the text make, such as the Mellifont reference just mentioned. The key to this miracle, which both makes the miracle happen and provides its substance, is talk. This is, after all, an *acallam* 'conversation,' and each of the voices involved in this conversation has its own special kind of authority. The most important of the dialogues that occur in the text (there are, in fact, several) is between Caílte—who, according to the chronological schema of medieval Irish historians, flourished along with his fellow heroes in the third century after Christ—and St. Patrick, the renowned fifth-century missionary to Ireland. When the holy man and his retinue first see Caílte and a few other Fenian survivors approaching, they are, the text tells us, right away very much aware that these are not contemporary Irishmen:

---

[9] Nuner, 231–32; and Proinsias Mac Cana, "The Rise of the Later Schools of *Filidheacht*," *Ériu* 25 (1984): 126–46.

[10] Mac Cana, 138, n. 47; Alan Harrison, "*Séanadh Saighre*," *Éigse* 20 (1984): 139–40.

At the time, Patrick was chanting the sacred scriptures, praising the Creator and blessing Ráth Droma Deirc, where Finn mac Cumaill had resided. The clerics saw the company approaching them and took fright at the big men with their big dogs, for they were not people of the clerics' time. Then arose the princely salmon, the pillar of lordship, the earthly angel, Patrick, son of Alprainn, apostle of the Gaels, and he seized the aspergillum to sprinkle holy water over the big men. For there had been a thousand legions of demons over their heads until that day, and those demons then scattered away from them upon every side and fled into the hills and chasms of the land.[11]

In the course of his extended discussions with Patrick and other latter-day notables, Caílte talks of himself and is talked of as one who has lived well past his time. When the Fenian is confronted by Scothniam, a beautiful otherworldly lover whom he jilted long ago and who is seeking redress, Patrick rather cruelly remarks: "It is a wonder for us to see the two of you: the girl who is young and lovely, and you, Caílte, a decrepit, bowed, crooked, grey, old man [*senóir*, as in the title of the text]." Caílte explains: "I know why: we are not people of the same era. She is of the Tuatha Dé Danann, and they are immortal, while I am of the children of Míl, and they are transient and mortal."[12]

Caílte's protestation of normalcy notwithstanding, there is obviously something unusual about his longevity, and it is never made clear in the *Acallam* how these people of different eras, the Fenians and Patrick, could have met and mingled. Yet such confusion about chronology may be more of a problem for us than for the author of the *Acallam*, who gleefully mixes together legendary characters from several different periods in the broad tableau of early Christian Ireland he presents.[13] Here, for example, the king of Ireland who is converted by

---

[11] Is ann sin do bhói Pátraic ac cantain na canóine coimdheta, ⁊ ic etarmholadh in Dúilemhun, ic bendachadh na rátha a roibhe Find mac Cumaill .i. Ráith Droma Deirc. Ocus atconncatar na cléirigh dá n-indsaighi iat-sum, ro ghabh gráin ⁊ egla iat roimh na feraibh móra cona conaibh móra leo, uair nir' lucht coimhré na comhaimsire dóibh iatt. Is and sin do éirigh in t-éo flaithemhnais ⁊ in t-uaithne airechais ⁊ in t-aingil talmaide .i. Pátraic mac Alprainn .i. apstal na nGaoidhel, ⁊ gabhus in t-esriat do chrothad uisci choisrictha ar na feraibh móra, uair ro bhúi mile léighionn do dheamhnaibh uas a ceannaibh conuic in lá sin, ⁊ dochuatar na demhna i cnocaibh ⁊ i scalpaibh ⁊ i n-imlibh na criche ⁊ ind orba uatha ar cach leath . . . (Stokes, 2–3).

[12] "Ingnad lind mar atchiamait sibh," ar Pátraic, ".i. inn ingen as í óc ildelbach ⁊ tusa, a Cailti," ar Pátraic, "at shenoir chrin chrotach cromliath." "Do fuil a adhbhur sin acum," ar Cailte, "⁊ ní lucht comaimsire sind, ⁊ do Tuathaib dé Danann iss í, ⁊ nemirchradach iat sein, ⁊ missi do clannaib Miled, ⁊ dimbuan irchradach iat" (ibid., 111).

[13] Máirtín Ó Briain, "Some Material on Oisín in the Land of Youth," in *Sages,*

Patrick is not Loegaire mac Néill, who normally plays the role, but Diarmaid mac Cerbaill, whom tradition places considerably later. Such undermining of chronology goes hand in hand with the *Acallam* author's fascination with the *síd* (the pagan otherworld), and the Tuatha Dé Danann (the people who populate it). It is repeatedly stated or implied in the text (as in the passage quoted above) that these beings are indifferent to time and timeless themselves, to the extent that even human characters in the *Acallam* who marry into the otherworld or are raised by supernatural fosterers have the option of escaping death by returning to the *síd*.[14] The Fenian heroes themselves, Caílte says, were wont to spend as much time with the Tuatha Dé Danann as with human beings,[15] and in the present of the story of the *Acallam*, the old Fenian freely commutes between this world, specifically the company of Patrick, and the otherworld, where he is welcomed as a contemporary and not as an "old man," and where his services as a warrior and hunter are much in demand.[16]

The continuous, infectious presence of the timeless otherworld in the *Acallam* almost mitigates the human time clash that underlies the text's premise: in the episode that features the forever fair, hopelessly "uncontemporary" Scothniam, for instance, both Patrick and Caílte end up on the same side of a metaphysical and temporal gap. This emphasis upon the otherworld complicates an even greater problem that is posed in the text: namely, the clash between cultures, pre-Christian (as represented by Caílte and the other Fenians) and Christian (as represented by Patrick). This problem, however, seems soluble, and the two sides are apparently reconciled: Caílte and his Fenian friends are exorcized, baptized, and saved; we learn from Caílte that Finn mac Cumaill, a seer as well as a warrior, believed in God, about whose existence he learned on several occasions through his mantic powers;[17] Patrick releases Finn and other kinsmen of Caílte from hell;[18] and Caílte becomes the helpful and beloved companion of Patrick, who relies upon him for sundry chores, such as finding water for mass baptisms[19] and

---

Saints and Storytellers. Celtic Studies in Honor of Professor James Carney, ed. Donnchadh Ó Corráin, Liam Breatnach, and Kim McCone. Maynooth Monographs 2 (Maynooth: An Sagart, 1989), 185–86.

[14] Stokes, 13, 134.

[15] Ibid., 147.

[16] Ibid., 44–53, 189–203.

[17] Ibid., 41, 52, 68–69, 74, 75–76.

[18] Ibid., 117.

[19] Ibid., 3–4.

robbing graves in order to procure wealth for the Church.[20] Even the Tuatha Dé Danann are admitted into the Christian fold, at least in the person of Aillenn, the *síd* woman whom Patrick marries to the king of Connacht in what is described as the first marriage ceremony he performed in Ireland.[21] Sinisterly underlying the ecumenical friendliness that seems to pervade the *Acallam*, however, is a subtext that has been explored by Richard Sharpe and Kim McCone,[22] who have reconstructed for us an antagonism specifically between the *fénnidi*, marginal hunter-warriors mythologized in the Fenian cycle of stories, and the Church, in the eyes of which both the real and the mythical *fénnidi* constituted a particularly pernicious native institution. McCone has suggested that the *Acallam* represents a rehabilitation of the Fenian tradition in the wake of the the increasing obsolescence of the aforementioned antagonism, which had kept mention of the Fenian heroes and their adventures to a minimum during the earlier (that is, pre-twelfth-century) period of Irish literature.[23] That the tension at least vestigially lingers in the *Acallam* can be inferred here and there—for instance, from the loaded exchange in which Diarmaid mac Cerbaill, the king of Ireland, proposes a very generous fifty-fifty split of provisions with Patrick's retinue, and the saint responds:

"Not so, for there are more of you; let the food be divided into three portions, of which a third goes to the Church as is its due." And so it was done. "Well, King of Ireland," said Patrick, "Let not those two [Caílte and Oisín] deprive you of your share of heaven." "How could that be, holy Patrick?" asked Diarmaid. "On account of the great deal of attention you pay to them," said the saint.[24]

According to Patrick, if not according to the author of the *Acallam*, *fianaigecht* (lore about the Fenian heroes) is to be taken in measured doses lest it threaten one's spiritual health.

Clearly, then, this most luxuriant of medieval Irish texts presents

---

[20] Ibid., 31.

[21] Ibid., 219.

[22] Richard Sharpe, "Hiberno-Latin *Laicus*, Irish *Láech* and the Devil's Men," *Ériu* 30 (1979): 75–92; Kim McCone, "Werewolves, Cyclopes, *Díberga*, and *Fíanna*: Juvenile Delinquency in Early Ireland," *Cambridge Medieval Celtic Studies* 12 (1986): 1–22.

[23] McCone, 1.

[24] "Ni hamhlaid," ar Pátraic, "ór lia dáibhsi, ₇ roinnter ar trí iat, ₇ tabar a trian donn eclais, ór as í sin a cuit féin." Ocus dorónad amhluidh. "Maith, a rí Eirenn," ar Pátraic, "ná benudh in dias út do chuid nimhe dítsa." Cidh é-sein, a naem-Pátraic?" ol Diarmuid. "A mhéd dobeiri dot uidh iat," ar Pátraic (Stokes, 66).

us with a heady mixture—or, perhaps we should say, "dialogue"—of different times, different cultures, and different genres: place-name lore, heroic tale, hagiography, prose, and verse. But there is another dialogue, or attempt at dialogue, that is prominently on display here, one which has been barely remarked on by scholars, but which is fundamentally connected with these other contrasts and is at the very heart of the composition of the *Acallam*. For this text purports very self-consciously to be a transcription of the lore, tales, and poems transmitted by Caílte to Patrick and others in the era when writing came to Ireland along with Christianity. Therefore the *Acallam* supposedly contains a series of oral performances rendered into a literary form.

I am certainly not maintaining that there is necessarily anything in this text or any of the other Irish texts mentioned in this paper that is in fact a transcription of orally composed prose or verse. But there are very few other medieval European works that maintain this conceit of oral provenance in such a sustained and analytic manner. The premise of the *Acallam* is not arrived at easily and requires divine intervention (of a Christian kind, that is!). Almost immediately after they meet, Patrick begins to pump Caílte for information and stories about Finn and his men. Caílte's storytelling and recitation of poems leaves the saint with mixed feelings: "Were it not for us the downfall of religion, the neglect of prayer, and the foresaking of dialogue (*acallam*) with the king of heaven and earth, the time spent talking with you, warrior, would seem short";[25] and, "that would be diversion for our mind and spirit, were it not a destruction of piety, a negligence of prayer, and an abandonment of praising the Lord."[26] Fortunately for us, the hooked but guilt-ridden Patrick consults a higher authority:

> They stayed there until the morning of the next day, at which time Patrick donned his vestments and went outside onto the lawn. Following him were sixty priests, sixty psalmodists, and sixty bishops, sowing faith and religion throughout Ireland. Two guardian angels came to Patrick at that time, Aibelán and Solusbrethach. He asked them whether it were the wish of the King of Heaven and Earth that he, Patrick, be listening to stories of the fían. The angels responded emphatically in unison:

---

[25] "Mun budh coll crábhaidh,₇ mun bud maindechtnaige urnaigthi, ₇ mun budh tréigen acallmha rígh nime ₇ talman dúind, ro bo gairit linn t'acallaimsi, a ócláich," ar Pátraic (ibid., 4).

[26] "As gairdiugud menman ₇ aicenta dúin sin acht min bhudh coll crábaid, ₇ min bhudh maidnechtnaighi urnaigthi, [₇ min bud trécon etarmolta in Coimdedh] dhúin é" (ibid., 9).

"Dear holy cleric, no more than a third of the stories that they used to know do the old warriors tell you, on account of their forgetfulness. Let these be written by you on the tablets of poets and in the decrees of the learned, for it will be entertaining for both the masses and the nobility of later times to listen to these tales." Then the angels left him.[27]

With this vindication of his Fenian fieldwork ringing in his ears, Patrick proceeds to baptize Caílte and his companions, and then continues in his role as enthusiastic audience. The saint responds to Caílte's first storytelling performance as a baptized Christian with an unqualified expression of glee: "Well do your stories suit us, as does your company."[28] But now there is a new dimension to Patrick's pastime in the company of the old Fenian. After the latter tells the tale of how Finn admonished the wayward *fian* lad Mac Lugach, Patrick exclaims: " 'Good the tale you have told us. Where is Broccán the scribe?' 'Here, holy cleric.' 'Take up your book, inkhorn, and pen, and write down that story.' And Broccán did so at once."[29] Patrick's ordering his scribe to take dictation becomes an irregular form of punctuation throughout the rest of the *Acallam*, marking Caílte's verbal performances and signalling either shifts from one episode to another, or moves from one place to another. This scribal imperative takes on a "national" and secular character when Patrick and Caílte visit Tara and meet Diarmaid, the king of Ireland, who, after Caílte chants a massive poem about the history of the Tara *fian*, asks:

"Where are the poets (*filid*) and the shanachies of Ireland? Let this be written in the tablets of poets, the recensions of sages, and the decrees of the learned, so that each may take back to

---

[27] Ocus do bhátur annsin co táinic maden arnamárach, gabais Pátraic a eirredh uime, 7 táinic ar in faithchi amach, 7 trí fichit sacart, trí fichit sailmchétlaid 7 trí fichit naeimescub 'na fharrad ac silad creidmhe 7 crábaid sechnón Eirenn. Ocus doriachtadar a dhá aingel fhorcoiméta cum Pátraic ann sin .i. Aibelán 7 Solusbreathach, 7 fiafraighios dibh in budh méid le rígh nime 7 talman beith dosom ag éisdecht re scéla na Féinne. Frecrait na haingil dosom co comnart cubaidh: "A anum, a naeimchléirigh!" ar siat, "ní mó iná trian a scél innisit na senlaeich út ar dáigh dermait 7 dichuimhne [orra]. Ocus scríbhthar [na scéla sin] letsa i támlorguibh filed 7 i mbriat[h]raibh ollaman, ór budh gairdiugudh do dronguibh 7 do degdáinibh deridh aimsire éisdecht frisna scéluib sin." Ocus do imt[h]igset na haingil [uada] iarsin" (ibid.).

[28] "Is tairisi linn do scéla 7 tú fein budhesta" (ibid., 11).

[29] "As maith in scél sin (ro indi)sis dúin; cáidhe Brocán scríbhnid?" "(Sunn), a naeimhchléirigh," ar Brocan. ["Tabair do lebar 7 t'adharc 7 do pend cugat, 7] scríbhthar an scél út lat." Ocus dorinne Brocan acétóir (ibid., 18).

his own territory and home his share of all that Caílte and Oisín have told of great deeds of courage and heroism, and of
the place-name lore of Ireland."[30]

Both church and state, clerical and native orders of learned men (both
apparently equally literate) take up the task of recording Caílte's oral
lore with a vengeance. Patrick is even careful to make sure that the stories Caílte tells while he is away are recorded after their paths cross
again:

> Patrick asked Caílte for news [or "stories"] since the time he
> left him till the time he came back to him, and Caílte told him
> the truth. "Well, Broccán," said Patrick, "let Caílte's accounts
> be written down and preserved by you, lest they go to waste,
> so that they may be a diversion for both the masses and the
> nobility for the rest of time."[31]

How, we may ask, does Caílte does respond to this adulatory tidal
wave of ink? In a self-contained episode of the *Acallam*, in which
Caílte meets St. Colmán Ela (late sixth/early seventh century),[32] we see
a replay of the opening of the *Acallam* itself, except here Caílte is given
the opportunity to comment on the activities that seem to characterize
the new age in which he finds himself—that is, reading and writing:

> Then three clerics came there and launched their curragh to
> catch some fish. They were reciting the divine offices for the
> canonical hours. Caílte saw them. As he listened to them, he
> spoke this poem: "Seldom did my head's ear hear reading (*léi-
> genn*) over a lake; there was a time when more often did I listen
> to the murmuring (*dordán*) of fine women. If someone had a pen,
> long would he be at writing them down; for, as wretched as I
> am now, I have experienced a multitude of wonders. My journey
> from Tralee was slow, long did I tarry; books of learning (*liubair
> léighind*), rarely did I hear them read aloud." Then Colmán Ela
> and Eoganán came out and saw the big men [Caílte and his
> companions] and their big dogs at their hands. Colmán said,

---

[30] "Caid a filet sin 7 senchaide Eirenn? Scribthar i tamlorgaib filed 7 a slechtaib
suad 7 a mbriathraib ollaman [sud,] co mbere cach a chuid lais da crich 7 da ferann
bodein da cach ní dar' indis Cailti 7 Oissin da morgnimarthaib 7 gaile 7 gaiscid, do
dindshenchus Eirenn" (ibid., 73).

[31] "Ocus maith, a Brogain," ar Pátraic, "scribthar 7 lesaigther let scela Cailti
nach dechat a mudha, corub gairdiugud do drongaib 7 do degdáinib deirid na
haimsire iat" (ibid., 217).

[32] Ibid., 81–86.

"Truly, that is Caílte of Finn's retinue; now he belongs to Patrick's retinue."[33]

Most likely the poem attributed to Caílte in this passage was not composed by the author of the *Acallam* and was not even originally associated with Caílte, who in the text is *not* approaching Colmán's dwelling from any place called Tralee. In his study of the story of the ill-fated lovers Cael and Créide as presented in the *Acallam*, James Carney has convincingly argued that the poems attributed to them, like many of the poems contained in the *Acallam*, are from different contexts altogether.[34] Nevertheless, the fitting together in the Colmán episode of verse, speaker, and situation is ingenious. The *dordán* "murmuring" that the poetic speaker contrasts with *léigenn* "reading" conjures up the *dord fiansa* or *dord fian(nachta)*, a sound made by Caílte and his fellow hunters of old to flush out their game, a Fenian calling card to which pointed reference is made elsewhere in the *Acallam*.[35] Furthermore, the implied invidious comparison of culturally produced sounds that is operating in this poem—perhaps, just perhaps, one might prefer to listen to the sweet warbled nothings of women rather than to prayers recited by clerics—evokes the acoustically coded tension that flares up between Patrick and Oisín in another literary *acallam*, the "Dialogue between Oisín and Patrick," a poem that enjoyed great popularity among scribes from at least the sixteenth century on.[36] The following is from Gerard Murphy's translation, slightly revised: "Oisín, your slumber is long: rise up and listen to the psalms, now that your activity and prosperity are over; you used to do battle in fierce war." (Oisín responds:) "My activity and prosperi-

---

[33] Is ann sin tangadur tri maic ecalsa do muintir na cleirech, ⁊ do chuirset a curach amach do gabail éisc, iat ac denam a n-uird a trath, ⁊ atconnairc Cailti iat, ro bói icc á n-eistecht, ⁊ adubairt in láid: Ba hannam re hé mo chind / cloistecht re léigind os lind, / ba minca lim ro bói than / eistecht re dordan degban. / Gebé nech ica mbiad pend / fada do biad 'ga scribenn, / is truag mar atussa bos / is mor d'ingantaib fuarus. / Mall mo thurus ó Thráig Lí / fada atú 'ga furnaidí, / liubair léighind, mór in mod / a n-eistecht lem ba hannam. Is andsin tainic Colman Ela ⁊ Eogan[án] amach ⁊ atchondcadur na fir mora ⁊ na coin mora ina lamaib. "Is fír," ar Colmán, "[i]s é Cailti siut, ⁊ do muintir Fhind hé," ar-si Colman, "⁊ is do muintir nóemPatraic fos dó" (ibid., 82).

[34] James Carney, "Two Poems from *Acallam na Senórach*," in *Celtic Studies. Essays in Memory of Angus Matheson*, ed. James Carney and David Greene (London: Routledge and Kegan Paul, 1968), 22–32.

[35] Stokes, 22, 25, 183.

[36] See Pádraig Ó Fiannachta's discussion of the evolution of this text in his article "The Development of the Debate between Pádraig and Oisín." *Béaloideas* 54–55 (1986–87): 183–205.

ty are over since Finn no longer has a battalion. After them I care not
for clerics, nor is music sweet to me." (Patrick rejoins:) "You never
heard such good music from the beginning of the great world till to-
night. You are old, stupid, and gray, though once you used to reward
learned men on hilltops." (And Oisín:) "I have heard music better
than their music, though you praise the clergy highly: the chatter of
the blackbird of Leitir Laoi and the sound made by the *dord fian*."[37]
It is clear from these verses, as from the poem attributed to Caílte in
the *Acallam*, what the source of clerical "music" or utterance is: the
written word. That the new medium is perhaps ultimately incompati-
ble with what Oisín and his ilk have to say or represent is more or
less stated in a quatrain of a poem addressed by Oisín to Patrick,
which is preserved in the Scottish Book of the Dean of Lismore: "If
choice Raighne lived, and Caol Cródha, son of Criomhthann [two
Fenian heroes], your book would not long hold together, O man who
reads from a Bible."[38]

Of course, such a radical impasse caused by an unwillingness of the
old and oral to be contained by the new and literary is not really to be
found in the bemused Caílte's thoughts on the fishing and reciting clerics on the lake, or for that matter anywhere else in the *Acallam*. His only
mildly challenging response to clerical literacy and knowledge is perhaps more directly comparable to the similarly competitive yet basically
cooperative attitude exhibited by the poet-madman (*geilt*) Suibne of the
medieval text *Buile Shuibne* "The Madness of Suibne" when he first
meets the saint who is to become his amanuensis:

> Suibne went to the place where Moling was, Tech Moling. At
> that time Moling was reading aloud the psalter of Coemgen to
> his community. Suibne came up to the brink of the well in the
> sight of the cleric and began to eat the watercress. "You're

[37] A Oisín as fada do shúan / eiridh súas is éisd na sailm / ó thairnic do lúth
is do rath / do chuirtheá cath a ngleó garbh. / Do tháirnic mo lúth is mo rath / ó
nach mairionn cath ag Fiond / i ccleircibh ni fhuil mo spéis / nó ceól da n-éis ní
binn liom. / Ni chúalais a ccomhmaith do ceól / ó thús domain mhóir gus anocht
/ tá tú arsaidh aimglic líath / gé do dhioltá clíar ar cnoc. / ... Do-chúal ceól as
fearr no an ceól / ge mor mholus tú in chlíar / sgalgarnach luin Leitreach Laoí /
's a' faoídheadh do-níodh in Dord Fian (Gerard Murphy, ed. and trans., *Duanaire
Finn. The Book of the Lays of Fionn*, vol. 2, Irish Texts Society 28 [London: Irish Texts
Society, 1933], 204, trans. 205).
[38] Dá maireadh Raighne roghdha (?). / is Caol Cródha mac Criomhthainn, / ní
bhiadh do leabhar lé chéile, / a fhir léigheas a bíobla (Neil Ross, ed. and trans.,
Heroic Poetry from the Book of the Dean of Lismore, Scottish Gaelic Texts 3 [Edinburgh:
Scottish Gaelic Texts Society, 1939], 118; the translation quoted here in a slightly
revised form is on page 119).

eating early, dear *geilt*," said the cleric. It is then that Moling said, and Suibne responded [here follows a dialogue poem]: "It is early, dear *geilt*, for proper observance." "It may be early for you, dear cleric, but it is already tierce in Rome." "How do you know, dear *geilt*, when it is tierce in Rome?" "Knowledge comes to me from the Lord every morning and every evening."[39]

After their exchange, the saint with the book and the madman from the forest become fast friends. Moling enjoins upon Suibne to come to him every evening so that Moling can write down Suibne's poems and accounts of his adventures, and Suibne agrees to do so.[40] (It is worth noting that he became a *geilt* as punishment for, among other irreligious things, trying to destroy a cleric's book.)[41]

Moling does not thoroughly domesticate the wild-man poet; he gives him leave to roam through Ireland during the day, just as Patrick does not stop Caílte from satisfying his *wanderlust*, even if it takes him into the realm of the Tuatha Dé Danann. It is significant that Caílte, like the *geilt*, needs to roam. After a series of tales early on in the *Acallam* in which Caílte highlights for Patrick the sad story of the end of the Fenians and their era, the oral informant experiences burn-out and declares: " 'Tomorrow it will be time for me to go away, dear holy Patrick.' 'Why will you leave?' asked Patrick. 'To seek the hills, spaces, and landmarks where my friends, my foster-brothers, the chief *fénnid*, and the stalwarts of the *fiana* of Ireland used to be with me—for too long, I think, have I been in the same place.' "[42] Caílte's ultimate destination in this excursion away from the Patrician juggernaut is the *síd* of Ess Ruaid, where he is warmly wel-

---

[39] Táinic Suibhne roime fo dheóidh conuige an baile i raibhe Moling .i. Teach Moling. Ba hisin tan sin robói psaltair Chaoimhghin i ffiadnuise Moling aga dénamh do lucht an aiceapta. Táinic iarumh Suibhne for sraith na tioprat i fiadhnuisi an chléirigh 7 rogab ag ithe biorair. "As moch-longadh sin, a ghealtagáin," ar an cléirech; conadh ann adbert Moling 7 rofreagair Suibhne é: Mochthráth sin, a ghealtagáin, / re ceilebhradh cóir. / Gidh moch leat-sa, a chlérecháin, / tánic tert ag Róimh. / Gá fios duit-si, a ghealtagáin, / cuin tig tert ag Róimh? / Fios tig dhamh ón Thigerna / gach madain 's gach nóin (J. G. O'Keeffe, ed., *Buile Shuibne,* Mediaeval and Modern Irish Series 1 [Dublin: Dublin Institute for Advanced Studies, 1931], 72–73).

[40] Ibid., 75.

[41] Ibid., 2–3.

[42] "As mithigh damsa imthecht amárach, a anam, a naemPatraic." "Crét um a n-imthighi?" ar Pátraic. "D'iarraid cnoc 7 céite 7 dingnadh in bhaili ir-rabutar mu choicli 7 mu chomaltada 7 in flaithfénnid 7 maithi Fian Eirenn am fhochair, ór is fada lim beith a n-aein inad" (Stokes, 42).

comed by the otherworldly lord Ilbrecc.[43] In the otherworld Caílte
finds the spear of Finn mac Cumaill, the story of which is told at length
by Caílte to his *síd* audience. It was with this weapon, they and we
learn, that Finn won the leadership of the *fian*.[44] Through the telling
of this tale, the climactic episode in the cycle of tales about Finn's
boyhood deeds, Caílte, his gusto for storytelling renewed despite or
perhaps because of the absence of any scribes, brings back to life the
ongoing Fenian performance of story and verse that had petered out
in the company of Patrick.[45]

There is another visit to Ess Ruaid which takes place in the second
half of the *Acallam*, at a point when Caílte, having rejoined Patrick, is
feeling physically exhausted, not just psychologically and narratolog-
ically depleted as in the episode discussed above. During this second
stay in Ess Ruaid he is treated to a full-fledged regime of restoration under the supervision of the female physician Bébinn.[46] At the end of his
cure he feels like a new, or like the old, man. "Then the people of the
síd went out to the rapids of Ess Ruaid, took their clothes off, and went
in to swim. Then Caílte said: 'Why don't I go swimming too? After all,
my health has returned to me.' And so he plunged and swam in the
water."[47] Back in the *síd*, Caílte's hosts notice the difference as well:
" 'By our word,' said the people of the *síd*, 'we have never seen a
better-looking fellow upon the face of the earth than you; we suspect
that Finn himself looked no better than you.' 'Alas,' said Caílte, 'had
you seen Finn, you would have exchanged the world to get to know
him.' "[48] With the return of his nostalgia, Caílte recalls his commit-
ments to Patrick and literary posterity. He must go, he explains to the
otherworldly folk, and rendezvous with the saint at Tara, where he
had promised to give Patrick, the king of Ireland, and their respective
scribal communities more of the lore he has at his disposal.[49] " 'We

---

[43] Ibid., 44–53.

[44] Ibid., 47–50.

[45] See Joseph Falaky Nagy, "Compositional Concerns in the *Acallam na Senórach*," in Ó Corráin et al., 152–53.

[46] Stokes, 191–203.

[47] Is ann sin do eirgedur lucht in tshída amach co hur Essa Ruaid meic Mod-
huirn, ⁊ ro bensat a n-étaigi díb, ⁊ tangadur ar in n-es, ⁊ doronadur snám. Ocus
adubairt Cailte annsin: "Cid damsa gan dul do tshnám, uair tainic mo tshlainti
dam." Ocus doróni a mescad ar in uisci annsin (ibid., 201).

[48] "Dar ar mbreithir ám," ar lucht in tshída, "ní fhaccamar-ne riam óclach bud
fherr anaissiu ar tonnchlar in talman, ⁊ dar lind nír' ferr Find féin anáissiu."
"Truag, no sin!" ar Cailte, "damad hé Find do chífed sibsi dobéradh sib in drong
daenna uile ina fhaisneis" (ibid., 202).

[49] Ibid.

have an aid for you,' said the girl [Bébinn, Caílte's physician]. 'What aid is that?' asked Caílte. 'A drink for reviving memory will be sent to you at Tara, so that everything that you every encountered— waterfall, stream, or inlet, or battle or duel fought there—will be in your memory.' "[50]

This potion seems to be precisely what Caílte and the *Acallam* need, but it very conspicuously does not come from Patrick and the world he represents. In fact, we never hear of this potion again. Were it to be re-introduced outside the blissfully unlettered context of the *síd* of Ess Ruaid, perhaps it would prove to be too much of a "pagan" threat to what is scheduled to continue at Tara, namely, the writing-down of oral tradition. Just how long would the dialogue, both as event and as text, have gone on if Caílte had remembered all things past? Even as it is, the *Acallam* is "endless." Remember Caílte's challenge to the scribe in the poem quoted above: "If someone had a pen, long would he be at writing them down; for, as wretched as I am now, I have experienced a multitude of wonders." Caílte in the timeless otherworld finds the secret of youth and potentially becomes an unfailing source of recollections; but in the latter-day world of Patrick and his scribes, his memory is designated by Patrick's angels as valuable but finite and failing: the memory of an old man. How else could it be controlled and contained within a text? How else could the text be legitimated as an authentic representation of what was said? Yet Caílte, the other-world, and the author of the *Acallam* gently resist the authority of the text by stretching it out, or suggesting that it could be stretched out, beyond reasonable literary limits. Similarly, Caílte's lifespan is extended and finally left an open question, as if the author, or the scribes who copied the manuscript, did not have the heart to finish him or the dia-logue. Hence this is a text that, in its sympathy for the oral presentation and presenter it supposedly records, attempts to defeat its own finite-ness as a text, its own textuality.

Patrick and the learned men of Ireland are not the only ones in the *Acallam* who are eager to record what Caílte has to say. During one of his spells apart from Patrick, Caílte comes across an *airfitech* "musician" or "performer" of the *síd* with a mission:

"I am Cas Corach mac Caincinde, the son of an *ollam* [a high-ranking poet] of the Tuatha Dé Danann, and I myself am a

---

[50] "Ocus fil cobair accainde duit," ar in ingen. "Ca cobair sin?" ar Cailte. "Deoch cuimnigthi céille d'indlucud duinde duit co Temraig connach tecma duit es nó abhann nó indber nó a cath nó a comlann nach bia a cuimne accut" (ibid.)

candidate for *ollam*-ship. This is what brought me here: to learn
the knowledge, truth, stories, and accounts of the great deeds
of prowess of the *fian* from Caílte." Then he made music for
them and put them to sleep. [This is traditionally the way in
which a musician demonstrates his talent and his power to
control his audience.] "Well, dear Caílte," said Cas Corach,
"What answer do you give to my request?" "Everything which
you came for is yours, if you have the skill and the talent to
comprehend everything the *fian* accomplished of deeds of val-
or."[51]

According to this contract for transmission, Caílte may communicate
as much as the recipient can manage to retain. Here, let us note,
retention is not textual; it is rather a matter of one oral performer's
listening to the repertoire of another. Neither memory nor medium is
defined as finite in this relationship, and there is, perhaps as a result,
a warm interdependence to the subsequent relationship between
Caílte and Cas Corach that, at least for this reader, threatens almost
to overshadow or even belie the affinity with one another that Caílte
and Patrick display. The *airfitech* and the Fenian become a veritable
dynamic duo. In one episode, they rid the land of three wolves who
are actually *síd* women in disguise. It is Cas Corach who lures them
with his music-making and then convinces them to shed their wolf
skins, so that they may enjoy the music all the more. Thus exposed,
the women fall prey to Caílte's spear.[52] " 'Good the deed you have
performed, Caílte,' said Cas Corach. 'That was not the deed of an old
man (*senóir*), although it *was* handy to have your musician with you.'
(Caílte responds:) 'How was my deed any better than the deed of the
musician? For you were the one who enticed them out of their wolf
shapes into the shapes of humans.' "[53] In the company of Cas Corach, as in the company of the *síd* folk, the old warrior finds not only

---

[51] "Cas corach mac Cáincinde, mac ollaman do Thuaith dé Danann, ⁊ damna
olloman mé fein," ar eissim, "⁊ iss ed ro m-imluaid, d'fhoglaim fhessa ⁊ fhireolais
⁊ scelaigechta ⁊ morgnim gaiscid na Féinne ó Chailti mac Ronain." Ocus tar a eis-
sin doroine céol ⁊ airfided dóib, ⁊ ro chuir ina suan chotalta iat. "Maith, a m'anum,
a Chailti, ca fregra dobeire forum?" ar eissium. "Cach ní da tangais d'iarraid
d'fhagbail duit,⁊ da raib acut fein d'eladhain ⁊ d'intlecht cach ní dorindedur ind
Fhiann do gnimradaib gaile ⁊ gaiscid do denum" (ibid., 95).
[52] Ibid., 214–216.
[53] "Is maith in t-engnum dorignis, a Cailti," ar Cas Corach, "⁊ ní hengnum
senórach sin aniu, ⁊ ro bói ba (?) ⁊ roba maith do t'airfidech beith it fharrud." "Ocus
ca ferr in t-engnum dorigniusa na eng[num] ind airfidig .i. dorignis a mbrégad o
rechtaib con í rechtai dáine" (ibid., 216).

an eager audience that sets no limits on Caílte and his memories, but also the chance to be young and vital again.

It is remarkable that the main representative of the ranks of the *áes dána* ("people of art") in the *Acallam* is characterized primarily as an *airfitech*, a musician, and not as a *fili*, a poet. In this choice the text reflects the apparent fact that it was the lower orders of oral performers, such as the *airfitech*, who in story and song sustained the Fenian tradition into the era of the composition of the *Acallam*, when *fianaigecht* (stories about Finn and his *fian*) became literarily so acceptable and even fashionable. The elevation of the musician, moreover, indicates the fluidity of the artistic scene in the Ireland of the twelfth and thirteenth centuries, when, as we have already noted, the various orders of performers experienced reshuffling within their traditional hierarchy, as well as a realignment with a literary tradition reconstituted outside the monastic realm.

Cas Corach and his craft, like Caílte and the lore he conveys, need to be formally introduced to Patrick, and the *airfitech* must receive the saint's approval. It is given—indeed Cas Corach's is made the prince of the arts, and its practitioners the *crème de la crème* of the artistic world—but all this occurs with some hesitation on Patrick's part, reminiscent of his ambivalence toward *fianaigecht* itself. After the saint and his scribe Broccán have sampled some of the *airfitech*'s sleep-inducing performance, Broccán says:

> "Good is the artistry you have demonstrated for us." "Good indeed," said Patrick, "except for the little strain of *síd* magic in it; were it not for that, there would be nothing more like the music of the King of Heaven." "If there is music in heaven," said Broccán, "why shouldn't there be music on earth? It wouldn't be fair to banish music." "I wasn't suggesting that," said Patrick, "only that one not put too much faith in it."[54]

This caution, together with that issued to Diarmaid mac Cerbaill concerning his attachment to the Fenians cited earlier, is not only a (by now) half-hearted Christian party-line on "pagan" tradition and its perceived proponents, but also a token scribal finger in a leaking dam. The *airfitech*'s time has come, and his repertoire of Fenian tales

---

[54] "Maith ind elada sin dorónais duind," ar Brogan, "Is maith immorro," ar Pátraic, "acht muna beth sianargan in brechta sídhe inti, ⁊ nocho n[fh]uil ní bo chosmala re céol Rig nime inas acht muna beth sin." "Matá ceol a nim," ar Brocan, "cid nach biad i talmain, ⁊ ní cóir amlaid ind airfited do dichur," ar Brocan. "Ní apraim úm," ar Pátraic, "acht gan rochreidim dó" (ibid., 99).

and *laíde* (quasi-narrative poems) overwhelms the literary scene in the centuries following the composition of the *Acallam*.

In sum, the *Acallam*, usually treated as a rather superficial literary work by its few modern commentators, reveals a penetrating awareness of the compatibilities and incompatibilities between oral and literary processes of transmission and preservation, an awareness that matches or even exceeds that of modern-day Celtic scholars. Here in the *Acallam* we see hermeneutic models presented and developed that are not very far removed from those which we in literary and oral traditional studies today develop and ponder. In the world of this text, oral performance and writing become strange bedfellows, like Caílte and Patrick: there is both attraction and repulsion, cooperation and annexation. Furthermore, the oral performer draws his inspiration from sources other than those of the scribe and the reader, and this creates a dynamic tension. The written text inevitably limits the vitality of the oral performance, which strains to break free, while oral performance threatens the fixity and form of literary composition. We also learn that transmission—oral, literary, or oral-to-literary—involves both entropy and renewal. And, whether or not there is such a thing as a "transitional text" in reality, here in the *Acallam* we are certainly treated to one in theory.

In focusing on this particular text, I did not mean to give the impression that it is only in the *Acallam* that we see such issues raised and discussed in the medieval Irish literary milieu. The consciousness exhibited here reflects the several centuries of scribal activity that preceded and followed the composition of the *Acallam*, a literary tradition which was rooted in the culture of early Christian Ireland and which coexisted synergistically with an ongoing oral tradition. The story and stories of the *Acallam* constitute only a part of what I would call a literary "mythology" of transmission and transition through which the scribal community and its audiences explored, legitimated, questioned, and relegitimated the foundation and nature of their written tradition. Stories such as the various hagiographical analogues to the *Acallam* (that is, accounts of miraculous meetings between saints and long-dead warriors or primeval sages), the tale of how the text of the *Táin Bó Cúailnge* ("Cattle Raid of Cooley") was recovered, the anecdote about how Cenn Faelad lost his "brain of forgetfulness" and became a scribe, along with the many other literary narratives that center on the process of transmission, form a multi-layered totality that deserves to be examined as such.[55] All too often has the medi-

---

[55] See Padraig Ó Riain, "Conservation in the Vocabulary of the Early Irish

eval Irish author been characterized as a juggler or bungler of sources trying to "con" us, or as a naif whom we condescendingly second-guess. In fact the men of letters behind the *Acallam* and the Irish literary tradition knew what they were doing, appreciated the difficulties of what they were doing, and often wrote about those difficulties. Given the gap of time and culture, however, these literati seem like strangers to us. Perhaps the *Acallam* can help to make them more familiar, by serving the modern community of scholars as a latter-day Caílte: a friendly old survivor, who forces us to rediscover the past and assess our understanding of it anew.

Church," in Ó Corráin *et al.*, 363; Edgar M. Slotkin, "Medieval Irish Scribes and Fixed Texts," *Éigse* 17 (1977–79): 437–50; and Nagy "Close Encounters of the Traditional Kind in Medieval Irish Literature," in *Celtic Folklore and Christianity. Studies in Memory of William W. Heist*, ed. Patrick Ford (Santa Barbara and Los Angeles: McNally and Luftin, and the UCLA Center for the Study of Comparative Folklore and Mythology, 1983), 129–49.

GAIL IVY BERLIN

Memorization in Anglo-Saxon England: Some Case Studies

I n Anglo-Saxon England, the problem of memorization is one that would have concerned both singers in meadhalls and monks in monasteries. In both realms, a good memory was a valued possession. The king's thane in *Beowulf* who recites Beowulf's adventure with Grendel is praised for the extent of his memory. He is

> guma gilphlæden, gidda gemyndig,
> se ðe ealfela ealdgesegena
> worn gemunde.[1]

> (a man laden with glory, mindful of songs, who remembered a great many old traditions, a large number.)

Similarly, those engaged in a religious life were deeply concerned with memorizing. Throughout the Middle Ages, both in England and on the continent, schools encouraged the memorization of psalms as a

---

[1] Frederick Klæber, ed., *Beowulf and the Fight at Finnsburg*, 3rd ed. (Lexington, MA: D. C. Heath and Company, 1950), ll. 868–870a.

rudimentary form of education. Monks were required to memorize psalms one through one hundred fifty in order. We are told, for instance, that John of St. Albans (bishop from the late twelfth to early thirteenth centuries) knew the psalter entirely by heart.[2] More advanced students memorized other portions of the Bible. Pierre Riché has collected two examples of men with exceptional powers of memory. "Abbot Achivus of Aguane could remember practically everything he read and knew almost all the books of the Bible; Cassiodorus cited his monks the example of a blind man who knew all the sacred texts."[3] England could boast comparable scholars. Eddius Stephanus reports that St. Wilfred (c. 634–709) "read the Scriptures and had a wonderful memory for their text."[4] Several centuries later, Hugh of St. Avalon is praised for similar skills. Geraldus Cambrensis reports that Hugh of St. Avalon, Bishop of Lincoln from 1186–1200, "had the Bible so in hand that scarcely any part of it could be read in his presence but he would recite several of the preceding and following passages with faithful and exact recollection."[5]

At least two possible systems of memorization prevailed in Anglo-Saxon England after the introduction of Christianity: one derived from native tradition, and the other from literate monastic practice. They imply different conceptions of what it is that is memorized (oral performance or written text) and different techniques of memorization. Examples of people engaged in memorization that have come down to us, however, do not always fall neatly into the categories of "oral" or "literate." Monasteries fostered both the lettered and unlettered. Oral poets could easily hear written texts read aloud. Among those who did receive some schooling, lettered and unlettered students would have had to employ somewhat differing tactics for memorizing. I will examine in particular these different methods of memorization and the varied notions of what end product may count as an adequately memorized "text."

---

[2] Cited in David Knowles, *The Monastic Order in England*, 2nd ed. (Cambridge: Cambridge Univ. Press, 1966), 471.

[3] Pierre Riché, *Education and Culture in the Barbarian West: Sixth Through Eighth Centuries* (Columbia, SC: Univ. of South Carolina Press, 1976), 465–66. I am deeply indebted to this book for my knowledge of educational practices in the Middle Ages.

[4] Bertram Colgrave, ed. and trans., *The Life of Bishop Wilfred by Eddius Stephanus* (1927; repr., Cambridge: Cambridge Univ. Press, 1985), 25.

[5] Richard M. Loomis, ed. and trans., *Gerald of Wales: The Life of St. Hugh of Avalon*, Garland Library of Medieval Literature, Series A, vol. 30 (New York: Garland Publishing, Inc., 1985), 11.

Memory and the Learned

The fragility of memory and the utility of writing in bolstering this faculty are common concerns of Anglo-Saxon writers. The author of an Old English charter concerning the lease of lands includes a Latin preface lamenting the unreliability of memory:

> OMNIBUS NAMQUE SAPIENTIBUS NOTVM AC MANIFES-
> TVM CONstat . quod dicta hominum uel facta pro multiplici-
> bus criminum perturbationibus et cogitationum uagationibus
> frequenter ex memoria recedunt nisi litterarum apicibus et cus-
> todie cautela scripturarum reseruentur et ad memoriam reuo-
> centur.[6]

> (It is known and manifest to all the wise that the words and deeds of men frequently slip from memory, through the manifold agitations caused by wicked deeds, and as the result of wandering thoughts, unless they are preserved and recalled to mind in the form of words and by the precaution of entrusting them to writing.)

This charter suggests that the dependence on memory alone is not as secure as the combination of words recalled plus written transcript. Writing does not replace the act of recalling words; it supplements memory.

Similarly, King Alfred's Old English version of Augustine's *Soliloquies*, a dialogue between Augustine and Reason, associates writing and memory:

> Þa cwæð heo [Reason]: is þin gemind swa mihtig þæt hit
> mage eall gehealden þæt þu geðengst and hym bebeotst to
> healdenne?
> Þa cwæð ic [Augustine]: nese, la nese, ne min ne nanes man-
> nes nis to þam creftig þæt hit mage eall gehæaldan þæt him
> me on befæst.
> Þa cwæð heo: befæste hit þonne bocstafum and awrit hit.[7]

> (Then said Reason: Is your mind so mighty that it can hold whatever you think and entrust it to hold? Then I said: Ah, no, indeed not, neither my [memory] nor any man's is so skillful

---

[6] Agnes J. Robertson, ed., *Anglo-Saxon Charters* (Cambridge: Cambridge Univ. Press, 1939), charter XIX with Robertson's translation, 34–37.

[7] Thomas A. Carnicelli, ed., *King Alfred's Version of St. Augustine's Soliloquies* (Cambridge: Harvard Univ. Press, 1969), bk. I, ll. 13–17, 49.

that it can hold all that I entrust to it. Then she said: Entrust it then to letters and write it.)

Writing and memorization were closely associated in the medieval schoolroom as well. Riché gives a valuable account of elementary education. He observes that children began their education by learning the alphabet, which they copied upon their tablets. From there, they progressed to syllables and then to nouns.[8] This technique is demonstrated in Bede's account of how John, bishop of Hexam, cured a mute: "Say A, the mute said A, and B, he said B, and so he answered the bishop by giving him the name of each letter. The bishop then continued by asking him to read the syllables and words."[9] Next, students would undertake memorizing the Psalter, which their teacher copied down for them. More advanced students went on to study Scripture. The education of the Anglo-Saxon saint, Guthlac, reflects this pattern. Felix, the author of the prose *Life of Guthlac*, tells us that

> when indeed, after having been taught his letters, he set his mind to learn the chanting of the psalms, then the divine grace sprinkled this same man's [Guthlac's] fertile heart copiously with the moist showers of heavenly dew. Cared for moreover by the best teachers and aided by heavenly grace, he was instructed in Holy Scriptures and in the monastic discipline.[10]

The clearest statement of what techniques of memorization were known to the Anglo-Saxons derives from Alcuin. His *De Rhetorica*, written in the form of a dialogue between Alcuin and Charlemagne, stresses the connection between memory and writing. After Alcuin explains the importance of memory as "the treasury of our thoughts and reflections," Charlemagne asks, "Are there not other precepts which tell us how it can be preserved and strengthened?"[11] Alcuin responds, "We do not have other injunctions upon this subject, except exercise in memorizing, practice in writing, and application to studious activity. We should of course avoid drunkenness, which does the

---

[8] Cited in Riché, 462–63; my translation.

[9] Charles Plummer, in *Venerabilis Baedae: Opera Historica*, vol. 1, bk. V (1896; repr., London: Oxford Univ. Press, 1975), chap. 2, p. 284. All quotations from Bede's *Ecclesiastical History* will be taken from this edition.

[10] Bertram Colgrave, ed. and trans., *Felix's Life of Saint Guthlac* (1956; repr. Cambridge: Cambridge Univ. Press, 1985), chap. XXII, p. 85.

[11] William Samuel Howell, ed. and trans., *The Rhetoric of Alcuin and Charlemagne: A Translation with an Introduction, the Latin Text, and Notes*, Princeton Studies in English, vol. 23 (Princeton: Princeton Univ. Press, 1941), sec. 39, p. 137.

greatest possible injury to all scholarly pursuits."[12] The advice given here, aimed at a literate audience, again associates memorization with the practice of writing and with sheer persistence, ingredients which are mentioned and praised repeatedly in the various accounts of memorization that have come down to us.[13]

Writing and repetition help to form the memory of St. Godric, a good account of whose elementary education we possess. The *Libellus de Vita et Miraculis S. Godrici* by Reginald of Durham informs us that Godric spent some time at the church of St. Mary in Northumberland where he learned his letters along with the school children.

> Ubi ea quæ prius didicit, arctius memoriæ infixit, et quædam quæ antea non cognoverat, ibi audiendo, legendo, atque psallendo apprehendit; nam ea quæ pueris sæpius eadem repentibus audivit, tenacius memoriæ infigere curavit.[14]

> (There, those things which he had previously learned, he impressed more firmly in memory, and certain things which formerly he had not known, there by hearing, reading, and reciting psalms, he apprehended, for those things which he learned through hearing the boys repeating them very often, he took care to fix tenaciously in his memory.)

This method of rote memorization Godric applied to learning psalms, hymns, and prayers.[15] Memorization for Godric, then, presumably involved a written text, as of the psalms, which was consequently absorbed through a process of listening, reading, reciting, and repeating, as one member of a group. We may take Godric's experiences as being typical of those of a beginning student.

The *Life of Leofgyth*, written by Rudolf of Fulda in 836, provides us with an example of the techniques of an advanced student, giving us a sense of her accuracy in memorizing as well. Leofgyth assisted St. Boniface in his attempts to convert Germany to Christian belief. Although

---

[12] Ibid., 139.

[13] Alcuin's account indicates clearly that the classical systems of artificial memory as expressed in such works as the *Rhetorica ad Herennium* did not survive into the Anglo-Saxon period. For further information on systems of memory, see Frances A. Yates, *The Art of Memory* (Chicago: Chicago Univ. Press, 1966); Mary J. Carruthers, *The Book of Memory: A Study of Memory in Medieval Culture* (Cambridge: Cambridge Univ. Press, 1990).

[14] J. Stevenson, ed., *Libellus de Vita et Miraculis S. Godrici, Hermitæ de Finchale* auctore Reginaldo Monacho Dunelmensi, Surtees Society (London: J. B. Nichols and Son, 1847), chap. 16, sec. 45, p. 60.

[15] Ibid.

she passed much of her later life as the abbess of Tauberbischofsheim, she had been educated in England. Rudolf gives the following report of her abilities:

> She applied herself to the pursuit of reading with such diligence that, unless she were occupied with prayer or refreshing the body with food or sleep, the divine Scripture was never out of her hands. For, since she had been educated from early infancy in grammar and in the study of the other liberal arts, she tried to attain to the perfection of spiritual knowledge with such great earnestness in meditation that, as natural gifts combined with diligence, she became most erudite by the double gift of nature and industry. For with a keen mind she went through the volumes of the Old and New Testaments, and committed divine percepts to memory. And she added also the sayings of the holy fathers and the decrees of the canons, as well as the laws of the whole ecclesiastical system in full perfection.[16]

Far more advanced in her studies than Godric, Leofgyth no longer depends on the act of copying or on group recitations. Her natural ability for retaining texts is sharpened by intensive reading instead.

This technique appears to have been effective, for Leofgyth's exceptional abilities were tested by her students. Their duty was to read from the Scriptures to her as she slept:

> And, marvelous to relate, they could not omit one word, or even one syllable, in their reading, without immediately being corrected by her although she slept. For, as those to whom the duty had been allotted themselves said afterwards, when they saw her to be sleeping deeply, they often deliberately made a mistake in reading to test her, but never could they escape detection.[17]

This example indicates that Leofgyth was capable of accurate verbatim memory of an extensive fixed text.

Verbatim memory, however, may not always have been the goal. A case in point may be found in Ælfric's three versions of the Pater

---

[16] Dorothy Whitelock, ed. and trans., *English Historical Documents c. 500–1042* (New York: Oxford Univ. Press, 1955), 722. All further references to Rudolf of Fulda's *Life of Leofgyth* will be taken from this text. *The Metalogicon* of John of Salisbury (twelfth century) likewise cites natural ability and exercise as keys to developing a good memory (Bk. 1, chap. 11).

[17] Whitelock, 786.

noster. Before turning to these texts, however, a few words about memorizing the Pater noster are necessary.

The Pater noster, like the Creed, was a text all Christians, literate or not, were required to learn. Early in the eleventh century, King Canute passed legislation requiring his subjects to learn the Lord's Prayer[18] while the homilist Wulfstan encouraged people to learn it in Latin if possible, in English if not.[19] Works such as Wulfstan's "Sermo de Baptismate" encouraged parents to teach their children the Pater noster and Creed as soon as possible:

> And æfre swa þæt cild raðost ænig ðing specan mæge, tæce man him sona ealra þinga ærest pater noster and credan.[20]

> (And as soon as that child most readily can speak anything, let someone teach him immediately, first of all things, the Pater noster and Creed.)

And again:

> Pater noster 7 credan mymerian þa yldran 7 tæcan heora gingran mid riht geleafan.[21]

> (Elders should remember the Pater noster and Creed and teach [them] to their youngsters with proper belief.)

That these injunctions were heeded seems likely. We are told, for instance, that St. Godric learned the Pater noster while still in the cradle (*ab ipsis cunabulis ante didicerat*).[22]

---

[18] Agnes J. Robertson, ed. and trans., *The Laws of the Kings of England from Edmund to Henry I* (Cambridge: Cambridge Univ. Press, 1925), Canute's Code of Laws, chap. 22, p. 170.

[19] Dorothy Betherum, ed. *The Homilies of Wulfstan* (1957; repr., Oxford: Clarendon Press, 1971), 7a, 166. All citations from Wulfstan's homilies will be from this edition.

Bede's letter to bishop Ecgbert also advises that all under the bishop's care memorize the Pater noster in Latin or in their native tongue. Indeed, Bede himself made English translations of the Pater noster and the Creed for priests who knew no Latin, although these have not survived. (See sec. 5 of "Epistola Baedae ad Ecgbertum Episcopum," in *Venerabilis Baedae Opera Historica*, ed. Charles Plummer [1896; repr., Guilford and London: Billing and Sons Ltd., 1975].) The Council of Clovesho in 747 likewise called for memorizing the Pater noster and Creed in the vernacular. (See Arthur Haddan and William Stubbs, *Councils and Ecclesiastical Documents Relating to Great Britain and Ireland, Edited after Spelman and Wilkins*, vols. 1–3, (Oxford: Oxford Univ. Press, 1869–78), 3:365.

[20] Ibid., 8c, 142–43.

[21] Ibid., 10c, 168.

[22] Stevenson, 4.140.

The parents themselves could have learned the Pater noster in a variety of contexts. Laymen could have encountered the prayer as catechumens, since it was considered necessary to understand the Pater noster and Creed in order to be worthy of baptism.[23] They could also have learned about the Pater noster during the *Prone*, which Milton Gatch defines as a "vernacular office in which the Gospel was explained, announcements were made about the season, the people were catechized, and prayers were bidden."[24] Or they themselves could have been taught by their parents or godparents. The chain of transmission, then, stretches away from the clergy and into family. The above passages thus provide evidence for a memorial oral tradition distinct from the native oral tradition,[25] which, while initially based on a written text consciously memorized, ultimately need not have remained entirely dependent on that text as it passed on from the clergy, to parents, who may well have been unlettered, to children, just able to talk, and, in time, on to their children. However, neither is memorial oral transmission likely to have been entirely divorced from textual tradition since the clergy, no doubt, periodically refreshed the memories of their charges.[26]

While injunctions to learn the Pater noster are plentiful, precise instructions on how this was actually done are not forthcoming; however, since children were encouraged to learn it as soon as they could speak, we may assume that the process of memorization was not considered taxing and that it involved oral repetition. We know, too, that it was often sung, a technique that helped bolster memory.[27] With what degree of accuracy or fixity was the text retained? Such a question can best be answered by a comparison of multiple texts known to be by the same author. While we have numerous copies of the Pater noster in Old English, Ælfric is the only author who has left us three distinct

---

[23] Betherum, 8c, 20.

[24] Milton McC. Gatch, *Preaching and Theology in Anglo-Saxon England: Ælfric and Wulfstan* (Toronto: Univ. of Toronto Press, 1977), 51.

[25] Alan Jabbour likewise distinguishes a primarily memorial oral tradition from oral-improvisational and textual transmission. See his "Memorial Transmission in Old English Poetry," *Chaucer Review* 3 (1969): 177.

[26] Ælfric, in his "Letter to Wulfsige," advises clergy to teach the Pater noster "swa he oftost mæge" (as often as he can). See Benjamine Thorpe, ed. and trans., *The Homilies of the Anglo-Saxon Church. The First Part, Containing the Sermones Catholici, or Homilies of Ælfric*, 2 vols. (1844; repr., New York: Johnson Reprint Corp., 1971), 62. All subsequent references will be to this edition.

[27] See the entries under Pater noster in *A Microfiche Concordance to Old English*, comps., Antonette di Paolo Healy and Richard L. Venezky (Toronto: Center for Medieval Studies, Univ. of Toronto, 1980).

versions of the prayer. Two occur in his homily "De Dominica Oratione," a work which explains the prayer to laymen. The third version
appears at the close of his Second Series of Homilies preceded by the
words "Her is geleafa and gebed, and bletsung, læwedum mannum,
ðe ðæt leden ne cunnon"[28] (Here is belief and prayer and blessing
for ignorant men who do not know Latin). The texts of all three versions are close, and in many cases wording is exact, yet none is a verbatim copy of the others. All three texts are printed below. For ease
in comparison, I have placed each of the seven petitions on a new line
and italicized significant variations.

Ælfric: "De Dominica Oratione" version one

Þu, *ure* Fæder, þe eart on heofonum,
Sy þin nama gehalgod.
Cume þin rice.
Sy ðin wylla *on eorðan swa swa on heofonum.*
Syle us to-dæg urne dæghwamlican hlaf.
And forgyf us ure gyltas, swa swa we forgyfað *ðam þe*
    wið us agyltað.
And ne læd ðu na us on costnunge.
Ac alys us fram yfele. Sy hit swa.

Ælfric: "De Dominica Oratione" version two

Ure Fæder þe eart on heofonum.
Sy ðin nama gehalgod.
Cume ðin rice.
Geweorðe þin willa *on eorðan swa swa on heofonum.*
Syle us *nu* to-dæg urne dæghwamlican hlaf.
Forgif us ure gyltas, swa swa we forgifað *þam mannum*
    þe wið us agyltað.
Ne geðafa, ðu God, þæt we beon gelædde on costnunge.
Ac alys us fram yfele.

Ælfric version three (Conclusion to the Second Series of
Homilies)

Ðu ure Fæder, þe eart on heofenum,
Sy ðin nama gehalgod.
Gecume þin rice.
Sy ðin willa *swa swa on heofenum swa eac on eorðan.*

---

[28] Thorpe, 258–75.

Syle us todæge urne dæghwomlice hlaf,
and forgif us ure gyltas swa swa we forgyfað þam ðe
  wið us agyltað.
And ne læd þu na us on costunge.
Ac alys us fram yfele. Sy his swa.

Three types of changes occur among these versions: reversals of
phrasing, additions to the text, and variations in diction. Reversals in
phrasing occur in version three. This version is nearly identical to the
first, except for the substitution of "Gecume" for "Cume" (petition
two) and for a reversal in phrasing in petition three where "swa swa
on heofenum swa eac on eorþan" replaces "on eorðan swa on heofenum." Additions and variations in diction provide the most striking
differences between versions one and two, both of which appear
within one homily. In two instances, version one gives the more expansive wording, preferring the personable "Ðu ure Fæder" where version
one has simply "Ure Fæder." Version one also creates a smoother transition to petition five with "And forgyf" where version two has merely
"Forgyf." Version two contains an addition as well, the pleonastic
phrase "*nu* to-dæg" (my emphasis). Two noteworthy changes in diction also occur in version two. It uses the weightier verb "geweorðe"
where version one has "sy" in petition one, and renders the diction
more explicit in petition five by substituting "þam mannum þe" for
the relative pronoun "þam þe." The variations between versions one
and two become more dramatic in petition six. Through direct discourse and use of the passive, version two expands the wording of
the first version from "And ne læd ðu na us on costnunge" (And do
not at all lead us into temptation) to "Ne geðafa, ðu God, þæt we
beon gelædde on costnunge" (Do not allow, thou God, that we be led
into temptation). The changes result in a line that differs in diction,
syntax, rhythm, and emphasis.

The differences among versions cannot be attributed to scribal
error, for all versions are complete and correct insofar as they reproduce adequately the meaning of the Latin. Nor can they fairly be im-
puted to differences in translation. The differences more probably result from the workings of memory. A clear instance of this occurs in
the introductory section of Ælfric's Homily "De Dominica Oratione"
which suggests that Ælfric composed from memory rather than by
examining texts spread open before him. The homily opens with an
account of Jesus teaching the apostles to pray, using the words of the
Pater noster. This passage contains a paraphrase of the Bible, not a
translation, combining the introductory narrative from Luke with the

prayer given in Matthew. This kind of conflation would more likely result from mutations of memory than slips in copying. And, if Ælfric practiced what he preached, then presumably he had himself memorized the Pater noster. It is unlikely, therefore, that he would have translated the text afresh each time he wished to write it out.

The differences may, I believe, be attributed to two causes. The first is quite simply a desire for dramatic emphasis. After the opening paraphrase of the Bible, the rest of the homily is devoted to a line-by-line explanation of the Pater noster. Ælfric cites each petition of the prayer individually, and supplies each with appropriate commentary. The differences in wording may be intended to hold the audience's attention by increasing the drama of the presentation. Secondly, the variations among texts may indicate that Ælfric had a more fluid notion of what could count as an adequately memorized text than we have at present. For Ælfric, presentation of the sense mattered more than exact wording. The variations that are so clearly tolerated here could indicate the persistent influence of oral culture, for, as Bruce A. Rosenberg points out, "precision ... is a product of writing."[29] For Ælfric, then, the written text served as a kind of anchor, not as a template.

Memory and the Unlettered

King Alfred's acts of memorization are those of an unlettered man guided by the learned. Asser's *Life of King Alfred* contains two widely cited passages on Alfred's gifts of memorization that suggest two distinct systems of memorization. After praising Alfred's desire for wisdom, Asser observes that

> by the shameful negligence of his parents and tutors he remained ignorant of letters until his twelfth year, or even longer. However, he was a careful listener, by day and night, to English poems, most frequently hearing them recited by others, and he readily retained them in his memory.[30]

Following a few words on Alfred's skill as a hunter, Asser gives an account of how Alfred's mother had offered a book of English poetry to whomever of her sons could learn it most quickly. Alfred asks,

---

[29] Bruce A. Rosenberg, "The Complexity of Oral Tradition," *Oral Tradition* 2 (1987): 87.

[30] See chap. 22 in Simon Keynes and Michael Lapidge, trans., *Asser's Life of King Alfred and Other Contemporary Sources* (Harmondsworth, England: Penguin Books, 1983), 75. All subsequent references will be to this edition.

"Will you really give this book to the one of us who can understand it the soonest and recite it to you?" Whereupon, smiling
with pleasure she reassured him, saying: "Yes, I will." He immediately took the book from her hand, went to his teacher and
learnt it. When it was learnt, he took it back to his mother and
recited it.[31]

Both of these passages concern the memorization of vernacular verse.
But in the first passage, King Alfred seems to have been present at traditional verse performances. He learns by hearing, most likely by means
of what Albert B. Lord refers to as the "principle of unconscious remembering."[32] Lord, writing of Yugoslav bards, explains that "the formulas and the diction of the poetry, the elements that enter into making
of verses, are not more consciously memorized or even 'remembered'
than the phrases and structural elements of any other kind of
speech."[33] In this way, Alfred could have absorbed the principles of
the Old English oral formulaic system style.

More often, however, Asser associates the learning of English
poetry with books. We are told that even while engaged in governing, Alfred found time for "reading aloud from books in English and
above all learning English poems by heart," which he did with "great
application to the best of his abilities."[34] His children Edward and
Ælfthryth "have attentively learned the psalms, and books in English,
and especially English poems, and they very frequently make use of
books."[35] Similarly, Alfred's memorization of the book with the attractive capital is more correctly associated with written rather than oral tradition, although Alfred is literate in neither Old English nor Latin at the
time of the incident. In this instance, he is not a member of an audience,
effortlessly soaking up traditional patterns. Instead, he sets about inten-

---

[31] Ibid., chap. 23, p. 75.
[32] Albert B. Lord, "Memory, Fixity, and Genre in Oral Traditional Poetries," in
Oral Traditional Literature: A Festschrift for Albert Bates Lord, ed. John Miles Foley
(Columbus, Ohio: Slavica Publishers Inc., 1981), 452.
  Useful discussions of memorization in oral tradition may be found in Eric
Havelock, *The Greek Concept of Justice* (Cambridge, MA: Harvard Univ. Press, 1978),
esp. chap. 3, "The Psychology of Rhythmic Memorization," 38–54; Ruth Finnegan,
Oral Poetry: Its Nature, Significance and Social Context (Cambridge: Cambridge Univ.
Press, 1977), esp. chapters 3 and 5; Walter J. Ong, *Orality and Literacy* (London:
Methuen Press, 1982), 57–68; Bruce A. Rosenberg, "The Complexity of Oral
Tradition," *Oral Tradition* 2 (1987): 73–90; Albert B. Lord, "Characteristics of Orality," *Oral Tradition* 2 (1987): 54–72.
[33] Lord, 451.
[34] See chap. 76 in Keynes and Lapidge, 91.
[35] Ibid., chap. 75, p. 91.

tionally and consciously to memorize a written text with the help of a teacher who, apparently, reads aloud to him.

Alfred devoted considerable time to learning various prayers which he then had copied into a book. Asser reports that "he learnt the 'daily round', that is the services of the hours, and then certain psalms and many prayers; these he collected in a single book, which he kept by him day and night, as I have seen for myself."[36] In his devotion to his handbook, from which "he derived no small comfort," he resembles Leofgyth who almost always kept divine Scripture in her hands.[37]

This book is a curiosity. Since Alfred was illiterate at the time he first began collecting it, others had to copy it for him and, presumably, read it to him. Nonetheless, the possession of such a book put him on a par with other literate students. Like them, he possessed written copies of texts he had memorized, although the copies had not aided in the process of memorization. As such, his handbook seems to have served as a kind of auxiliary memory to which he would have had access only through his instructors. Alfred was dependent on intent listening as his primary means of memorization. Asser's language emphasizes the point: We are told that "he was a careful listener, by day and night"; that he listened "eagerly and attentively" when Holy Scripture was read; and that he attended to a passage being read aloud to him from a book "with both ears."[38] For Alfred, learning was a process that could only take place among others.

Apparently, Alfred conceives of writing down what he has in memory to be a joint exercise as well. In his Old English translation of Augustine's *Soliloquy*, Reason tells Augustine that in order to write down what he has entrusted to memory, he will need "a private place free from all other distractions, and a few familiar and learned men with [him] who would not at all hinder [him] in his work but would assist [him]."[39] Keynes and Lapidge point out that "Alfred's translation here is entirely opposed to the sense of Augustine's original, where the stress is on 'pure solitude' (*solitudo mera*) as the condition necessary for composition."[40]

While help in composition may be unusual, help in memorization was common practice. Riché, writing of Gaul in the eighth century,

---

[36] Ibid., chap. 24, p. 75.
[37] Ibid., chap. 89, p. 100.
[38] Ibid., chap. 22, p. 75; chap. 76, p. 91; chap. 88, p. 99.
[39] Carnicelli, bk. I, ll. 19–21, p. 49.
[40] Keynes and Lapidge, 300 n. 6.

notes that the "*Rule* of the Master required that monks who were not *psaltarati* [that is, who did not know their Psalter by heart] were to provide themselves with tablets covered with the Psalms when they traveled so that when they stopped, they could sharpen their memory either alone or with the help of a brother."[41] Eddius Stephanus' *Life of Bishop Wilfred* provides another pertinent example. During a visit to Rome during which Wilfred prayed for the ability to learn and teach the story of the gospel, he met the archdeacon Boniface. Boniface became his friend and teacher, coaching him until he learned the four Gospels perfectly (*perfecte didicit*).[42] It is clear that Wilfrid did not need Boniface's help simply to read the Gospels, for Eddius Stephanus informs us that Wilfrid had often spent his time in praying, fasting, reading, and keeping vigils, and further that he had both read and memorized all of the psalms twice, once in Jerome's revision and once "from the fifth edition, after the Roman use."[43] The fact that Wilfrid is literate does not make memorization any less an activity for two.

While Asser's *Life of King Alfred* re-emphasizes the importance of writing as a form of memory even for the unlettered and alerts us to the practice of memorization as a group activity, it tells us nothing about the accuracy of Alfred's memory. But this is not surprising since Asser was primarily interested in Alfred's desire for learning, not in his feats of memorization.

The story of Cædmon presents us with the case of another unlettered man who learns Scripture from learned tutors; however, his situation and the demands made on his memory are quite different from those of Alfred. Cædmon's story appears in Bede's *Ecclesiastical History*[44] and has often been used to furnish evidence for the memory and skills of a traditional oral poet.[45] Cædmon, an unlettered cowherd, flees from festivities in the beerhall when he sees the harp approaching him, indicating that it is his turn to sing. He retires for the

---

[41] Riché, 464.

[42] Colgrave, chap. 5, p. 12.

[43] Ibid., chap. 3, p. 9.

[44] Plummer, bk. IV, chap. 24, pp. 258–62.

[45] Useful studies of Cædmon include: N. F. Blake, "Cædmon's Hymn," *Notes and Queries* 207 [n.s., 9] (1962): 243–46; Donald Fritz, "Cædmon: A Traditional Christian Poet," *Mediaeval Studies* 31 (1969): 334–37; Donald K. Fry, "The Memory of Cædmon" in *Oral Traditional Literature: A Festschrift for Albert Bates Lord*, 282–93; Francis P. Magoun, "Bede's Story of Cædmon: The Case History of an Anglo-Saxon Oral Singer," *Speculum* 30 (1955): 49–63. See also Jeff Opland, *Anglo-Saxon Oral Poetry: A Study of the Traditions*, (New Haven: Yale Univ. Press, 1980), 106–20.

night, falls asleep, and dreams of a man who calls him by name and demands that he sing about the creation. Cædmon does so, singing a song of praise for God in the traditional Old English alliterative style, a song which he remembers and expands upon awakening. But while Cædmon has clearly learned to sing Christian poetry in an oral style, Bede just as clearly takes trouble to disassociate Cædmon's poetry from secular oral tradition. We are told that Cædmon had at no time learned anything about singing ("nil carminum aliquando didicerat") and that his skill in poetry came as a gift from God and not through men or the instruction of a man ("non ab hominibus, neque per hominem institutus"). He learns stories not in the traditional way of listening attentively to other oral performances, but by having stories from Scripture explained to him by learned teachers. Even the language that Bede uses to describe Cædmon's memory associates its workings clearly with literate monastic practice. After learning a passage from Scripture, Cædmon would retire until the next day. "But all which he could learn through hearing, remembering it and ruminating like a clean animal, he converted into sweetest song."[46] ("At ipse cuncta, quae audiendo discere poterat, rememorando secum et quasi mundum animal ruminando, in carmen dulcissimum conuertebat.") The chewing of words is a common monastic metaphor. Jean Leclercq points out that

> the repeated mastication of divine words is sometimes described by use of the theme of spiritual nutrition. In this case the vocabulary is borrowed from eating, from digestion, and from the particular form of digestion belonging to ruminants. For this reason, reading and meditation are sometimes described by the very expressive word *ruminatio*. For example, in praising a monk who prayed constantly Peter the Venerable cried: "Without resting, his mouth ruminated the sacred words."[47]

Cædmon digests and assimilates words before he can transmute the explanations of Scripture into verse. This pause for rumination is similar to the case of a Yugoslav oral poet, cited by Lord, who requires a day before hearing a song and performing his own version of it. The singer, Sulejman Makić, when asked whether he could pick up a song

---

[46] Plummer, bk. IV chap. 24, pp. 259–60.

[47] Jean Leclercq, *The Love of Learning and the Desire for God: A Study of Monastic Culture,* (1961; repr. New York: New American Library of World Literature, 1962), 78.

right away, replied, "Yes, I could sing it for you right away the next day." When asked what he thought about during the intervening day, he replied, "It has to come to one. One has to think ... how it goes, and then little by little it comes to him, so that he won't leave anything out."[48] Lord attributes this pause to the singer's desire to practice.[49] Jeff Opland attributes Cædmon's day-long retreat to his need to memorize his song, thus distinguishing him from improvisational singers.[50] It is difficult to prove, however, that such memorization necessarily resulted in a fixed text, particularly since even the written copies of Cædmon's hymn that have come down to us contain significant variation.[51] We do not possess a clear idea of what Bede knew about the process of oral composition; however, in this passage, he associates Cædmon's withdrawal before performance with meditation and rumination (the process of absorbing words and making them one's own), and perhaps with the usual literate methods of composition which required solitude.

If the account of Cædmon's composing is disassociated from oral tradition, his process of learning poetry is distinguished from it as well. Cædmon learns stories from learned men who explain passages of Scripture to him. But Bede also points out two methods by which Cædmon does *not* learn to sing. Bede reports that Cædmon learned the art of singing "not from men nor [was he] instructed by a man, but he received the gift of singing through divine grace."[52] ("Namque ipse non ab hominibus, neque per hominem institutus, canendi artem didicit, sed diuinitus adiutus gratis canendi donum accepit.") The precise meaning of these words is difficult to pin down. Bede may be contrasting group recitation with one-on-one instruction. Or, the theory that I prefer, he could be referring to learning from the performances of many men as opposed to learning from a single instructor. If so, this passage may allude to a distinction which Bede observed between oral and lettered methods of learning, much as Alfred sometimes learned English poetry from the oral performances of others and sometimes from the instruction of a single tutor.

How good was Cædmon's memory? Clearly the demands made

---

[48] Albert Lord, *The Singer of Tales* (Cambridge, MA: Harvard Univ. Press, 1960), 26–27.

[49] Ibid., 26.

[50] Opland, 114.

[51] See Katherine O'Brien O'Keeffe, "Orality and the Developing Text of Cædmon's Hymn," *Speculum* 62 (1987): 1–20.

[52] Plummer, bk. IV, chap. 24, p. 259.

on it differ from the demands made on the memories of others discussed so far. His task, of course, was not merely to memorize but to transform material from prose paraphrase of Scripture to verse for performance. Judging by the list of Cædmon's compositions that Bede leaves us, most of the material he turned to song was narrative in structure (Genesis, Exodus, the events in Christ's life), while some would have been more descriptive in nature (accounts of the Last Judgment or the joys of heaven). It seems in general that Cædmon's job was simply to retain the gist of the story, what the ancients would have called *memoria ad res* (memory for things). Bede's words confirm this observation: Cædmon turns "all that he *could* learn from hearing" into song (my emphasis).[53] He may not have learned it all.

In sum, the degree of precision required in memorization was variable, depending primarily on the purpose for which a piece was memorized. Leofgyth's memory was so exact that she herself could have served as a reference book in a land where books were scarce. Ælfric's memory was also precise, but he felt free to alter the words of a well known text for dramatic effect. Cædmon's memory was that of an oral poet who needed to retain only a general sense of events in Scripture. Techniques of memorization, whenever possible, engaged both eye and ear. Each memorizer here cited, whether lettered or not, made use of some kind of vocalization in memorizing, whether singing, reciting, repeating in unison, or reading aloud. And each, whether lettered or not, made use of or had access to writing as a first step in the formation of memory.

---

[53] Ibid., 260.

ESHA NIYOGI DE

From Theater to Ritual: A Study
of the Revesby Mummers' Play

T he mummers' plays, recorded in England since the seventeenth
century but suggestive of an ancient and continuing tradition,
bring a unique form of theater.[1] Although nominally "plays," to a
modern audience, they are only vestigially dramatic. The works are

---

[1] For a chronological survey of recorded texts of the English mummers' plays,
see Alex Helm, *The English Mummers' Play* (Woodbridge, Suffolk: D. S. Brewer,
1981), 7–10. Alan Brody lists some vague references from the fifteenth and sixteenth
centuries to mummers, morris dancers, and players, but also notes that these may
not refer to the mummers' plays per se because their stock characters are never
grouped together, nor do they mention the crucial death-rebirth sequence. See his
The English Mummers and Their Plays: Traces of Ancient Mystery (Philadelphia: Univ.
of Pennsylvania Press, 1969), 10–13. Both Helm and Brody agree that "the earliest
known accepted reference" to the mummers' plays is to be found in a manuscript
(ca. 1800, Trinity College, Dublin) which supposedly reproduces an earlier work
dated ca. 1685. Despite the lack of documented evidence in England, Helm and
Brody both agree that the mummers' plays originated in *primitive* seasonal rites and
also appeared in some form in English village ceremonies before they were first set
down: "If it can be accepted that the roots of the action probably took hold in
primitive times, there is a long gap between them and the first mention in [the] MS
.... We can only assume that there was something before the 1700s which had
begun, even by then, to harden off into the [largely farcical] form which remains
today." See Helm, 7.

performed in a semi-circular space instead of on a stage, contain thin
plot lines that are interrupted by completely irrelevant characters and
action, and rely heavily on direct audience-address. The acting style
is arbitrary. Words are either "treated with almost mystical reverence,
no matter how nonsensical they may appear, or are dealt with simply
as skeletal ideas which guide the plays to the action and leave [the
actors] free to improvise as freely as they please."[2] Indeed, the plays
frequently evoke a sense of mystery; however, by trivializing the central death-rebirth sequence, they seem to interject this "mystical reverence" with blasphemy. The resurrection motif recurs in these plays
and play-fragments, but often in illogical juxtaposition with combats
and weddings. This mysterious combination of elements seems to
point beyond the farce and entertainment to a sub-theatrical "text"
that exists not only in spite of, but almost in order to, undermine the
fragmented, quasi-representational theater in which it appears.

The reason for their untheatricality requalifies the works. In texts
that have been set down, the underlying meaning is often diffused
through farce. At the same time, the men who perform these plays are
acting out the "remains of what was an urgent magic necessity to ensure that life would go on, ... To a primitive society whose future depended on maintaining growth of all things in the summer months, it
was necessary to assist the cycle."[3] Insofar as ritual is a "collective
articulation" that seeks, by imitating the rhythm of nature, to gain at
least invocative power over that rhythm, the men are performing a
quintessential ritual.[4]

Students of the mummers' plays generally agree that the substance of these works lies not in their spurious theatricality but in
their embodiment of "life-cycle ritual[s]."[5] However, few critics explore in the plays the tension between representational theater and
ritual performance. I suggest that under the influence of contemporaneous religious and secular drama, folk rituals organize themselves

---

[2] Brody, 27.

[3] Helm, 6.

[4] According to Robert Potter, "The action of ritual [is] a collective articulation
[that is formulated from] past experiences and individual responses." In seeking to
"control nature by sympathetically imitating its order," ritual seeks to place individuals within the rhythm of nature, and convey a "general significance" to the life
of the individual. See The English Morality Play: Origins, History, and Influence (London: Routledge and Kegan Paul, 1975), 10–11.

[5] Margaret Dean-Smith, "The Life-Cycle Play or Folk Play: Some Conclusions
Following the Examination of the Ordish Paper and Other Sources," Folklore 69
(1958): 244.

into plays that employ plot lines; at the same time, they seek to escape that constitutive urge. In this paper, I study the conflict that obtains.[6]

In their urge to resist theatrical plot, the mummers' plays resemble both the early medieval liturgical drama of eleventh-and twelfth-century England and the mysteries that grew to popularity in the fourteenth century. Both the liturgical drama and the mystery cycles are imbued with "tensions between ritual performance and representational action"; Robert Weimann detects similar tensions in the mummers' plays.[7] In the doctrinal liturgical drama, for instance, setting, action, and dialogue are largely discrete. Because setting "belongs to the wider patterns of church symbolism," it is set apart from the representational dialogue and action. The dialogue, in turn, directly interrupts the central processional movement "to the symbolic focal point."[8] While the liturgical drama is a "ritual incarnation of the Christian mass," the mysteries are the "mimetic representation of Christian myth."[9] Therefore, they are more prone to confine an audience in realistic details such as Noah's taming of a recalcitrant wife in the Wakefield Play of Noah or the machinations of an incorrigible shepherd boy in the Wakefield Second Shepherd's Pageant. However, they also use frame-rupturing devices such as audience addresses or monologues. For example, Noah's family squabbles are preceded by his lengthy monologue on the history of mankind. Similarly, we see Christ, in the Wakefield Play of The Resurrection of the Lord, turn purposefully to remind the audience that he has redeemed sinful man by shedding his own blood.[10] In each instance, the monologue pointedly directs attention away from the particular, contextualized tale toward a larger cyclic order. By employing many themes "identical with these same days in the English church year," the mysteries are able to connect themselves to that order; and, because they complement the

---

[6] In his chapter on the folk play, Robert Weimann undertakes a brief but illuminating discussion of this "tension" between the "effective magical purpose of . . . ritual embodiment," and the "affective communicative function of . . . a representational mode of impersonation." Because the folk play failed to "comprehend in one vision, the non-representational embodiment of the rite and the sensuous representation of reality," Weimann concludes, it gradually "withered away, leaving vestigial dramatic and verbal formulae. . . ." See *Shakespeare and the Popular Tradition in Theater*, ed. Robert Schwartz (Baltimore: The Johns Hopkins Press, 1978), 17.

[7] Weimann, 58.

[8] David Mills, *Medieval English Drama: A Casebook*, ed. Peter Happe (London: Macmillan [1969] 1984), 38.

[9] Weimann, 58.

[10] See David Bevington, *Medieval Drama* (Boston: Houghton Mifflin, 1975).

actual church service, the liturgical plays constantly work within it.[11]

That rhythmical order is clearly seasonal. Not only does it move in symphonic fashion—from the birth of Christ, through his death, to the Resurrection—but, as Hassel has shown in his investigation of the Elizabethan church year, it links every major religious festival to a secular seasonal counterpart (one form of which could be a mummers' play).[12] Just as the liturgical drama and the mystery play maintain their profound power over the common man by reflecting the seasonal order of the English church year, the mummers' plays maintain a similar hold, by making deep associations through their death-rebirth sequence, which is suggestive of Christmas and Easter festivities. Like the early liturgical drama and the medieval mystery cycles, then, only more directly, the Mummers' Plays rupture their crudely improvised theatrical plots to gesture at the cyclic whole.

To study the mummers' plays within a model of early Christian drama is to study theater for something other than the standard formulations of sequential plot and character; in effect, it is to look for the counter-representational tendencies that urge theater to move away from a recording of atomistic reality and toward a ritualistic sense of total, multi-significative life (encompassing birth/death, fertility / harvest, youth / age, fulfillment / emptiness). This underlying tension between representation and ritual in the mummers' play shares a basic impulse with the non-representational elements of drama that were popular in the Middle Ages and the Renaissance—an impulse to subvert linear theater in order to empower a sub-theatrical meaning that is communal rather than narrowly realistic and context-dependent.

Of the extant versions of the English mummers' plays, the Revesby Play supplies one of the few relatively suitable models for such a study. Although not recorded until 1779, the Revesby Play incorpo-

---

[11] R. Chris Hassel, *Renaissance Drama and the English Church Year* (Lincoln: Univ. of Nebraska Press, 1979), 6–7.

[12] Hassel describes several such secular celebrations "tightly interwoven" with religious occasions in the Renaissance court (13). These include the festival mummings performed by the Shrovetide and Christmas Lords of Misrule and their retinue of beasts and fools that were traditionally associated with seasonal processions, and all the egg-throwing and rolling contests held at Easter, which also had a "Pace-Egging tradition of boys ... performing the old Mummers' Play of Saint George and the Dragon"(Hassel, 13–14).

Glynne Wickham explains that the seasonal order of the Christian year sprang from its associations with preceding pagan customs. He notes that Gregory the Great had already paved the way for this incorporation by instructing St. Augustine at Canterbury to purify pagan temples and use them as churches, since the shock of transition would otherwise be counterproductive. See *The Medieval Theater* (New York: St. Martin's Press, 1974).

rates the three major types of mummers' plays (the hero-combat, the wooing ceremony, and the sword ceremony) which were being performed at that time but also long before this date. For the most part, these mummers' ceremonials are recorded elsewhere only in scattered bits and pieces.[13]

The action of the Revesby Play has two parts.[14] In the first part, the Fool's five virile sons, led by Pickle Herring, threaten and finally kill their aged father—ostensibly for an inheritance, but ceremonially as a harvest—in the course of a sword dance. Before the execution, which takes place amid much farcical byplay, the Fool fights a hobby horse and a dragon. The second part of the action sees a reborn Fool engaged (in rivalry with Pickle Herring and the other sons) in wooing Cecily. The play closes with Cecily's selection of the rejuvenated Fool over a now-aged Pickle Herring. The quête or processional circle then leads all the characters of the play out to the audience for the collection. Both this procession, which embodies a form of ritual exchange (the distribution and gathering of "luck"), and the round dances that have been interspersed in the action, are either led by the Fool, or center around him. Both include the audience in the action.

The text of the Revesby Play is comprised largely of comical patter. Even when the dialogue supports the action (as in the words of the dying Fool, who promises to rise and dance again, or in his wooing of Cecily), any such use of "representational" dialogue to explain and interpret symbolic action creates theatrical problems. In one instance, representational language is used to state a cause for the Fool's death (the sons' greed for inheritance), serving only to divert the attention of the audience from the resurrection and wooing sequence. The principal, ceremonial actions take place a-textually, either undertaken directly by the Fool or intimated through his activities; in fact, the Fool is as often outside the plot—commenting upon the action

---

[13] For the classification of the mummers' plays into these three types see E.C. Cawte, Alex Helm, and Norman Peacock, *English Ritual Drama* (London: English Folklore Society, 1967).

The Revesby Play itself is a conglomerate version from all the three ceremonies. It takes from the hero-combat the fights with the hobby horse and the dragon; from the sword ceremony the sword dances, the lock of swords, and the Fool's death; from the wooing ceremony the young woman and the wooing sequence; and from all three the rebirth sequence. For a history of the Revesby Play and its analogy with contemporaneous plough plays, see Michael J. Preston, "The Revesby Sword Play," *Journal of American Folklore* 85 (1972): 51–57.

[14] All quotations derive from the text provided by E. K. Chambers, *The English Folk Play* (Oxford: The Clarendon Press, 1933), 105–120. The extant manuscript probably was recorded in October 1779 at Revesby, at the home of Sir Joseph Banks. For a description of the manuscript see Preston, 51–57 and Helm, 25.

of the plot, chattering with the audience, leading the characters and audience in round dances—as he is within it.

Of some use in studying the ritual role of the Fool in the Revesby Play is Mikhail Bakhtin's theory of the conflicted nature of what seems outwardly to be a unitary language system. According to Bakhtin, any living language is only theoretically unitary.[15] In actuality, a language is a dynamic of sociopolitical signs, within which forces of "verbal-ideological" centralization wage incessant struggle with a multitude of unsystemic forces. These "centrifugal" forces, which invariably destabilize the "centripetal" or systemic forces, include a variety of "social dialects, characteristic group behavior, professional jargons ... street songs, folk sayings, anecdotes ...."[16] Bakhtin's construction of language as the site of intersecting, conflicted socio-ideological signs theorizes the dynamic of plot construction in the Revesby Play. It suggests that the language of the linear plot strives to arrange the work into a systemic literary artifact but is repeatedly interrupted in that dynamic by signs freely arising from, and involved with, the ritual base of the mummers' play.

Clearly, the application to a theatrical work of a linguistic model such as that of Bakhtin is somewhat suspect; the language system he considers is less complex than an expression such as theater, which uses several voicings of such a language in addition to a full body of signs in theater and in its embedded ritual. Despite the multiplicity of signs inherent in theater, however, Bakhtin's concept of dialogism illuminates the Revesby Play insofar as that play is centralized in the character of Pickle Herring, a representative for the other sons of lust for life and of decay. The centripetal plot movement from youth to age depicted in Pickle Herring's tale is disrupted by the Fool's centrifugal gestures, which reinterpret the limited reality exposed by Pickle Herring's story. With the round dances that are either performed to songs or in silence as well as with the final silent quête, the Fool conveys reality into a ritual that lies beyond language systems—glossia— of all sorts.

The Revesby Play opens with the Fool as Prologue and Commentator. He is critical of his own drama of death and rebirth even before that drama can begin. By calling it a "pleasant sport" performed by a group of "jovial boys" (12, 29) he not only underlines the festive nature of the action to follow but also encourages the audience to

---

[15] See M. M. Bakhtin, *The Dialogic Imagination: Four Essays,* trans. Caryl Emerson and Michael Holoquist, ed. Michael Holoquist (Austin: Univ. of Texas Press, 1981), 270.

[16] Ibid., 273.

look upon it from the outside only as a sport. The Fool then initiates the action, calling in his five sons. With this Calling-On Song, he transforms himself from the author reviewing and arguing the contents and purpose of his own work to an actor within the work. Thenceforth, he becomes the subject of the linear plot.

The aged Fool of the play's first part is simultaneously a threat to Pickle Herring's vulnerable youth and a forewarning of the deterioration that must overtake Pickle Herring later in the action. Like Pickle Herring, the old Fool suffers seasonal decay and progresses toward death. His decline into old age, moreover, is a ritual sign of contamination that needs to be ritually purged by death. That purgation is brutally if comically acted out by the triumph in the course of the sword dance of the young sons over the old Fool. By performing the sword dance and ritual execution, the Fool's sons expedite his centripetal decay. Moreover, by ceremonially executing the aged Fool, the youthful sons also prefigure the inevitable ritual end of their own youthfulness. The hobby horse and dragon, who meet and fight the Fool in the first part of the play, perform toward the Fool a function very similar to the sword dancers / sons. They come to him as threats of death that hasten the Fool's decay. Indeed, both animals generically contain elements of decay. The worm hardly can avoid being Christianized "as" the serpent, the Dragon of evil that, in Christmas mummers' plays, fights St. George. As a recognized fertility figure who is ritually killed in many folk plays, the hobby horse also indexes the decay that is one essential component of the fertility cycle.[17] Both in their ritual signification and in their specific uses in the Revesby Play (their appearance in combination with the declining Fool and their fights with him) then, the animals reinforce the fable of seasonal decay that is confirmed in the actual decadence of the Fool.

Even within the generally centripetal construct of the first part of

---

[17] For the Hobby Horse as a fertility figure in a life/death bracketing see Violet Alford, *Sword Dance and Drama* (London: Merlin Press, 1962). See also R. Vuia, "The Roumanian Hobby Horse, the Calusari," *Journal of the English Folk Dance and Song Society* 2 (1935): 97–117; Brody, 63–64; Helm, 17–19, 29–30, 43–47.

For the Dragon as a ceremonial figure endowed with divine powers see G.E. Smith, *The Evolution of the Dragon* (Manchester: Manchester Univ. Press, 1919). Weimann argues that the Dragon's powers of life-giving may be deduced more conclusively from its "dancing and disguised function" than from its "legendary background"(38). I would agree that animal disguise associates the dragon (along with its companion, the hobby horse) with the disguised animals of traditional seasonal processions and therefore with the magical fertility of nature. In the Revesby Play they thus are reflections of the Fool who undergo the same process as the Fool, even if within the action the Fool is to them what his sons are to the Fool: threats of death.

the Revesby Play, however, both the Fool and the animals centrifugally resist the linear movement of the seasons portrayed by the story
of Pickle Herring and the other sons. For instance, the Fool periodically disrupts the centripetal plot by calling the characters and the
audience to join him in round dancing ("Come, follow me, merry
men all" 61). These interruptive dances led by the Fool in a sense "interpret" for the audience the theatrical action insofar as they transfer
to it the therapy of the life-renewing magic embodied in the potent
circle of the dance. The sword ceremony is another instance where
this same "interpretive" function is performed.

By producing the Fool's death, the circle and the threat of the
sword dance seem to approve the linear. They actually deny it, however; a curved line refuses direction. The sword dance only *appears* to
be threatening; the swords that lock together over the head of the
Fool actually form a quintessential ritual (linked) circle that ensures
the Fool's eventual rebirth. During the dance, the sons are not agents
of decay; instead, they are virile components of the crucial circle. Because the sword dance is fundamentally a fertility-promoting sun-
charm, in performance it iconizes for the audience the circularity of life
/ death, fertility / harvest that lies at the heart of all the activities of the
central Fool of the Revesby work. Whereas every circle dance led by the
Fool or performed around him suggests this magic of renewing life,
however, only the sword dance actually shows it to the audience. Just
before he is ceremonially executed by the sword dancers the Fool promises to "rise and dance again"; very soon he keeps his promise, thereby
explaining to the audience much of the meaning underlying the ceremony itself and the play as a whole.

Similarly, the hobby horse and dragon appear to buttress the plot
of linear decay but erupt irrelevantly into the play mostly in order to
disturb that linear process. Because the Fool's fights with the animals
end with his triumph over them, they also guarantee the Fool's eventual triumph over the decay engraphed by the plot. Furthermore, the
animals generically parallel the Fool himself in their embodiment of
both seasonal decay and the promise of renewal. Although they enter
the Revesby Play only in connection with the declining Fool, in all
other mummers' plays they are recorded to have been inevitable participants in the fertility-enhancing quête. As such, the animals operate as
autonomous, yet relevant, "icons" that, like the circles and the dance,
record in microform the centrifugality or multiplicity indexed by the
play. Whereas the play itself seems practically divided—in death and
in rebirth—both the Fool and the animals are the common factors
between the two. While the animals in decay or in intimated fertility
remain only peripheral to the action, however, the Fool is central to it.

Throughout the play, the Fool is engaged in disrupting the centripetal plot of decay in which he himself is also a participant. However, the openly centrifugal and frame-rupturing activities of the Fool are in the foreground only in the second portion of the play, which follows the rebirth and leads to his wooing of Cecily and the celebratory circle of the quête. The Fool's rebirth is the turning point of the action. Indeed, as Helm suggests, the ritual sword dance that brings on the death-rebirth itself could be a life-giving rather than life-robbing activity. Helm notes that the lock of swords that traditionally is placed above the victim's head seems like an "inept and clumsy" means of execution; instead, "if the role of the Lock could be inverted it could be looked upon basically as a means of restoring life rather than taking it."[18] He suggests that the lock conceivably "could be a symbol of the female principle placed over the head of the male performer to complete the union."[19] If the lock is an emblem of a life-giving female principle, it serves as the means for progressing beyond the forms of decay active in the first part of the Revesby Play to the signs of revitalization in the second. Against the linear plot that depicts the aging of the sons (notably of the eldest, Pickle Herring) then, the Fool's magical renewal and conversion from age to youth register the boldest denial that they represent any action other than a ritual death-rebirth.

At first it can appear that the plot's linear movement toward decay continues undeterred by the Fool's rebirth: the second half of the play shows the decline from youth to age of Pickle Herring and the other sons. But it is soon evident that the aged Pickle Herring and his brothers appear in the second part of the play solely to be rejected by the young woman and her mate. Because all the sons now are suitors of Cecily, her rejection of Pickle Herring becomes a rejection of all the sons in their tacit lineation into irreversible age. Moreover, Pickle Herring not only is rejected by Cecily, he is openly ridiculed by his rival (the reborn Fool) for unbecoming amorous gestures ("Nay, old rogue, I thee defy" 401). In being objects of rejection, the Fool's sons clearly show what they are: indexes to the decay of fertility that is in-

---

[18] Helm, 26.

[19] Ibid., 26. Helm derives several examples from Europe to show that the lock was used in many instances "as a platform to hoist notable characters as well as their Leader"(26). He concludes that in Europe the lock might have had a different significance from the execution theme popularly assigned to it in England. Helm also suggests that the Doctor associated with the magical cure in many English mummers' plays is a "rationalization of a later date"(Helm, 26). If that is so, then the Revesby version has retained the use of the lock in its original form, as the means for restoring life rather than only terminating it.

herent in any linearly seasonal (rather than ritual) function of the
Fool. It follows that they must be ritually discarded by both the
woman and her rejuvenated companion, the Fool, before the ritual
wedding can take place.

As the female principle engaged in discarding decay in order to
nurture new life, the youthful Cecily centers the rebirth portion of the
play (necessarily, she has no place in the first part). She fulfills her
role when, in a resonantly literary January-May sequence, she spurns
aside a "silly, old" Pickle Herring who has failed to realize that
"youthfull years and frozen age / Cannot in any wise agree"(380–
381). This rejection of Pickle Herring can be traced to European fertility ceremonies that showed the ritual rejection of older women or
men by the young.[20] But, as Brody puts it, the action of the play
cannot end with an act of rejection, for there is "yet another mimetic
action to be performed, an action that is vital to the magical nature of
the ceremony in terms of fertility": the ritual wedding.[21] As agent
and center of that fertility ritual, the woman embodies the restorative
female principle that is emblematized in the lock of swords that antic-
ipates her actual appearance in the play. She enters the action as a
principle of nature that exists beyond the linear movement of the seasons and is an index to the Fool's inherent power to transcend linear-
ity. As such, she accompanies the reborn Fool in leading the characters and audience in the life-perpetuating, celebratory quête that concludes the play.

Because the Fool is centrifugally indexed in the several meanings
and functions of the Revesby action (age and youth, death and
magical life, acceptance of decay and transcendence of it), even as he
is identified with the audience outside the play (as Prologuer and

---

[20] A traditional wooing ceremony presents a young woman principally to reject
a suitor in favor of the Clown (Helm, 11). In many wooing sequences she is coun-
terposed with an old woman who also encounters some form of rejection, mostly
by the fertility figure of the Fool. Citing Sir James Frazer (*The Golden Bough*, 1911–
15), Brody likens the rejection to the "Scottish custom of fashioning two female
figures [the Corn Maiden and the Old Wife] out of reaped corn ..."(Brody, 107).
The former is fashioned from the last stalks of the harvest while the latter often is
made from earlier cuts of corn. The Corn Maiden "is retained by the farmer all
year, but as soon as he is finished with his own field he passes the Old Wife on to
a slower neighbor"(Brody, 107). Although several of Frazer's theories are now in
question, they are, as Brody would have it, "rich with suggestive insight." Whether
or not the Young Female indeed is the spirit of the new corn, her role seems to
suggest a similar ceremonial rejection of the old and the decadent in order that the
new can take root and, more generally, a ceremonial celebration of the self-renew-
ing year and the seasons.

[21] Brody, 108.

Commentator, whose interpretations rupture the plot), he in his turn can involve an audience in all the functions and meanings of the play.[22] Exactly because of his multiple and overlapping functions, the Fool also confounds the standard stratification of theatrical communication as it is described by Kier Elam. According to Elam, theatrical communication is comprised of codification, transmission, and receipt.[23] The Fool encompasses all those functions. He is the principal actor and the author-director. Paradoxically, in a reversal of the usual placement of an actor in the action, he as the "decoder" is situated outside the theatrical circle. Conversely, the actual audience is drawn (once more by the Fool) into active participation in the action. As such, the Revesby Fool achieves a deeply ritualistic facility and meaning. He approaches Marcel Mauss' description of the *personnage* or *total role* that is assumed by a select member of the community in certain ritual enactments in primitive cultures: "In primitive society, a complete character is made explicit and given a fixed 'sanctified' social reality through ritual, and particularly ritual dance and drama ....[The] *personnage* serves as a complete, schematized typification."[24] This centering of the Fool's functions permits the Fool to attain a totality unavailable in full-fledged theatrical figures, a totality that encompasses the (life-denying

---

[22] Of immediate use in describing the dissemination of the central Fool function into relevant yet discrete units of theater is Umberto Eco's formulation of the "undercodes" discernible in certain texts. Eco defines "undercoding" as the "operation by means of which in the absence of reliable, pre-established rules, certain macroscopic portions of certain texts are provisionally assumed to be pertinent units of a code in formation." See Umberto Eco, *The Theory of Semiotics* (Bloomington: Indiana Univ. Press, 1976), 135. Kier Elam, in distinguishing these undercodes from generally understood dramatic codes, describes them as the "potent dramatic and theatrical conventions ruling the structure and understanding of plays and performances [that is, the rules that distinguish tragedy from comedy, etc.]" See his *The Semiotics of Theater and Drama* (London: Methuen, 1986), 52. Undercodes point to "emerging patterns" in theatrical texts (Elam, 54). Therefore, undercoding, "is the formation of rough and approximate norms in order to characterize a [theatrical] phenomenon which is not fully understood or which is only vaguely differentiated [by the audience of a given text]"(Elam, 55).

Insofar as the Revesby Play is at all literary, it is held together by the recognizable codes of a theatrical plot (with a beginning, middle, and end). However, the actual action of the Revesby Play far exceeds its skeletal plot. First, it includes circular dances and other elements, which disrupt the sequence of the plot; and second, it distributes attributes of the central "actor" a-sequentially into all the environing characters. The coded "linear plot" of the Revesby Play, then, is constantly juxtaposed with "undercoded" elements. Vaguely distinguishable by an audience, these magnetize the witnessed action toward its ritual performance.

[23] Elam, 35.

[24] Quoted by Elizabeth Burns, *Theatricality: A Study of Convention in the Theatre and Social Life* (London: Longman, 1972), 122.

and life-renewing) functions attributed variously to the other characters in the play. He must be all, even though the parts may not be very coherent; any distinct functioning of the parts would unmake the ritual whole. Relatedly, as it enters the ritual performance in mutual action and participation, the audience too becomes whole in and through the Fool.

Thus, atomistic theater is magnetized by the Fool into a configuration in which linear or centripetal theater opens itself toward centrifugal or multi-significative ritual (although never completely so). But the movement initiated by the Fool does not end with him. It moves beyond all such components of theater as the animals and even the Fool, into the extra-theatrical round dance. By magnetizing all the separate roles that constitute the play, the repetitive movement of the dance erases all vestiges of individuation, whether characteristical or linguistic. It is performed either in silence or to the accompaniment of the Calling-On Song ("Come, follow me merry men all") sung by the Fool and bearing affinities with the ritual (phallic) songs sung in ancient seasonal processions.[25] Such dances, unencumbered by any dissemination toward representation, are ritualistic in form: they show communal activity that is "compulsive [and] purposive," designed to enhance "virility in man and fertility in cattle and crops."[26] As Susanne Langer explains, the circle dance is "an envisagement of a world beyond the spot and moment of one's animal existence, [a] conception of life as a whole, continuous, superpersonal life, punctuated by birth and death."[27] The circle dance, then, both completes the function of the Fool as "pure" theater and virtualizes that function as ritual.

With the incursion of the final procession which encompasses both actor and audience in one life-enhancing circle, the action begun by the Fool moves beyond him into the center of a cycle shared by actor and audience: the supremely centrifugal life-cycle containing multiplicitous meanings or signs of human life, in their concord of separation and reintegration, of death and life. In itself the cycle both is the originating source of ritual and the end of interpretation. The Revesby

---

[25] Brody likens both the Calling-On Song and the Finishing Song that sometimes accompanies the quête to the antiphonal, ritual song (the "phallic" *komos*) that supposedly formed a part of the ancient fertility ritual underlying Aristophanic comedy. Underscoring their ritual aspect, Brody points out that the Finishing Song often contains elements of invective (associated with the enhancement of fertility) and invocation, frequently through the agency of the Hobby Horse (Brody, 67–71).

[26] Alford, xiii.

[27] See Roger Copeland and Marshall Cohen, eds. and comps., *What Is Dance: Readings in Theory and Criticism* (Oxford: Oxford Univ. Press, 1983), 38.

Play accordingly can offer the audience the impression that within the work centripetal (or artificially linear) theater recedes until it almost reforms as multi-significative ritual. As such, the action at last assumes some of the conditions of ritual such as the circles and dance, the recognition of time and the seasons concurrent with the transcendence of the seasons, and the subjectivity of the ritual performer complementing the objectivity of the ritual audience. Even as the Fool himself in all those functions (subject/object, suffering actor/ transcendent audience) is nothing other than himself, so also the audience at the close of the Revesby Play is itself but also *is* within the ritual action embodied in the play.

Because the given "signifiers" of the Revesby Play never are ordered syntactically as if in a terminable grammatical "sentence," they continue to be bi-significative in and also among themselves but always within the great bi-significations of nature: life/death, fertility / harvest. As such, they can achieve only slight signifying with theatrical rules or codes. Instead, they point across a threshold, or *limen*, to a vast area of "signified" that lies beyond all codification and receipt. This includes any codification in language or glossia.[28] Just as mumming in itself originates in a silent perambulation with the unsignified purpose of distributing luck, so the final luck-distributing ritual circle of the quête forms within a potent silence that remains characteristically liminal.

---

[28] For a description of the threshold, or *limen*, in social initiation rituals, see Arnold Van Gennep, *The Rites of Passage*, trans. Monika B. Vizdom and Gabrielle L. Caffee (Chicago: Univ. of Chicago Press, 1968), 189. Van Gennep characterizes the primary stages of such rituals as separation from previous surroundings, and reincorporation into these surroundings. Between these two stages of a social initiation rite lies the stage of transition—of the threshold. The rites characteristic of this transitional stage intimate the giving up of an old life in order to "change form and condition, to die and to be reborn" (Van Gennep, 189).

JEREMY DOWNES

Or(e)ality: The Nature of
Truth in Oral Settings

H ans Vaihinger, and more recently the radical constructivist
philosophers, have taken as a basic epistemological stance that
"truth" is a culturally relative conceptual tool, "an adaptation in the
functional sense."[1] As Vaihinger so neatly puts it, "What we generally call truth ... is merely the most expedient error."[2] In the light of
current critical discussion of oral noetics, and orality in general,[3] I
would like to make a brief preliminary exploration of the way truth
is established and received in oral settings. The definition of truth as

---

[1] Ernst Von Glasersfeld, "An Introduction to Radical Constructivism," in *The Invented Reality*, ed. Paul Watzlawick (New York: W. W. Norton and Co., 1978), 20.

[2] Hans Vaihinger, *The Philosophy of "As if,"* trans. C. K. Ogden (New York: Har-
court Brace and Co., 1925), 108.

[3] Jan Vansina remarks that although anthropologists "have realized the crucial
value of the notions of space and time and have studied them ... similar information is lacking, in far too many cases, for the notion of the historical truth" in his
Oral Tradition as History (Madison: Univ. of Wisconsin Press, 1985), 131. Walter J.
Ong, though he notes that literate folk "regard oral peoples ... as dishonest in fulfillment of promises or in responses to queries," does not discuss the nature of
truth within primary oral cultures in his *Orality and Literacy* (New York: Methuen,
1982), 170.

"expedient error" allows two major advantages in the study of orality. First, by calling the status of *all* truth into question, such a definition breaks down the "Great Divide" so often created between so-called "primitive" and "advanced" cultures.[4] Second, and more important, is Vaihinger's emphasis of truth as an eminently *useful* concept, a "system of ideas which enables us to act and to deal with things most rapidly, neatly, and safely."[5] According to such a view, truth, in oral or literate settings, operates as a fundamental conceptual tool, as a guide to action within the world, and thus ultimately as a means of survival.

Once the essential utility of truth is recognized, it becomes clear that there are different kinds of truth suitable for different occasions. For example, the sharp distinction drawn between orality and literacy is greatly overshadowed by the profound similarities between such cultures; however, the distinction is "true" insofar as it serves a useful purpose, encouraging us to recognize those important differences which do exist. Graham Oddie provides a similarly useful distinction between "legisimilitude" and "verisimilitude" in his recent *Likeness to Truth*. The following passage becomes especially illuminating if we substitute "oral poet" for Oddie's "physicist" and "science":

> A physicist ... is not interested in recording every accidental fact that he notices and incorporating it into the body of his hypotheses. Such additions may well bring him closer to the whole truth, and so his reluctance to include them seems to suggest that the whole truth is not his goal.... Rather, science aims at the truth about the laws of the universe, and so what is required is ... a somewhat different concept, which could be called "legisimilitude."[6]

Thus, we have two different kinds of "expedient error": verisimilitude, or a likeness to the "whole truth" of every "accidental fact," and legisimilitude, a conformity with the laws of the universe. Note that here I am expanding Oddie's scientifically-oriented model of the universe to comprehend the more relativistic "worldview" of the anthropologists. The oral poet aims to conform with the laws of his or her own universe, not with the laws of ours. It is also worth noticing that legisimilitude and verisimilitude are not always in agreement but

---

[4] The term was first used in this application by Ruth Finnegan in her *Oral Poetry* (Cambridge: Cambridge Univ. Press, 1977).

[5] See Vaihinger, 108.

[6] Graham Oddie, *Likeness to Truth* (Boston: D. Reidel Publishing Co., 1986), 131.

can, as Oddie points out, "pull in two different directions."[7] As an illustration of this, imagine a child first trying to catch a football as it bounces. Though the child has developed a set of legisimilar expectations, a worldview, concerning the behavior of spherical balls, these expectations will be of little use when confronted by the "accidental fact" of the football's markedly different (i.e., erratic) behavior. As Oddie suggests, "a step in the direction of the whole truth may well be a step away from the truth about natural necessity."[8] While *we* may know better, still, according to the *child's* worldview, it is a "natural necessity" that the ball bounce the way other balls have bounced. By developing Oddie's distinction along these lines, we can see legisimilitude and verisimilitude as two alternate bases for the establishment of truthful narratives, though, of course, both kinds of truth inevitably mix within a given narrative or discourse.

In the Anglo-Saxon poetic corpus we are fortunate to have two sharply contrasting narratives of the same event, one of which is clearly true, the other almost as clearly untrue. I refer, of course, to the confrontation between Beowulf and Unferth (lines 499–603).[9] This scene, in which the hero and his antagonist recount differing versions of Beowulf's swimming contest with Breca, provides an excellent example of the establishment of truth by legisimilitude, the aspect of truth I would like to emphasize most, since it is the less familiar.

Perhaps the most fundamental influence on the legisimilar aspect of this or any text[10] is the patterning effect of the human mind, the desire for truthful narratives to make sense. In large part, conformity with the laws of the worldview is a product of having the same mind as everyone else and thus, as Jan Vansina puts it, a product of the "known tendency of the mind in memory to construct a coherent discourse.... Sequential ordering is imposed and the ordering made easier by patterning successive accounts in one of the basic ways the mind patterns—by opposition, or by strong sequential association."[11]

---

[7] Oddie, 134.

[8] Oddie, 134.

[9] All citations of *Beowulf* are based on Fr. Klaeber, ed., *Beowulf and the Fight at Finnsburg*, 3d ed. (Lexington: D. C. Heath and Co., 1950). All translations are my own.

[10] I use the term "text" in spite of its affinities with *textus* and the production of books, because I feel it is the most relevant term applicable to oral productions, especially poetic oral productions (as compared to the oxymoron of "oral literature"). It seems particularly applicable to Old English poetry, where words are *soðe gebunden*, "bound with truth," and there is an exchange or play in *wrixlan* that suggests the constructive play of weft and warp, as well as the play of swords.

[11] Vansina, 171.

Such cognitive patterning is inevitable in any human discourse, naturally, but in oral texts these patterns tend to be much more obvious.
Both Unferth and Beowulf order their narratives in much the same
way, first addressing the other by name, next describing the adventure in sequence: the boast made, the voyage on the sea, the actual
contest, and the outcome; finally, both speakers return to the subject
at hand, Beowulf's suitability for the upcoming contest with Grendel.
While the sequential ordering is thus very similar, the use of opposition in these passages differs. Unferth develops quite clearly the contest between Beowulf and Breca: *"Eart þu se Beowulf, se þe wið Brecan
wunne ...?"* ["Are you that Beowulf, who struggled against Breca
...?" (line 506)]. Beowulf, on the other hand, rejects this opposition in
favor of other (and greater) ones, the contest of the two men against
the sea, and of Beowulf with the denizens of the sea. As Beowulf
says, there is no rivalry between Breca and himself: *No ic fram him
wolde* [Nor did I wish to go from him (line 543)]. Regardless, it is
clear that both Unferth and Beowulf can speak within the truth to the
degree that they can produce coherent, sensibly organized discourse.

A far more interesting influence on the establishment of legisimilar truth is the political context of the narrative. Truth is not determined entirely by the interaction of the individual human mind with
its environment. Rather, as Emile Durkheim has made abundantly
clear, concepts of any kind are *collective* representations. Moreover,
Durkheim, like Vaihinger, recognizes the specific "adequacy" or ex-
pediency involved in the formation and maintenance of concepts:
truth, or for that matter any concept, is a functional device, verified
by the continued experience of its usefulness, and authorized by its
initial acceptance into the collectivity.

> A collective representation presents guarantees of its objectivity
> by the fact that it is collective: for it is not without sufficient
> reason that it has been able to generalize and maintain itself
> with persistence. If it were out of accord with the nature of
> things, it would never have been able to acquire an extended
> and prolonged empire over intellects.[12]

I would like to stress for a moment this idea of the conceptual
"empire over intellects," emphasizing that "the nature of things" includes, in fact is dominated by, the social system, the hierarchy of human interaction. This idea, that the power relations of a community

---

[12] Emile Durkheim, *The Elementary Forms of the Religious Life*, trans. J. W. Swain
(1915; repr. New York: The Free Press, 1965), 486.

govern that community's understanding of reality, and especially of truth, is not really new. As Cicero suggests, "It may be that the rulers of states, with an eye to the practical side of life, created this belief ... that there was one king in heaven," with the consequence that "all people in decrees—passed of course by their rulers—have expressed their agreement that nothing is superior to monarchy, since they believe that all the gods are ruled by a single divinity."[13] This ability to create truth (and even divinity) by means of the argument from authority, as with other arguments explicitly related to the bases of power, is generally less heavily masked in an oral society than in a literate one. As Vansina notes,

> [i]n Mande land (Guinée, Mali) truth is appreciated according to the antiquity of the family of the professional who speaks: the older, the more truthful. A correlation between truth and rank seems to occur in some stratified societies: the higher the rank of the speaker the truer what he says, even if he speaks about the past. For the Kuba, truth is guaranteed by the state councils.[14]

In this century we may be particularly aware of the degree to which "state councils" control the establishment and presentation of the historical reality, but it should come as no surprise that the Anglo-Saxon lord and his thanes exerted a similar degree of control. As Leslie Perelman has remarked concerning *Beowulf,* "a character's representation in direct discourse appears to be largely dependent on both his social and moral status."[15] In Anglo-Saxon poetry in general, the distinction between the foolhardiness of youth and the wisdom of age is commonplace. While Hrothgar is the most obvious example of this, we should also recall Byrhtwold, the old retainer of Byrhtnoth, the aged *snottor on mode* [the one wise in mind] of *The Wanderer,* and the *har hilderinc* [the gray-haired warrior] of *Brunanburh.* The status of these speakers as older, experienced men, and in most cases as men of rank, is a major factor in establishing the truth of their speeches. Moreover, though, it is hard to imagine a society that is not "stratified" in some fashion in terms of the production of truth; if it is not stratified on the

---

[13] Marcus Tullius Cicero, *On the Commonwealth,* trans. G. H. Sabine and S. B. Smith (Columbus: Ohio State Univ. Press, 1929), I:36.

[14] Vansina, 130.

[15] Leslie Cooper Perelman, "The Conditions, Consequences, and Structure of Direct Discourse in Beowulf: A Study of Speech Acts" (Ph.D. diss., Univ. of Massachusetts, 1980).

basis of age, lineage, and martial prowess, then certainly it will be on the basis of race, sex, or class.

To summarize, it is clear that the Durkheimian "collective representation" is a bit too idealistic. Rather than being a conceptual tool which guarantees "objectivity" by its "collective" nature, it is an *elite* representation which guarantees *functionality* within the social system, by virtue of the fact that it is produced by the bases of power within that social system. And the elite representation of such a heavily valorized concept as truth becomes one of the most powerful of political tools, insofar as it allows the dismantling as well as the establishment of monolithic social institutions.

Returning to the scene of *Beowulf*, truth is clearly being established along political lines as well as along those required for a coherent discourse. This kind of war of words, of challenge and response, is somewhat of a type-scene in itself, possessing analogues not only in the later Anglo-Saxon hagiographies and Christian epics, but in other oral societies as well.[16] As Vansina makes clear, "The use of messages is perhaps most dramatic in conflict situations. One fights with tradition ... debates turn around clan history and it is the use of decisive formulas that make points."[17] Recalling Unferth's position as *þyle* or spokesperson of Hrothgar, it becomes clearer still that, although knowledge among the Anglo-Saxons is not the "only permanent basis of power" as it is among the Nzebi, still this confrontation represents "a fight between masters of knowledge."[18] Klaeber points out that Unferth, "by his reference to the Breca incident [,] shows that he is the best informed man at court."[19] Furthermore, his position of authority at the very feet of Hrothgar stresses quite forcefully his ability to speak the truth. During the course of his narrative, he freely accuses Beowulf, a guest in the hall, of "pride" [*wlenco*] (line 508), of "foolhardy boasting" [*dolgilp*] (line 509), and of not having the "greater strength" [*mare mægen*] (line 518).

Beowulf's response, of course, does not consist of a logical, point by point rebuttal of Unferth's accusations. That would be a particularly literary sort of activity. Rather, the *soþ* or truth which he claims is established by a superbly balanced adherence to legisimilar patterning. As Vansina points out, the oral "repertoire is a blueprint of the

---

[16] Classical and Germanic analogues are outlined by Klaeber (149). More wide-ranging examples are found in Vansina (102ff.).

[17] Vansina, 102.

[18] Vansina, 102.

[19] Klaeber, 149.

political system,"[20] and Beowulf's sensitivity to the political context of his narrative is rather striking.

Beowulf's awareness of the operative political system at Hrothgar's court has often been noted here and in his analysis of the impending marriage (lines 2024–68). In this passage, it is apparent that he too is a "master of knowledge," as he indulges in an impressive display of the classical *argumentum ad hominem:*

> Hwæt, þu worn fela, wine min Unferð
> beore druncen ymb Brecan spræce,
> sægdest from his siðe!   (530–32)

> . . . . .
>   No ic wiht fram þe
> swylcra searoniða secgan hyrde,
> billa brogan. Breca næfre git
> æt heaðolace, ne gehwæþer incer,
> swa deorlice dæd gefremede
> fagum sweordum —no ic þæs [fela] gylpe—,
> þeah ðu þinum broðrum to banan wurde,
> heafod mægum; þæs ðu in helle scealt
> werhðo dreogan, þeah þin wit duge.   (581–89)

Indeed, my friend Unferth, drunk with your beer, you have spoken much about Breca, and said many things about his adventure. . . . But not a thing have I heard tell of such cunning in battle, such terror of swords, coming from you. Breca never yet in the sport of battle, nor you either, achieved so bold a deed with a bloodbright sword—nor do I boast too much if I say this—though you did kill your brothers, closest kinsmen; for that you shall suffer punishment in hell, clever though you may be.

Beowulf's own recounting of the episode, then, can be seen to gain in truth-value in proportion to the amount he can disparage his opponent. Opening with a personal attack on Unferth's inebriated state, he returns to this mode of establishing truth some fifty lines later with a still rounder assertion of his own knowledge in the face of Unferth's apparent ignorance. Unferth, it should be recalled, opens his challenge with a question, not a statement of known fact: "Are you the Beowulf who. . .?" Beowulf, on the other hand, though he has never heard of "skilled combats" fought by Unferth, clearly has heard that Unferth is a kinslayer. This shows a rather amazing

---

[20] Vansina, 120.

knowledge of the ins and outs of the Danish court, comparable to Hrothgar's antecedent knowledge of Beowulf himself. The accusation of Unferth as an agent of strife in an ideally harmonious social group (such as the family or, by implication, the comitatus) has of course been remarked on before, especially in terms of his name's etymological significance.[21]

Beowulf continues to undercut his opponent in the following lines (590–94), but here he is playing a more dangerous game. He must bring up the obvious fact that Unferth himself is afraid to face Grendel, but without humiliating Hrothgar, "protector of the Scyldings." It is a delicate situation, but Beowulf carries it off by his emphasis on the second person address as he invokes the obligation of the particular thane Unferth to defend a far more general *eower leode* [your people], and Heorot. In this way he neatly sidesteps the question of Hrothgar's ultimate responsibility. As an additional rhetorical ploy, if we do not regard the formulaic epithets as fixed, consider Beowulf's use of martial terminology in his characterization of the "victorious Scyldings" and the "spear-wielding Danes." His generosity and delicacy are reinforced as well even during his scathing attack on Unferth. Despite the general import of the speech, Unferth remains "clever" and "my friend," and by the end of the speech is re-assimilated within the community, where *Gæþ eft se mot to medo modig* [Any who wish may go boldly again to the mead-drinking] (603–4).

In oral societies, then, we see more overtly the establishment of truth from the position of power, whether that power resides in knowledge, rank, age, or force. Though literates tend to see the *argumentum ad hominem*, for example, as a fallacious means of establishing truth, we recognize its effectiveness nonetheless. In oral societies, such a means is not fallacious, but instead shows verbal prowess and knowledge, and thus establishes a greater right to a truthful narrative.

Thus, basic mental operations, in their organizational interaction with a "blueprint of the political system," generate a system of conventional laws whereby truth is established. In this, oral cultures are not far different from literate cultures. The third determinant of conventional legisimilitude, however, rests on the very technological difference between the two cultures, for in an oral culture, as Walter J. Ong points out, one must

---

[21] For a recent discussion, see Eugene Greene, "Power, Commitment, and the Right to a Name in *Beowulf*," in *CUNY English Forum* (New York: AMS Press, 1985), 133–40.

think memorable thoughts. In a primary oral culture, to solve effectively the problem of retaining and retrieving carefully articulated thought, you have to do your thinking in mnemonic patterns, shaped for ready oral recurrence. Your thought must come into being in heavily rhythmic, balanced patterns, in repetitions or antitheses ... in standard thematic settings (the assembly, the meal, the duel ...).[22]

These conventional ways of patterning, created to counteract the defects of human memory, act as a third and very powerful force in the determination of legisimilar truth. A new narrative, in order to be perceived as true, will have to accord with the form of other truthful narratives. This can be observed to a lesser extent in literate settings, of course; a scholarly article that abrogates generic conventions (in its choice of less than literary epigraphs, for example) is clearly less true (less "scholarly") than one which accords with those conventions. But generic conventions operate far more powerfully in the necessarily conservative milieux of oral cultures.[23] If a narrative were to stray perceptibly from the conventional laws of discourse, from the traditional ways of conveying truth, it would become not only untrue, but quite dangerous, changing as it would the very laws upon which the worldview and hence the culture itself is based.

Returning to examination of *Beowulf* in this light, then, it quickly becomes apparent that the way in which the narratives are told differ markedly. Few would dispute that Beowulf tells a better story: *his* swimming contest includes much swordplay, in a fierce battle by night with sea-monsters. A brief nod is made to the high-spiritedness of youth, but the bulk of Beowulf's narrative is a glorification of combat and the heroic ethos, couched in some of the most familiar and striking of poetic formulas.[24] We have already noted that the "contest" of Beowulf is not with Breca at all, but with the sea and its inhabitants—the fact that the swimming contest thus meshes more neatly with the principal events of the poem as a whole, the monster-fights, is probably not accidental. Moreover, while his narrative is thereby undoubtedly more memorable than Unferth's, due to its in-

---

[22] Ong, 34.

[23] Both Ong and Jack Goody stress this aspect of oral cultures. Goody basically equates the two terms: "members of oral (i.e. traditional) societies find it difficult to develop a line of sceptical thinking" (*The Domestication of the Savage Mind* [Cambridge: Cambridge Univ. Press, 1977], 43).

[24] Klaeber, pointing to "the admirable use of variation, the abundance of sea terms (lines 508ff.), the strong description of the scene" claims that these speeches "show the style of the poem at its best," 150.

clusion of conflict and its much greater use of concrete description
and variation, it is also more correctly formed with respect to the conventions of the oral tradition. As David K. Crowne analyzes this particular passage in his important article, Beowulf's use of "composition
by theme" here demonstrates "an excellence akin to that of Homer's"
and "an instance of the extreme flexibility with which the *Beowulf*-
poet is able to employ the theme."[25] This theme, of course, is that of
the hero on the beach, "a stereotyped way of describing (1) a hero on
the beach (2) with his retainers (3) in the presence of a flashing light
(4) as a journey is completed (or begun)."[26] Beowulf himself puts it
better, naturally:

> Næs hie ðære   fylle gefean hæfdon
> manfordædlan,   þæt hie me þegon,
> symbel ymbsæton   sægrunde neah;
> ac on mergenne   mecum wunde
> be yðlafe   uppe lægon,
> sweordum aswefede,   þæt syðþan na
> ymb brontne ford   brimliðende
> lade ne letton.   Leoht eastan com,
> beorht beacen Godes. . . .   (562–70)

> These evil-doers had not the joy of eating their fill, of taking
> me for their food, or of sitting at their feast on the seabottom;
> rather, by morning they lay high on the shore left bare by
> ebbing waves, wounded by blades, sent sleeping by the sword,
> so that never again would they hinder travelers from their
> voyage across the seas. Light came out of the east, the bright
> beacon of God. . . .

Crowne explains in his analysis that the retainers are transformed by
"a figurative description of the sea-monsters' sitting around the ban-
quet-table like a Germanic comitatus"; the performer can likewise
equate "the monsters' lying dead on the shore with the more usual
reference to a live troop." Similarly, voyages (coming or going) will no
longer be hindered by the sea-monsters.[27] This elegant use of theme
and motif, that is, of the laws of standard truthful narratives, should
make a strong impression on the audience, especially if another such

---

[25] David K. Crowne, "The Hero on the Beach: an Example of Composition by
Theme in Anglo-Saxon Poetry," *Neophilologische Mitteilungen* 61 (1960), 362–372: 369.
[26] Crowne, 368.
[27] Crowne, 370.

performance is within immediate memory. And of course, Unferth's account is literally pale by comparison:

> Þa hine on morgentid
> on Heaþo-Ræmes   holm up ætbær;
> ðonon he gesohte   swæsne eþel,
> leof his leodum,   lond brondinga.   (518–21)

Then one morning the sea washed him up in the land of the Heatho-Ræmas; thence he, dear to his people, sought his beloved homeland, the land of the Brondings.

No *Leoht eastan com*, nor is this a "bright beacon of God." Rather, a pale "morning" seems to be the best that Unferth can manage. The retainers are practical non-entities, as they are quite abstract, and happen to be in a country some distance from Breca's landing place.

It could be argued, of course, that since Breca is not a hero, he cannot receive full heroic treatment; that, of course, is exactly my point. Beowulf, by his brilliant (if not flashy) conformity with the laws of representation has firmly established the truth of his story, and himself as a hero, eminently fit to challenge Grendel. Moreover, to underscore the truthfulness of his narrative, the highest ranking member of the audience is immediately described as having "placed trust in his aid" [*geoce gelyfde*] (608).

While legisimilitude in all three of its aspects is thus clearly necessary to the creation of a truthful narrative, it is likewise clear that the demands of legisimilitude can affect one's understanding of concrete historical reality to an enormous degree. Vansina, attempting to retrieve the real events that lie behind oral historical accounts, notes that "traditions adhere to the 'great man' school of history. They thereby fundamentally distort the nature of historical processes but in a way diametrically opposed to all evidence that stems from direct traces of the past."[28] We can see this process operating in living oral traditions, where inventions and heroic qualities will coalesce about a single exemplary figure, and all villainous qualities and actions will be gathered to his or her opponent. As in the case of Beowulf and Grendel, for every hero there must be an equal and opposite monster. This shift toward idealization is a movement away from verisimilitude toward greater legisimilitude, and is "a process that is revealed very quickly in tales or other artistic genres, much slower perhaps in historical accounts."[29] It should be remembered, however, that the

---

[28] Vansina, 108.
[29] Vansina, 106.

legisimilar ideal type and the verisimilar character or personality of day-to-day reality are separated by a difference of degree only: the description of character is a functional adaptation to current reality. For example, Shakespeare and Milton are much more "heroic" to us today than they were to their contemporaries, who held widely divergent opinions of them depending on their kind and degree of interaction.

Historical reality then, undergoes a process akin to that which affects the jagged bit of dirt that bothers an oyster; an initial and perhaps uncomfortable reality is transformed through repeated performance into a polished and much more comfortable truth. The situation can then arise, naturally enough, that narratives based in legisimilitude, and therefore true, may not necessarily be perceived as "factual" in terms of quotidian reality.

> When Trobrianders (New Guinea) hear assertions that run counter to their everyday ideas ... the words of the ancestors, while true, should still be backed up by a trace of the event visible in the landscape. Otherwise the tradition is true, but not factual.[30]

I would like to explore this notion of the "trace" a bit more, because it seems to me to operate a bit differently, or at least with a different emphasis, in Anglo-Saxon poetry. The "trace of the event visible in the landscape" is an obvious verisimilar device. Dennis J. Tedlock provides an interesting example in a Zuni tale that explains why ducks waddle rather than walk straight: "Asked whether this tale were true, Andrew (a Zuni story-teller) said, 'Yes, that's true. Ducks really walk that way.'"[31] As Aristotle understood it, Tedlock goes on to explain, this is a paralogical argument: "Just because we know the truth of the consequent we are in our minds led on to the erroneous inference of the truth of the antecedent."[32] This kind of argument from the truth of the consequent can of course be found in Anglo-Saxon poetry. *The Ruin*, for example, argues from the visible trace of the decaying Roman ruins to the splendor of the city at its height, and to the cause of its downfall.[33] Likewise, in the speech of

---

[30] Vansina, 129.

[31] Dennis J. Tedlock, *The Spoken Word and the Work of Interpretation* (Philadelphia: Univ. of Pennsylvania Press, 1983), 165.

[32] Tedlock, 165.

[33] We need not give full credence to R. F. Leslie's argument (in his introduction to *Three Old English Elegies* [Manchester: Manchester Univ. Press, 1961], 2–28) that the poem describes actual conditions of the ruins at Bath. Clearly pointing to Roman construction, however, are the use of tile, metal reinforcing bands, and of course, the *hyðelic* (convenient) hot public baths which the poet describes within the ruins.

Beowulf already examined, there are verisimilar anchors to the legisimilar pattern he establishes: the "trace" of a living Unferth is a
strong argument for Unferth's relative cowardice in defense of Heorot. However, Beowulf's argument also hinges upon an *invisible* trace,
or rather, on the trace of absence. The real "trace" of the humiliation
of the Danish court lies in the absence of the thanes and retainers
killed by Grendel.

The elegiac reputation of Old English poetry is much remarked
on, and this reputation, it seems to me, rests upon that poetry's profound recognition of absence as conditional of narrative truth. *Beowulf*
as a whole is true, partly because the Geatish kingdom is no more.
The ultimate locus or rhetorical topos of absence is naturally the
gravesite, and the descriptive system of things absent at the place of
most absence, at the Anglo-Saxon barrow, tumulus, or *eorðscræfe*, is
overwhelming. Beowulf's barrow, with its multiple remembrances of
things past, is also the site of the lay of the last survivor. *The Wife's
Lament*, with the added verisimilar touch of the oak tree, takes place
at an *eorðscræfe*, as does Guthlac's hermitage.

The Wanderer, moving toward a legisimilar meditative emphasis,
combines the rhetorical topoi of absence in its contemplation of both
gravesites (lines 23, 83–84) and ruin (lines 62–98). The famous *ubi sunt*
passage, of course, in the mind of "one who deeply contemplates this
wall-foundation and this dark life" (lines 88–89), poignantly illustrates the truth of former joy by the trace of its absence:

> Standeþ nu on laste   leofre duguðe
> weall wundrum heah,   wyrm-licum fag.   (97–98)

> The wall wondrously high, stained with snakepatterns, stands
> now as a trace (or in the track) of that beloved company.

Contemplation of the wall-foundation thus leads in *The Wanderer*, as
in the lay of the last survivor, to the simultaneous establishment and
lament of the things which must have been:

> "Hwær com mearh? Hwær com magu? Hwær com maðum-giefa?
> Hwær com symbla gesetu? Hwær sindon seledreamas?
> Ea-la beorht bune! Ea-la byrnwiga!
> Ea-la þeodnes þrymm! Hu seo þrag gewat,
> genap under nihthelm, swa heo na wære!"   (92–96)[34]

---

[34] Cited from John C. Pope's edition in *Seven Old English Poems* (repr. New
York: W. W. Norton and Co., 1981), 28–32.

"Where now is the horse? Where the young man? Where is the treasuregiver? Where the banquet-seats? Where now are the joys of the hall? Alas, the bright cup! Alas, the mailed warrior! Alas, the lord's glory! How that time has fled—vanished in the helm of night—as if it never were!"

Throughout Anglo-Saxon poetry, but especially in *The Wanderer* (with its movement toward abstract contemplation), the evidence shows clearly enough that rhetorical topoi of absence such as the barrow and the ruin become *legisimilar* means of establishing the truth about things absent, although at the same time they appear to refer to the trace of that absence visible in the everyday landscape. With such a cultural emphasis on the things that are not, the speedy conversion of the Anglo-Saxons to the Christian faith is somewhat easier to understand. Thus, the barrow in Anglo-Saxon poetry occupies a position somewhere between the extreme legisimilitude of heroes and monsters, and the opposing pole of extreme verisimilitude. Yet there are a number of ways to keep an idealized legisimilar narrative more "factual," more realistically earthbound. The environmental trace, which allows a tale ascribed to a particular item to be deemed true, is a good one; even better, however, is the "inscribed" trace, or proof, presented as evidence that the tale told is true. The distinction here is between a trace inherent in the mere present state of things, and the newly achieved trace of a changed state. That proof is necessary, or at least helpful, in establishing the truth in an oral society, can again be seen in *Beowulf*, where it is best exemplified by Grendel's hand:

> Þæt wæs tacen sweotol,
> syþðan hildedeor   hond alegde,
> earm ond eaxle ...   (833–35)

That was a clear token, after the one brave in battle had laid down the hand, the arm and shoulder...

The arm is a "token" of Grendel's defeat, a sign of a change in Danish fortunes; it is also a *wundor*, much like a religious relic in the latter Middle Ages, a proof to the chieftains who come from far and near to gaze upon it and hear the story. Grendel's head and the hilt of the *ealdsweord eacen* [great sword of old (line 1663)] function similarly, to corroborate Beowulf's account of the battle beneath the mere.

The treasure which Beowulf presents to Hygelac also works as a proof, but here we have the added verisimilar anchoring of witnesses, not only in Beowulf's retainers but in what "many men now know of that famous encounter" (line 2000). The importance of witnesses is seen even more often in the use of formulas such as "we have heard" or "I heard"; though the oral performer is not an immediate witness, the formula and the tradition suppose a regressive chain of performers and auditors, culminating in the original event and its witnesses.

Tedlock points out that truth can also be established, or lent at least, by "the description of the technology and ritual employed by the characters."[35] Especially significant for *Beowulf* is the fact that characters "almost never perform their more fantastic actions without going through some sort of technical or ritual procedure."[36] In *Beowulf*, the three most "fantastic" elements, those most idealized or distorted from concrete historical reality, are the monster fights. Before his combat with Grendel, Beowulf goes through a ritual (and technologically necessary) "disarming of the hero" (lines 671–74); the parallel (and equally necessary) ritual of arming occurs just before the hero's descent into the mere (lines 1441ff.). Here we have the additional ritual of the exchange of swords: the loan of Hrunting, and the later substitution of the *ealdsweord eacen*. Perhaps the most interesting use of this particular verisimilar device occurs before Beowulf's fight with the dragon:

Heht him þa gewyrcean   wigendra hleo
eallirenne,   eorla dryhten,
wigbord wrætlic;   wisse he gearwe,
þæt him holtwudu   helpan ne meahte,
lind wið lige.   (2337–41)

The protector of warriors, lord of earls, commanded that a splendid warshield, all of iron, be made for him; well he knew that timber, a shield of linden wood, could not help him against fire.

Though the dragon itself is "fantastic," in that (while alive) it is beyond the limits of human measure or pattern, as Daniel Calder has shown,[37] still an iron shield is a sensible, realistic precaution, establishing far more firmly the truth of the narrative within the constraints of quotidian common sense.

Other kinds of verisimilitude exist, particularly those we might call performative verisimilitude. As Tedlock notes,

in seeking to create the appearance of reality a narrator has recourse to a number of devices which stretch the limits of ver-

---

[35] Tedlock, 173.
[36] Tedlock, 176.
[37] Daniel G. Calder, "Setting and Ethos: The Pattern of Measure and Limit in *Beowulf*," *Studies in Philology* 69 (1972): 21–37.

bal description or transcend them, including gesture ... quotation, onomatopoeia, and the linking of the story to the actual context of its narration.[38]

Within the scope of this paper at least, these devices must remain untested against the pulse of Anglo-Saxon poetry. Though we can certainly imagine a performer gesturing toward the mead-hall door at the point in the story where Grendel smashes it open, this is purely conjecture. Moreover, the variations in tone, volume, and length of pause, that Tedlock stresses throughout his work, and which could easily affect the truth content of the narrative, must likewise be omitted from the present discussion, tempting though they are. The narrator's use of quotation of characters is, of course, very common among Anglo-Saxon poets as a verisimilar device. As this paper, by example, attempts to show, it is here, in the direct discourse of the characters, that we can begin to look for substantial performative differences. Looking back at the confrontation between Unferth and Beowulf, can we begin to see distinctions of tone, volume, presentation? Does Unferth, *beore druncen*, slur his words?

Such questions obviously fall outside the scope of this paper, which as I have said, only begins to explore the nature of truth. Principally, I have tried to avoid the too-frequent dichotomization of oral and written, focusing rather on an epistemological framework that allows the two types of culture to be seen as fundamentally similar in their establishment of truth. Second, I have tried to shed light on cultural differences of emphasis, on the formal memorability so crucial to oral societies, and on the political and contextual considerations so often repressed in a literate culture. The distinction I make between legisimilitude and verisimilitude, despite the fact that one persistently shades into the other, has been, if not completely accurate, at least an expedient error.

---

[38] Tedlock, 166.

SAMUEL KINSER

Wildmen in Festival, 1300–1550

One of the favorite figures of masquerade in medieval and Renaissance courtly festivals was a person dressed in a long-haired, fur-like costume called the wildman. In 1392 King Charles VI of France and his courtiers donned such costumes at a Christmas-season ball. Their costumes caught fire from the torches and the king narrowly escaped death; contemporary manuscript illuminations show the startling scene.[1]

Wildmen did more than cavort at courtly balls like this, or pose along the streets when feudal princes, at the outset of their reign, made their triumphal entries into the chief towns of their realm.[2] They also danced at locally centered occasions, in mountain villages and in small and large towns, especially during the Twelve Days of

---

[1] See e.g., Richard Bernheimer, *The Wildman in the Middle Ages* (Cambridge, MA, 1952), pl. 23, and Timothy Husband, *The Wild Man, Medieval Myth and Symbolism* (New York, 1980), 33, for two manuscript versions of the scene which came to be called *le bal des ardents*.

[2] Cf. the entries at Paris (1389, 1431, 1461), Marseille (1516), and Saint Jean de Maurienne (1548), discussed in chap. 7 of my *Managing Majesty: Princely Entries and the Political Imagination, 1400–1600* (forthcoming).

Christmas (December 25–January 6) and during Carnival, the festive period preceding Ash Wednesday and Lent. They still do so in the Alps and in scattered localities in Eastern Europe.[3]

In this paper I will deal primarily with the wildman's appearances in late medieval and Renaissance Carnivals in order to explore the hypothesis, often proposed, that there is a special affinity for figures of wildness in this old seasonal festival. What the affinity between wildness and Carnival might be needs clarification; different forms of this affinity also need to be distinguished.

Carnival was a time of masquerade. But from the fourth century onward men who masked themselves in furs to look like animals had been denounced as possessed by the devil. In the sixteenth century Protestant reformers took up the polemic, blaming the survival of animalistic Carnival disguises on the abominable lenience of the Catholics. Thomas Kirchmeyer in his *Regnum papisticum* (1559) made a list of such disguises in the German Carnivals of his time, a list translated into bad verse by one Barnaby Googe in the late sixteenth century:

> Some like wilde beastes doe runne abroade in skinnes
> that divers bee
> Arayde, and else with lothsome shapes, that dreadfull
> are to see:
> They counterfet with Beares and Wolves, and Lions
> fierce in fight,
> And raging Bulles. Some play the Cranes with wings
> and stilts upright.
> Some like the filthie forme of Apes, and some like
> fooles are drest,
> Which best beseeme these Papistes all, that thus keepe
> Bacchus feast.[4]

I will touch upon maskers pretending to be animals and birds, but there is not space to explore their connection to the fool-figure which Googe mentions in the penultimate line. We will concentrate on the first figure, the wildman who is dressed in diverse skins. In medieval literature and festive practice this personage has two origins.

---

[3] *Carnavals et Fêtes d'hiver* (Centre Georges Pompidou exhibition catalog, no editor indicated) (Paris, 1984), 24 and 29, show the occasions at Bischofshofen, Austria, on January 6, and at Mohacs, Hungary, on the Sunday before *mardi gras*, which precedes Ash Wednesday.

[4] Thomas Kirchmeyer (Latinized as Naogeorgus), *Regnum papisticum* (n.p., 1559), trans. by Barnaby Googe, *The Popish Kingdome* (London, 1570; repr., London, 1880), fol. 48r.

Wild people may be persons who have deserted civilization for one reason or another, like the early Christian saints living in the desert, "hairy anchorites" whose only clothing was the long body-hair which they grew; and also like those wise men driven so mad by the corruption of civilization that they sought refuge in the woods. In the tales of Geoffrey of Monmouth and Robert de Boron, King Arthur's magician-counselor Merlin is an example of the latter; in some manuscript illuminations he is shown in the same hirsute garb as Charles VI and his courtiers.[5] The idea that wildmen result from a loss of manners and sociability, or, in the Christian case, from a gain in morality, is characteristic of literature and art by and for feudal and Christian elites. Of course some of the iconography connected with anchoritic saintliness was known to broad groups of Christians. John the Baptist, shown in long hair, was a favorite subject of altarpiece painting and sculpture. It is possible that the Christian idea of devout men in the wilderness may thus have touched festive practice; by and large, however, the wildmen appearing in Carnival derived from a different idea.

This second idea of wild people is that they never possessed culture, that they in fact constitute separate, strange races unlike "us." Here the wildman is an image not of alienation from society, but of something beyond and other than society: this is the image exploited in Carnival. It is helpful to distinguish the real, ideal, and festive settings of this idea of wild people as a strange, primitive race.

By "real" I mean that persons living between 1300 and 1550, the time period discussed here, thought that wild people really existed, living singly or in families in remote, forested, mountainous areas in many parts of Europe. In an extraordinary sequence on facing pages in the manuscript *Psalter of Queen Mary*, illuminated between 1300 and 1325, such a "real" wildman was depicted as the object of a royal hunt.[6]

By "ideal," with reference to wild people, I mean that no one ever saw a wild man, woman, or child. Depictions like that in the Queen Mary Psalter are ideal in the sense that they are created from an amalgam of ideas about what it would be like for humans to live outside or in opposition to social ways. This ideal or ideational quality of

---

[5] On the hairy anchorite, see Charles Williams, "Oriental Affinities of the Legend of the Hairy Anchorite," *University of Illinois Studies in Language and Literature* 10 (1925): 195–248, and 11 (1926): 427–93. See the illustration of Merlin as a hairy wild man in Husband, *The Wild Man*, 61.

[6] Ibid., 3–5.

thought about wildmen, which made such thought as difficult to dis-
prove as to prove in an era where both science and geography offered
ample space for strange races to exist,[7] was redoubled by festivity.

Festive activity is not a place where beliefs are tested but where
they are exhibited, extended, and reinforced. Festive behavior is lei-
sure-time activity; in contrast to work-a-day situations, the festive am-
biance affords space for the emergence of non-pragmatic, generalized,
and deep-lying elements of belief. That is why, quite aside from its
color and joyousness, it is a significant site of human expression: it allows and even solicits the exhibition of otherwise unexpressed or politely suppressed thought and feelings. Unlike works of art and philosophy, which are similar sites of expression, somewhat distant from
everyday preoccupations and hence capable of revealing underlying
realities, festive expressions are strongly collective. There is less room
in them than in individually constructed artifacts for personal patterning of forms.

In the festivity of Carnival, then, the idea of strange races living
far from society—and yet geographically nearby, in mountains and
woods—is made tangible by the irruption of wildman maskers into
and through the streets and even into the houses of villagers and
townspeople. From this situation derives my initial hypothesis: there
is a parallel between wildmen as people who disrupt—not deny—the
social bounds, bursting in from outside, and Carnival as a festival
which disrupts but does not deny the Christian moral economy.

Carnival precedes Lent, and is indeed the prelude to Lent. It
occurs, like Lent, in the early spring upon dates that are determined
by the movable date of Easter. The Christian calendar specifies Lent
as a time of penitent waiting for the supreme mystery of the Resurrection which occurs at its close. But the development of Carnival in
the period just before Ash Wednesday expresses the counter-Lenten,
but not necessarily anti-Christian, idea that early springtime is also a
time of festive joyousness, a time when the gifts of nature—above all,
ample food and drink—should be recognized and enjoyed. Carnival's
relation to Christianity is ambivalent, and so also has been the Church's attitude to it, sometimes tolerating and other times condemning it.

Carnival disrupts the Christian calendrical schema, directing attention not to the spiritual drama of Christ's death and resurrection but
to the material drama of nature's imminent rebirth in spring. As such,

---

[7] On this aspect of the subject see, together with Husband and Bernheimer (note
1), John B. Friedman, *The Monstrous Races in Medieval Art and Thought* (Cambridge,
Mass., 1981).

Carnival also disrupts social life. In the spiritual sense it disrupts with its raucous, bodily self-indulgence a social scene which should be the theater of Christian restraint and piety. In the material sense it disrupts with its reckless merrymaking the sober husbanding of resources which is so needed during the winter season and especially in early spring. Because Carnival, like the wildman, has a disruptive relation to society, the wildman figure developed with particular breadth in this festival.

I shall divide the many versions of Carnival wildness into three symbolic modes: the diabolic wildman, the fertilizing wildman, and the coercive wildman. The body of my paper is devoted to explaining these differences and their mutual influence on each other.

Consider the illustration of fur-clad figures in a Parisian manuscript of the rhymed comic epic, *Le Roman de Fauvel*, made about 1350. It depicts a chärivāri, a ritual usually performed in medieval times by masked figures at night during the Twelve Days of Christmas or at Carnival-time.[8] With raucous music and fiendish howling, chärivāris "celebrate" anomalous or dishonorable marriages, like that of the rascal Fauvel to the young lady "Vainglory" in this tale. The leader of the masked throng is shown in two of the illustrations. He is called a "giant" in the text and shows no hairy costume; for the moment, then, let us not call him a wildman. But his followers include seven wildmen, that is, persons with hairy bodies but human faces. There are eight persons with hairy face marks but hairless, humanoid bodies or feet. These are a variant of the wildman: they simply invert the placement (face versus body) of the animalistic disguise. They have muzzles like those of bears and lions. Their representation is generalized; they dance along with the others. There are 59 figures in the throng. Their gestures are no less varied and complex than their costumes. Nearly all the gestures, like many of the costumes, illustrate Mikhail Bakhtin's observation that Carnival's inversions substitute low, bodily symbols for high, spiritual ones. Carnival, he says, glorifies the "bodily lower stratum."[9] Indeed it does so here: Five naked and bald men are in the throng, one "shows his

---

[8] This manuscript has recently been reproduced in facsimile with extensive introductory essays devoted to its artistic, literary, and musical aspects, by Edward Roesner, François Avril, and Nancy Regalado: *Le Roman de Fauvel in the Edition of Mesire Chaillou de Pestain* (New York, 1990). The author of the chärivāri passage, interpolated by Raoul de Chaillou (d. 1337) in the *Roman* by Gervais du Bus, does not specify the seasonal date of the fictional chärivāri. See fols. 34r–36v.

[9] Mikhail Bakhtin, "Images of the Material Bodily Lower Stratum," chap. 6 in *Rabelais and His World* (Boston, 1968).

bottom," another "breaks wind." Some throw salt and even feces; others break windows. All these gestures are amply documented among Carnival pranks; they are not restricted to chäriväri rituals. Half of those in the illustrations have drums, fiddles, bells, pots, cymbals, or wagon-spokes with which to perform the "rough music" characteristic of chäriväris and of Carnivals generally. One of the wildmen carries a flag and another wears a tunic with "little cowbells." These two accouterments will be seen in several of our later examples.

The story elevates the figures to superhuman—but also to subhuman—status. The masked throng has the same character as the hero of the tale Fauvel, who is a humanoid horse: it is both human and inhuman, natural and unnatural. "I believe," confides the author, "that it [the leader] was Hellequin and that the others were his household (sa mesnie), who follow him, all enraged." Some of the wildmen indeed grimace and gnash huge teeth in the illustrations, but others in the group look harmless enough, especially the children trundled along in baskets and wagons. Men and women of all ages, bearded and bald, monks, nuns and lay, masked and unmasked, grin, grimace and gambol arm in arm. Such promiscuity is the most prominent feature of the illustrations.

It is the promiscuity of the dead. This literary depiction of festive wildmen among all manner of other people has a supernatural dimension. Hellequin in medieval lore was the leader of an angry or unhappy throng of dead souls (we recall the gnashing grimaces of some in the throng; it is a *Wüttisher*, an "enraged army," as it was called in some fifteenth- and sixteenth-century sources). The largely oral tradition which, we suppose, developed this representation was first recorded in 1091 by a Norman monk named Ordericus Vitalis. Walking in the countryside near Chartres at night a young man known to Ordericus was terrified to see what he called Hellekin's household (*familia hellequini*) riding in a whirlwind across the sky, carrying in their wake some recently dead persons who were recognized by the terrified cleric.[10] The demonic leader of the dead is called a king (*li rois Hellekins*) in Adam de la Halle's play, *le Jeu de la Feuillee*, written about 1260.[11] Hellekin, a "hell-raiser" in late medieval and modern Dutch parlance, is the devil as bedeviler of the recently dead, the improperly buried or evil dead.

---

[10] Ordericus Vitalis, *Ecclesiastical History*, as quoted in Otto Driesen, *Der Ursprung des Harlekin* (Munich, 1905), 24–25.

[11] Adam de la Halle, *Le Jeu de la Feuillee*, line 604 (many editions).

Are the wildmen who are so prominent among the chärivāri
throng of maskers in the *Roman de Fauvel* natural or supernatural? To
pose the question as an alternative is absurd. The natural and supernatural were inextricably mixed, both for devout and learned Christians and for less devout average persons who were full of ethnically
derived superstitions and tales about a world understood through
myth and pragmatic experience more than through science or theology. Wildmen were, because of their remote habitat in the mountains
and deserts—indeed, their inaccessible habitat, since seeing them was
always a matter of hearsay—uncanny, preternatural, possibly supernatural parts of nature. The wildman's distant, dim home was like
that of the dead, that quintessential group of natural yet supernatural
beings. For nearly all of us in the twentieth century, as in the eleventh or fourteenth, death is more than a natural event. People "go"
somewhere when they die, and from that place they sometimes
"come back." There is no subject more fraught with oral tradition;
we, like the people in late medieval times, have inherited a vast body
of legend about the ghostly dead, and especially about the unquiet
dead who, because they left the world of the living in a violent and
unfinished manner, are compelled to return to visit those whose lives
have been left ragged by their departure.

Amalgamating the recent dead and wild men in a single demonic
throng, as in the chärivāri passage in the *Roman de Fauvel*, was therefore intensely—but given the comic context, also ridiculously—fright-
ening. It wasn't funny, however, to churchmen. To pretend to be a
wildman was nearly as awful and diabolic as to pretend to be a
ghost. Thus preached Caesar of Arles in the 530s in a sermon concerning New Year's Day which was copied and recopied by other
Christian preachers in succeeding centuries:

> What is so mad ... as to be clothed in the manner of wild beasts
> and to become like a goat or a stag, so that a man who was
> made in the image and likeness of God becomes a sacrifice to
> the demons? By these means that contriver of evil [the devil] in-
> troduces himself, so that he can dominate minds gradually cap-
> tivated by the [repetitious?] similarity of these amusements.[12]

Wildman maskers are possessed by the devil. One thousand years
later these diabolic wildmen were not just maskers, but were real.
Geiler von Kaysersberg, a popular preacher at Strassburg, included in

---

[12] Caesar of Arles, *Sermons*, vol. 3 (Washington, DC, 1973), sermon 193, p. 31.

his Lenten sermons of 1508 about "real" wildmen not only references to the good kind—*solitarii* who were hairy, pious wildmen living in the desert—but to *diaboli* or "evil-spirited" wildmen: "You ask whether magicians can make real animals? These [magicians] are devils ... they have done it [i.e., made tame men into wild-animal men] just as men say they have."[13]

Unlike Geiler von Kaysersberg, the bishop of Aosta in 1467 was concerned less with spiritual than with material effects. He spoke not of real wildmen but, like Caesar of Arles, of the maskers imitating them:

> Men mask themselves, putting on bizarre clothing, attaching little cowbells [to it] [*tintinnabula vaccarum*] and putting the devil's horns on their heads. Disguised so, they run and roam through the streets and public places, spreading terror especially among women and children, and committing all manner of excesses. The view of these demons in effigy even drives some people mad.[14]

The demon's effigy is created by attaching cowbells and—no doubt—cow's horns to "bizarre" clothing: the animal signs are signs of the devil.

Mardi gras fell on February 10 in 1467, twelve days after the date of this description, which makes it at least possible that the bishop was referring to Carnival processions. The edict issued in 1562 by the city council of Solothurn, Switzerland, refers directly to Carnival. Again, a reference to devil's clothing is coupled with cowbells, already used as decoration by one grimacing wildman in the *Roman de Fauvel*: "*Hauri* [ghostly beings]," reads the edict, "shall no longer run about with devil's clothing and cowbells."[15]

Thus the state was no less concerned with the disruptive effects of festive wildmen than was the church. A generation before the bishop

---

[13] Geiler von Kaysersberg, *Die Emeis*, as quoted in Albert Hiss, "Umholde-Hexen-Gespenster, Volkskündliches aus Johannes Geiler von Kaysersbergs Predigt-sammlung Die Emeis," *Badische Heimat* 49 (1969): 90–91.

[14] Joseph Auguste Duc, *Histoire de l'eveché d'Aoste* vol. 5 (Turin, 1879), 21. Duc paraphrases the original Latin (with the exception of his citation of the cowbells), which has remained apparently unedited. The paraphrase is made from a letter, either one by the bishop of Aosta, François de Prez, to the duke of Savoy or more likely one by the duke to one or several of his officers, relaying the bishop's concerns, written at Pinerolo on January 30, 1467.

[15] Quoted in Hans G. Wackernagel, *Altes Volkstum der Schweiz* (Basel, 1956), 24, n. 2.

of Aosta addressed the complaint quoted above to the duke of Savoy, the supreme civil authority in his region, that duke himself issued an edict concerning maskers who take on the appearance of devils (June, 1430). Given the context of assimilating wildman masking to devilish masking, I would suggest that the reference is to the diabolic-wildman masker, who in this case seems to appear earlier in the wintertime:

> ... In some years on holy days and above all on Saint Catherine's Day [Nov. 25] or close to these dates, some despicable folk [*detestabiles quorundam*] change themselves into the appearance of devils [*in speciem diabolorum*] by donning deformed costumes [*habitus diformes*]. Carrying arms in and out of households, they run and roam through the streets and public places of our cities, villages, and rural areas, bringing ruin. And they violently accost peasants and various other simple, quiet people, and sometimes strike them, and force them to give them money, while heaping other injuries upon them which are offensive to God and men.[16]

The duke prohibited all such masking in his edict.

Since these maskers, then, risked state as well as ecclesiastical penalties, why did they dare? The answer seems to be that these rural, mountainous dwellers in Savoy and Switzerland were representing in ritual form what seemed to them a stronger power than church or state: the forces of nature generally.

Wildmen are beings with more than human strength. They are a force of nature, a force outside society. Because of the material character of that force they are seen as existing below and against the high spiritual force of God. When they invade the streets, homes, and even the physical collectedness of persons, striking them and extorting money from them—this of course was the well-known festive custom of quêting, or, as Americans say, "trick-or-treat"—they invoke in their victims feelings of social and personal vulnerability and limitation. The difference between the wild and the tame was sensed as nearly the same as that between the great and the small; wildmen reminded people of society's dependence upon surrounding nature, a nature filled with mysterious, dark powers.

---

[16] *Decreta Sabaudorum* (Turin, 1586), fol. 7r; the edict is partly quoted in Wackernagel, *Altes Volkstum*, 234, n. 2. The edict prescribed special punishment for clerics taking part in such manifestations, which of course indicates that they sometimes did so.

That dependence was, first of all, agricultural. In the nineteenth and twentieth centuries, folklorists have gathered many examples of peasant customs dedicated to the stimulation of crops through ritual propitiation. These rituals often involve wildman figures, persons wearing animal masks and furs and carrying sticks or clubs with which, for example, they may beat, like *kukeri* in Bulgaria, sterile fruit trees and grapevines to render them vigorous.[17] Such rituals have been assumed to be as old as European agriculture, older than Christianity. But they were unwritten rituals; orally transmitted, their form and presence can not be traced more than two or three generations. I have found only one example of agricultural rituals involving wildman maskers at Carnival-time before 1650, and this one is recorded for the relatively remote area of Graubünden in the Swiss Alps. Three sixteenth-century Swiss historians comment on the custom, each with different details, which indicates that they used different sources.

The Swiss wildmen were called *Stopfer*—"stickers"—because they carried big sticks or clubs with which they "run at full tilt against each other, mightily knocking and punching," as Gilg Tschudi wrote in 1528. They moved in groups from one village to the next, "making high jumps and doing other strange things." They jump and punch and stick, writes Tschudi, "so that their grain will do better." Ulrich Campell, writing about 1570, remarks that "it was believed that performance of this custom brought a fruitful year." This source and a third text by Johannes Stumpf, written about 1550, indicate that the custom had ceased, while Tschudi, writing in the 1520s, reports it as still present. Only one of the three sources specifies that the performance took place at Carnival: at that time the "inhabitants ... run through the villages disguised with masks, carrying clubs, and ... jingling bells." None of the three mentions the wearing of furs. Tschudi, on the contrary, says that they wore armor (*harnasch und gwör*, i.e., *Gewehr*) and that "they say that after they have taken off their armor and have terminated their affair, they can never jump so high and so far."[18] A twentieth-century anthropologist, dealing with a similar custom of dancing and leaping with heavy bells and sticks in present-

---

[17] See Waldemar Liungman, *Traditionswanderungen Euphrat-Rhein*, II (Helsinki, 1938), 792–95 on the *kukeri*.

[18] Gilg Tschudi, *Die uralt warhafftig Alpisch Rhetia* (Basel, 1538), unnumbered folio, corresponding to printer's gathering H i, verso; the rare text is transcribed from the earlier 1528 edition in Hans Moser, "Zur Geschichte des Winter-und Sommer-Kampfspiels," *Bayerischer Heimatsschutz* 29 (1933): 41. The German texts by Johannes Stumpf and Ulrich Campell are easily accessible in James Frazer, *The Golden Bough*, vol. 9 (London, 1936), 239, n. 2.

day Romania, concludes that the maskers believe the power of nature is engendered in them by their costumed ritual, making them capable of more than human deeds.[19]

The *Stopfer* with their masks, clubs, and bells were fertilizing wildmen. Like the diabolic sort, they broke into villages, disrupting everyday life. In larger towns where concern with agricultural productivity was less immediate, the aggressive aspect of their gestures had more meaning and impact than the bountiful, fecund one. In 1469, for example, the Nuremberg city council legislated against wildmen in terms similar to the duke of Savoy, enjoining "no one, especially not the wildmen," to run after people in Carnival-time, forcing them to "give money with cries, insults, and injury."[20] The maskers in question here were probably fertilizing wildmen rather than the ones with primarily diabolic overtones. I assert this because of their apparent similarity to the behavior and appearance of wildmen fifty years later at Nuremberg, when for the first time we have an illustration of wildmen's festive dress and accouterments.

Manuscripts illuminating the Carnival celebrations of 1518 there show a wildman in hairy nakedness, trotting along with an uprooted tree over one shoulder. The wildman is a giant, as denoted by his stature, compared to the normally sized man whom the wildman has snatched up and bound to his tree; stories and illustrations of how wildmen carried off men, women, and children to their lair are frequent in tapestries, stained-glass windows, and illuminated manuscripts made for the knightly class of the fourteenth and fifteenth centuries.[21]

The Nuremberg wildman of 1518 carried no arms, aside from the uprooted tree which might be seen as a sort of club. The *Stopfer* carried some definite weapons. This again may refer to a difference in environment. Unlike the landscape around lowland Nuremberg, nature in the mountains has itself an aggressive aspect. Nature is bountiful there not only in the vigor of agricultural crops but in wild

---

[19] Gail Kligman, *Calus* (Chicago, 1981). A Tirolian ethnographer, writing first-hand in 1909 about the custom of leaping by masked, fur-clad figures, says that it hung on in his area, although in "shrunken" form, "out of fear for a bad harvest . . . should these Carnival games . . . be omitted." See Moser, "Zur Geschichte," 41, quoting Ludwig von Hörmann.

[20] Quoted in Samuel Kinser, "Presentation and Representation: Carnival at Nuremberg, 1450–1550," *Representations* 13 (Winter 1986): 3.

[21] See the illustrations in Husband, *The Wild Man*, 65–82. The manuscript showing the 1518 Carnival wildman at Nuremberg is reproduced in *Carnavals et fêtes d'hiver*, 20.

and dangerous animals: hunting was a regular and important occupation. The hunter confronted nature in its own terms, wildly and aggressively. The weapons of the *Stopfer* suggest both the strong character of this nature and also the way mountain peasants dealt with it.

The *Stopfer* may also have worn armor because of their frequent employment as mercenaries in the large international armies of the fifteenth and sixteenth centuries: Swiss peasants' fighting ability had become legendary by the 1450s. The wildman seems to have become a symbol of the Swiss soldier's impetuous power, and self-consciously so. During the Carnival season of 1477 a group of "insolent youths" from Basel swept into neighboring Lorraine, robbing and pillaging; they may well have been the same as the mercenaries who are recorded as returning to Basel in 1477 with a banner "on which a hairy man [*vir pilosus*] is painted."[22] A similar way of associating the wildness necessary for high fecundity and effective soldiering is evidenced in the behavior of another group of Swiss mercenaries, those returning home during that same year, 1477, also at Carnival-time, after having served in the armies of Charles the Bold and Louis XI of France. These mutinous mercenaries moved through villages and cities, quêting "in grand style" and taking a banner with a sow, that is, a mother pig, as their emblem (fatty swine were a strong symbol of fecundity and rich Carnival food). The Solothurn edict about Carnival in 1562 evokes this same image two generations later: the *Hauri* with their bells and devil's clothing "shall no longer carry the sow banner around."[23]

We have arrived at the third wildman variant, that in which a coercive and domineering rather than a fecundating or a dreadful demonic element is most prominent. This third variant introduces a set of social parameters quite different from the other two, and I have hesitated about how to name it. When large groups of mercenaries adopted the sow and the hairy man as their emblems, they introduced a set of social dynamics quite at variance with the locally centered groups performing chäriväris, animal masking, and crop rituals. Wildness was now not the pitting of nature against society, but the opposition of one part of society against another. This oppositional part was "outside" locally centered society; it was rootless and nearly lawless, used to the catch-as-catch-can tactics of mercenary soldiering. The sow-banner and hairy-man-banner groups introduced the dynamics of class and regional conflict to wildman masking.

---

[22] Wackernagel, *Altes Volkstum*, 293, 311.
[23] Ibid., 241, n. 2.

It was not only peasants who in the fifteenth century, having stepped outside locally articulated society, found perhaps quite by accident that wildman festivity suited their new social condition, a condition based on the opposition of broad mass force to narrow local power. The merchants who in the small towns and cities of later medieval Europe possessed that narrow local power of course derived it not locally but regionally, nationally, and internationally from their commercial connections and from their entente with feudal elites. Wildman festivity became a way of expressing their power over society, just as it had for the sow-banner troops. Wild nature could thus become a symbol for this coercive force at the top no less than at the bottom of the social scale. The best example of elite use of the coercive wildman variant evolved in north France, where the elites of two neighboring towns, Valenciennes and Lille, took turns hosting a springtime festival called the Epinette. An *epinette* was a cage of twigs in which a fowl could be roasted: the "king of the Epinette" was a mock ruler elected on that day of grand, greasy eating, mardi gras.

At Lille the festival parades, jousts, and banquets planned on mardi gras *and* Ash Wednesday (!) by the new king and his court took place in May. In 1438 a large contingent of patrician burghers from Valenciennes, dressed as wildmen, came to Lille to share in the joyful proceedings. A contemporary manuscript explains that the wildmen with their typifying clubs were mounted on horses and were accompanied by others disguised as a variety of animals, lions, tigers, dogs, and birds. (The idea of wildmen as masters of the animals among whom they live is an old motif in elite literature.[24]) The herald of the wildmen from Valenciennes wore a bearskin, while the King of the Epinette, who advanced to greet him, was covered with mirrors and with swan and peacock feathers.[25] It would seem that the superiority of the town's elite was given such lavish form in this display that the ominous and forceful qualities of wildness must have receded before the rich spectacle of the wildmen's exoticism.

As the sixteenth century progressed, the differences among the three variants faded. For Kirchmeyer, Googe, and other Protestants,

---

[24] This is not to say that the wild man as master of animals had no roots in popular and oral traditions. The relation here as always between elite and non-elite, literary and oral *topoi* is circular and reciprocal. See Lutz Röhrich, *Sage und Märchen* (Freiburg, 1976), 147–95, for a rich collection of materials concerning this subject from all parts of Europe, from medieval times to the present.

[25] See Albertine Clément-Hémery, *Histoire des fêtes civiles et religieuses . . . du département du Nord* (Cambrai, 1836), 25–26, and Claude Fouret, "La violence en fête, la course de l'Epinette au bas moyen âge," *Revue du Nord*, 1982: 377–90.

wildman and wild-animal maskers were not people incarnating occult powers, possessed by the devil; they were simply fools. The supernaturally devilish was certainly at work in the world, but not in such simple, directly material ways. Belief in Hellekin and the army of the dead came to seem less sacrilegious than silly.[26] Communal stimulation of the crops by the high-leaping *Stopfer* died out. The marauding sow-banner groups were repressed. Emperor Charles V, overlord of Lille and Valenciennes, ordered the sumptuous festival of the Epinette drastically reduced in scale and splendor at the request of the citizens themselves, who were finding it difficult to find anyone wild enough to expend his fortune for the honor of being king of the feast.[27]

Myths faded, violence was controlled. Gradually the wildman became an ideologically and sociologically neutral figure. That is—to use terms which I have developed more fully elsewhere—the tension between presentation and representation in wildman performances declined.[28] Representation comprises predictable, controllable images, like those in the Nuremberg Schembart parades, made for the sake of impressive spectacle. The presentational kind of festive performance works actively and directly upon the material and social world, as in the case of the horned, bell-jingling maskers of Aosta in 1467, or the *Stopfer* in Graubünden. The *Stopfer* beat and shake the earth, encouraging it to produce; the horned fiends of mountainous Savoy rush through the streets and in and out of households, making their demonic presence physically felt. But the *Stopfer* and the Savoyan demons obviously *represent* no less than they *present*: there are ample symbolic dimensions to their costumes and gestures, which go beyond what their ritual performances are intended to accomplish in the way of fecundation and remembrance of the demonic dead beyond. That is why I speak of *tension* between presentation and representation in these performances.

But in the eyes of authority, in the view of settled, elite power, such tension is objectionable. It provokes unforeseeable behavior, uncontrollable violence. Elites and officials have, from the beginning of

---

[26] In the sixteenth century Hellekin became Harlequin in the Italian *commedia dell' arte*, as Driesen demonstrates (see n. 10). Nevertheless, people in rural Normandy still occasionally heard or saw Hellequin in the mid-sixteenth century. See Gilles de Gouberville, *Journal*, for April 14, 1553, quoted in Katharine Fedden, *Manor Life in Old France* (New York, 1933), 75: "Symmonet and Morisseau went shooting and got a hare. It was dark when they returned and they said that they had heard Helequin the Huntsman in the old wood."

[27] See the sources referred to in n. 25.

[28] See Kinser, "Presentation . . . ," 6.

the history of Carnival, sought to freeze its images, rituals, and symbols, and thus in fact to end the enlivening dynamics of presentation versus representation. By 1518 in Nuremberg, the wildmen who had been denounced a half century earlier for their unpredictable tactics had dwindled to a bug-a-boo giant. This Schembart wildman was simply an assemblage of familiar symbols of social disruption, rather than the cause of any such thing. Like the carefully apolitical surface of most twentieth-century television, images like these encouraged passive receptivity, a complacently unquestioning acceptance of the elite and official forces that were putting on the show.

The capacity to re-present an activity is a sign of one's ability to distance oneself from it. Between the fourteenth and sixteenth centuries, Europeans began to distance themselves from the myths and tales peopling mountains and woods with wild folk. The change was gradual and incomplete, something like that process of simultaneous belief and disbelief which Paul Veyne has described as taking place with respect to the gods and heroes of Greek myth between Herodotus's time and Pausanias's. By the time of Pausanias, Veyne explains, most Greeks possessed two ways of thinking about these figures, two "programs of truth" which allowed them, for example, both to believe and disbelieve in the tales of Homer.[29]

It was the same in Europe by 1500. In church the angels and devils were real; certain species of wildmen were truly naked and hairy and others were absolutely and undeniably vehicles of the devil, as Geiler explained. Outside church, in the marketplace, hairy, ape-headed devils were simply images of foolishness, part of a ship of fools, no different in essence from overly solemn demagogues like the Lutheran preacher Andreas Osiander, who indeed is associated with these maskers, as if his black frock and Bible were just one more silly Carnival costume on the Hell-float of 1539 in Nuremberg.[30]

A second program of truth which tested and sometimes ridiculed the first theologically derived one, a program humanistically critical, socially pragmatic, and morally skeptical, emerged after 1300 in many European locales. It was evinced not simply by a few heterodox writers—Boccaccio, Machiavelli, Montaigne, the seventeenth-century "libertine" thinkers—but by many hundreds and thousands of anonymous people, merrymakers in Carnival.

---

[29] Paul Veyne, *Did the Greeks Believe in Their Myths? An Essay on the Constitutive Imagination* (Chicago, 1988).

[30] For discussion of this occasion and its consequences, see Kinser, "Presentation . . .," 19.

Why did it happen at this time? Let us set aside for the moment the usual litany of secular, middle-class, and politically fortuitous causes of Renaissance rationalism and humanism, not because such causes are false but because their relative importance in determining such a vast and gradual shift of consciousness cannot possibly be ascertained, and always risks reading *our* mind-set, evolved in very different circumstances, back into the situation then. Let us simply suggest another element, it too immeasurable with exactitude. Mental horizons broadened in the fourteenth and fifteenth centuries due to better facilities of communication, above all written facilities. This broadening did not necessarily "liberate" people: just as good a case can be made—and it has been made—for the idea that it increased people's fears.[31] Human information increased, but reliable means of testing that information did not. Distinctions between wildmen and the devilish dead, human purposes and diabolic seizure, festive make-believe and monstrous reality multiplied and "contaminated" each other. The devil became more ridiculous *and* more feared, more remote *and* more powerful. Carnivalization of wildness did not, as Mikhail Bakhtin anachronistically suggests, empty people of their apprehensions by augmenting their capacity for laughter: it simply widened the boundaries of the laughable by augmenting information about the real. In this process, the articulation of reality's parts, the places of transition between the natural and supernatural, the grotesque and the commonplace, the mysterious and the self-evident became not sharper and clearer but that much more difficult to discern.

A second program of truth (was there *only* a second, and not a third, and a fourth? this remains to be investigated) emerged not because men and women stepped confidently out of the Middle Ages' superstitious shadows into the warm light of modern secular rationality, but because doubt found wider and wider fields to explore. New elements of reality leapt over the ramparts of settled opinion—like wildmen at Carnival time, disrupting things with their otherness.

---

[31] The classic presentation of this mode of consciousness, limited to northern Europe and the fourteenth and fifteenth centuries, and carefully avoiding head-on collision with Jacob Burckhardt's totally different picture of circumstances in Italy in the same period, is Johan Huizinga's *Waning of the Middle Ages* (Garden City, NY, 1954). See also Jean Delumeau, *La Peur en Occident* (Paris, 1984).

SAUL LEVIN

The Medieval Transformation
of the Jews' Oral Heritage

Although the Jews are known as "the people of the Book," it is worth pointing out that until the middle ages their religion relied enormously on oral tradition. Muḥammad's phrase ʔahlu (ʾ)l-kitābi (Qurʔān 4.153/152, and elsewhere), which would be more idiomatically translated "the Scripture people," took in the Christians and perhaps the enigmatic Sabaeans (2.62/59, 5.69/73, 22.17) as well as the Jews; and it earned them, if not a privileged, at least a tolerated status under Muslim rulers, whereas all other religions—being idolatrous—were in principle to be wiped out by holy war. While enjoying protection, the Christians had no occasion to change their treatment of their sacred texts; and of course the greater part of Christendom, in Europe, remained unconquered. The Jews, on the other hand, were strongly, if indirectly, influenced by the Muslims to fix their texts much more in written form than before. This took place in the Holy Land and Mesopotamia, but the results were gradually disseminated through most of the Diaspora. In time the European Christian scholars also got access, more or less, to all the Jewish texts in the original languages.

Most of the facts that I am going to mention are pretty well known to scholars of Judaism. But I can claim some originality in fitting them together to show the extent of the change in the verbal patrimony of the Jews.

The scriptures, for the sake of which Muḥammad respected the people, were not yet accessible to him in an Arabic translation. Neither did he know Hebrew, but he learned something about their contents from listening to Arabic Jews, as well as Christians. The Arabic culture, however rich in poetry, had little need as yet for writing. It was his prose discourses that marked an epoch in the Arabic language as well as in the new religion. For they were written down, not by himself but by devoted scribes, and presently gathered into a codex—the first great book in Arabic and by far the most valued. The codex of the Qurʔān was not arranged chronologically or by subject, but with the longest discourse first and those thereafter in descending order of length. That was destined to supply the Jews with a twofold model—in fact, more than twofold.

I must explain the paradox that the Jews, who (except perhaps for the distant Chinese) had the oldest book tradition in the world, yet took such fundamental lessons from the Arabs. When the Arabs after the death of Muḥammad conquered the Christian armies defending the southeastern provinces of the Roman empire, the Hebrew scriptures were the only literature still being copied and read on scrolls. Scrolls had been, in antiquity, the normal book-form, not at all peculiar to the Jews. But during several centuries of the Christian era, not only had the Christians used codices for the Old and the New Testament in Greek and for translations into other languages and for subsequent Christian writings; but also, as much as was preserved of pagan literature had been copied from scrolls into codices, and this too depended henceforth on transmission by Christians. It is no wonder that the Jews would not do the same, in spite of the convenience of the codex; for the scroll was the holiest thing in their possession. Containing the Tetragrammaton, the four letters of the divine name, it had to be reproduced with absolute accuracy, word for word, and then handled with the most exquisite care, according to rabbinical precepts.[1] To do anything else with the sacred text would have violated the hălăkăʰ, the obligatory ritual that bound the Jewish community from generation to generation.

Nevertheless, under Muslim influence the Jews found a way around the age-old restrictions. Without giving up the scrolls, they made copies on codices too. And once the text was in a codex, they

---

[1] Summarized in the post-Talmudic tractate Soᵂpəriʸm "Scribes."

added there a notation to remedy all the shortcomings of the ancient consonantal alphabet—whereas putting any of those extra marks on a scroll would have desecrated it. Furthermore, they likewise wrote down in codices the *unwritten* Hebrew text in six divisions that is known as the Mišnå^h. Within each division they arranged the individual tractates by length in descending order. And finally they subjected the Hebrew language for the first time to a grammatical analysis, based on the findings of Arabic grammar.

That is my introductory summary of the changes which in a sense transformed the Jewish heritage under the impact of Islam. The historical sources reveal what happened, and approximately when and where, but they tell little or nothing about why it happened, and why then and there. I must try to state the salient facts and to suggest the underlying causes, which will perhaps interest more people than the facts themselves.

Many recent authors have pointed out that the Jews were on the whole better off under Muslim rule and felt more secure; accordingly they were open to influence from Muslims as they had not been to influence from Christians. In part I agree, but Islam also put a new sort of pressure on the Jews to live up to Muḥammad's characterization of them as the "people of the Book." It took finesse for them to maintain the old and essential rabbinical distinction between the Miqrå', literally the "Reading," and the Mišnå^h or "Repetition." For the latter consisted of all the unwritten laws, upon which a great deal of Jewish observance depended; they had been kept unwritten and simply memorized, group by group. But now at last it became inexpedient to leave these authoritative laws unwritten; for that would have diminished the legitimacy of Judaism in the Muslims' eyes. Similarly in Persia after the Arab conquest the Zoroastrians systematically wrote down their texts, many if not most of which had been transmitted orally.[2]

---

[2] Bertold Spuler, *Iran in früh-islamischer Zeit*, Akademie der Wissenschaften und der Literatur, Veröffentlichungen der Orientalischen Kommission, Band II (Wiesbaden: Franz Steiner, 1952), 185:
> Die Zoroastrier suchten sich der neuen Lage anzupassen, indem sie sich als die Besitzer eines offenbarten Buches auszuweisen verstanden. Bisher waren die Gāthās, war das ganze Avesta vielleicht nur mündlich überliefert worden, wie das in so manchen morgenländischen Religionen mit heiligen Texten geschehen war. Damit hat man auch das Fehlen einer alten schriftlichen Überlieferung in dieser Religion erklärt, deren heilige Bücher vielmehr nur in ganz wenigen geheiligten Stücken vorhanden gewesen seien. . . . Erst nach der arabischen Eroberung scheint das Avesta allgemein zugänglich und den Arabern als 'heiliges offenbartes Buch' vorgewiesen

The claims of each religion had to face the counterclaims of powerful rivals. An impressive instance was the response of Christians to the Muslim challenge that their making and veneration of images was idolatrous, a betrayal of the heritage from Abraham and every true prophet. Most of occidental Christendom was too far from the main power of Islam to be shaken out of its devotion to the precious images. But in Byzantium and the East certain Christian emperors— and their soldiers—felt the issue more urgently: if they were offending God by transgressing one of his greatest commandments, they placed themselves in jeopardy of losing everything on the battlefield.[3] Torn between a deep attachment to the images and the dreadful taunt of idolatry, their successors eventually settled for the Byzantine compromise of holy pictures upon a surface, to the exclusion of sculpture.[4]

---

worden zu sein. Die Muslime haben diesen Anspruch anerkannt: die heiligen Schriften der 'Magier' wurden als solche respektiert. . . .

(The Zoroastrians tried to conform to the new situation, realizing that they had to show themselves in possession of a book of revelation. Until then the Gāthās—indeed the entire Avesta—had perhaps been only transmitted orally, as had happened in so many Oriental religions with sacred texts. Thus also the lack of an ancient written tradition in this religion has been accounted for: its holy books are said rather to have been extant only in a very few hallowed specimens. . . . Only after the Arab conquest does the Avesta seem to have become generally available, and to have been shown to the Arabs as 'a holy, revealed book.' The Muslims recognized this claim: the sacred writings of the 'Magians' were respected as such. . . .)

See also V. F. Büchner in *The Encyclopaedia of Islam*, s.v. "Madjūs" (Leiden: Brill, 1936): 3:97–99. A whimsical identification of Zoroaster with Abraham, of all people (ʔibrāhīm in Arabic), may have suggested that the Zoroastrian scriptures were older than the Mosaic books of the Jews. Later in India, where the Muslim conquerors confronted another religion with a myriad of sacred chants and other oral lore, the likening of the Brahmins (*brāhmaṇāh* in Sanskrit) to ʔibrāhīm was at least phonetically plausible. On this curious point I am indebted to a letter from Gerald Baker of *Science Frontiers*.

[3] See André Grabar, *L'iconoclasme byzantin*, 2d ed. (Paris: Flammarion, 1984), esp. 126–27; Cyril Mango in *Iconoclasm: Papers given at the Ninth Spring Symposium of Byzantine Studies, University of Birmingham, March 1975*, ed. Anthony Bryer and Judith Herrin (Univ. of Birmingham, 1977), 2–3.

[4] Even before the competition of Islam and the great iconoclastic struggle, Julian, bishop of Atramytium, had forbidden sculpture while allowing the worship of paintings: προσκυνητὰς ἐπὶ τῶν ἱερῶν ἐῶμεν εἶναι γραφάς, ἐπὶ ξύλου δὲ καὶ λίθου πολλάκις οἱ τὰ τῆς γλυφῆς ἀπαγορεύοντες οὐδὲ τοῦτο ἀπλημμελὲς ἐῶμεν, ἀλλ᾽ ἐπὶ θύραις. ("We allow figures to be painted on the holy places for adoration; but since we have often forbidden anything carved upon wood and stone, accordingly even this [i.e., painted figures] we do not allow except at the doorway.") See Paul J. Alexander, "Hypatius of Ephesus: A Note on Image Worship in the Sixth Century," *Harvard Theological Review* 45 (1952): 177–84, esp. 179 and 182: "There is, at least on the part of Julian, a much greater hesitancy towards religious sculpture than towards Christian paintings. This is interesting, in view of the al-

To Jews the validity of the oral To^{w}rå^h (or law), no less than the written, and the distinction between the two, was just as precious as the images were to Christians, although Jews were not at war with the Muslims and therefore were not particularly afraid of forfeiting God's protection. The most authoritative, though brief, rabbinical statement—the eighth followed by the ninth article in the creed of Maimonides (1135–1204)—sidesteps the matter:

I believe with perfect faith that the To^{w}rå^h as found now in our hands is the one given to Moses our teacher—peace be upon him.

I believe with perfect faith that this To^{w}rå^h will not be changed and there will be no other To^{w}rå^h from the Creator—blessed be his name.

So careful was Maimonides here *not* to divide the To^{w}rå^h into the written and the oral that he dispensed with asserting the paramount doctrine of rabbinical Judaism against the Karaite sect, which emerged around 765 and rejected the oral To^{w}rå^h. He left it out of the very creed of thirteen articles that he formulated to differentiate his religion from all who could not share it: Christians, Muslims, Samaritans, Zoroastrians, and anyone unduly influenced by the great philosophers of pagan antiquity.[5]

The earliest extant codices of the Mišnå^h are not datable so as to make it clear whether such codices were already in vogue before the first stirrings of Karaism. It is unhistorical to speculate that without the codex nothing like Karaism might ever have developed among the Jews. Before they accepted the codex, the writing of the Mišnå^h on a scroll was not entirely unknown, but censured as illicit.[6] In the new

---

most complete absence of religious sculpture in the Byzantine Church after the restoration of images."

[5] Maimonides himself was quite an Aristotelian, but not to the point of conflict with the essentials of Judaism.

[6] According to Rabbi John, c. A. D. 250 (Təmu^{w}rå^h 14b):

כותבי הלכות כשורף התורה והלמד מהן אינו נוטל שכר

("Anybody that writes *hălåko^{w}i* [oral laws] is like one who burns the To^{w}rå^h, and he that learns from them [i.e., studies the written *hălåko^{w}i*] gains no merit.") Similarly in Brahmin India: "Kumārila-bhaṭṭa (c. AD 730) [a former Buddhist and a zealous opponent of Buddhism] denounced the writing down of the Vedas as a sacrilege; he held that memorizing the Vedas from written texts was pointless since it brought no merit"; Benjamin Walker, *The Hindu World* (New York: Praeger, 1968), 2:558.

Within each of the six divisions of the Mišnå^h, the longest tractate was entered first in the codex, and the shortest one last—on the same principle of arrangement as in the Arabic Qur?ān.

age, ushered in by the Arab armies, the Mišnå^h was transmitted chiefly by means of the codex, although many still learned it—or parts of
it—by heart. I have called the change-over a transformation of the
Jews' oral heritage, but the oral custom lingered; and memory, while
no longer so absolutely necessary, was still much esteemed.

The Karaites, in a quite different way and to a degree that remains
in dispute, figured in the codification of the Holy Scriptures. This too
amounted to a transformation, for it involved far more than just a
new mode of sewing the pages of a book together, not on both the
right and the left edge but only on one edge, after writing on both
the obverse and the reverse of each page instead of leaving one side
blank. Apart from that, the text was changed from a consonantal skeleton of the words to a complete register of the entire sound of every
sentence, down to the finest details.

Few Christian scholars have ever understood how, in the age of
the scroll, oral transmission was indispensable to the Hebrew scriptures themselves. Jewish scholars too have gradually lost their grip
upon it, since the Hebrew text is now as fully accessible as anything
written in any language, or more so. But it was not like that in antiquity. The alphabet in its Semitic homeland consisted only of consonants, and books were not intended to be read by strangers guessing
or figuring out a possible way to pronounce the sequences of Hebrew
letters with unwritten vowel-sounds. Instead, any Hebrew book
needed a continual chain of readers who learned from one another to
use the letters as a reminder of how they had heard it being read. Indeed the text was fundamentally an *oral reading*, for which the Hebrew term is *miqrå*; the written consonantal skeleton was an aid to
recall it word for word.[7]

Over the generations the *miqrå* or "reading" of any valued Hebrew book had its own tradition, independent of the many slight
variants that differentiated one copy from another before the scribes
arrived at virtually absolute uniformity. But the Miqrå' developed its
own deviations, of which the most prominent and most frequent was
quite deliberate: not to pronounce the divine Tetragrammaton but to
substitute [ʔădonåy], the word for "Lord"—or rather "Milord." In
case that word was already in the text right in front of the Tetragrammaton, the substitute to be pronounced was [ʔělohim], the word for
"God."[8] Apart from this paramount deviation, recurring thousands

---

[7] See my article (in Hebrew) "The קר as the Primary Bible Text,"
הוות עדות ביאסריקה (Tel-Aviv: World Hebrew Union, 1972), 1:61–86, esp. 66.
[8] In English versions of the Old Testament, since the learned in England gained

and thousands of times, there were many others of intrinsically lesser import but still firm and obligatory. In a few instances a minor word written in the text was passed over in reading; the Aramaic term for this is *kəṯīᵛb wəlå' qĕriᵛ* "written but not read." The converse also occurred: a minor word inserted orally although not written.[9] These particular discrepancies went back, presumably, to a deviant copy from which the Miqrå' was learned; but the Miqrå' continued its own life, regardless of the disappearance of any such copy.

As long as the scriptures were read exclusively from scrolls, everything about the Miqrå' had to be taught orally. The best readers knew entire books by heart and were capable of reproducing the written text without an exemplar in front of them; but it was forbidden to write even the first word of a canonical book unless it could be copied letter-perfect from a previously certified copy.[10] The two traditions of the text, written and oral, were to be kept distinct, even though intertwined.

But the codex, not being for the Jews a traditional book, was not limited to the written tradition as the scroll was. Rather they exploited the codex to combine the two traditions on the same pages, by devising a written representation of the Miqrå'. They did not intend the codex to supersede the scroll, as it had long since done among the Christians. The Jewish reader used the codex at first to help achieve a flawless liturgical reading, for which a scroll was still required. He could practice the Miqrå' written down in the codex until he knew at least a portion of it exactly; then, as he read liturgically from the scroll without seeing the Miqrå', he would reproduce it orally. If he misread anything, the liturgy demanded only that the error be corrected immediately; a man with a codex stood near the reader of the scroll and was ready to correct him.

To register the Miqrå' on the pages of a codex, the primary need was for a notation showing the sounds that the ancient alphabet could not capture. The Jews were the last of the Semitic peoples to do this. They learned from the Syriac or Aramaic Christians and from the Arabs, and they improved upon their predecessors. Jewish readers temporarily resorted to two notations, known as the Palestinian

---

knowledge of Hebrew, it has been customary to print LORD and GOD in small capitals to represent the Tetragrammaton.

[9] See Robert Gordis, *The Biblical Text in the Making: A Study of the Kethib-Qere*, 2d ed. ([New York]: Ktav, 1971), 11, 147–48.

[10] Məḡillåʰ 18b, esp. אסור לכתוב אות אחת שלא מן הכתב ("It is forbidden to write one letter except from the exemplar.")

and the Babylonian, before the expert readers of Tiberias (on the Sea
of Galilee) worked out their own, which in time gained universal
authority among Jewish communities.

The triumphant Tiberias system actually owes the most to the
earliest Christian notation for Aramaic, the Nestorian, which dates
from around AD 600, if not earlier.[11] But the Nestorian notation had
one technical drawback: it consisted entirely of dots above or below
the letters—little dots, big dots, medium-sized dots, which were too
liable to be confused through blotting. That was not why the Jews
were so unreceptive to it for so long; but anyhow they changed their
minds only after their Muslim rulers had adopted a different notation, with other marks besides dots, for the Qur'ān. The Arabic
adaptation of the alphabet, though still consonantal, needs more
letters than its Aramaic source, because the Arabic language has more
consonant sounds. The additional letters were created by adding a
dot or two or three. Furthermore, Arabic penmanship had reduced
certain originally distinct Aramaic letters to an identical shape, so that
these also needed diacritical dots.[12] For vowels, therefore—to be precise, for two vowels [a] and [i]—the Arabs hit upon a new device,
elementary but brilliant: a short line above or below the letter. The
Jewish readers of Tiberias recognized the best features of the Nestorian and the Arabic systems—above all, that the dot and the line, the
simplest units for rapid supplementation of a given letter-text, could
be written in significantly different positions close to any letter and
thus indicate whatever sounds the Miqrå' called for.

A further part of the oral lore pertaining to the Miqrå' kept track
of how many times such-and-such a word—pronounced so-and-so
and spelled in one or more ways—occurs either in the entire sacred
corpus or in a section of it—particularly in the To^{w}rå^h or Penta-
teuch—or in a single book. Those custodians of the Miqrå'—the
Masoretes ba^{c}ăle^y hammåsoreł "masters of the tradition"—who had
nearly a concordance of it in their heads, were motivated not only by
loving curiosity for its own sake; they were especially on the alert for
whatever might occasion a misreading on the part of someone less
skilled. A disproportionate mass of their remarks called attention to
words that occur just once and hence were liable not to fall within the
Hebrew already known by the average reader. Such a person would

---

[11] J. B. Segal, *The Diacritical Point and the Accents in Syriac* (London: Oxford
Univ. Press, 1953), 25.

[12] E.g., ז [r] and ז [z] had both come out ﻯ —so the latter was distinguished by
marking it ﺞ.

be better off for the assurance that the word is indeed pronounced so-and-so. The need to be thus assured had grown when Hebrew as a vernacular language gave way gradually to Aramaic, from the fifth or fourth century BC on; after AD 200 Hebrew survived only in the school and the synagogue.

This sort of information about the words of the Miqrå' was the last addition to the Bible codex by the Masoretes of Tiberias, and only in the margins or at the end. Between the lines of the sacred text they made such marks as would serve to show the sounds of the Miqrå' itself, and one other mark—a tiny circle above many a word, usually signaling a marginal note on the number of its occurrences. This method precluded the intrusion of any Hebrew letter where it might be taken for part of a holy word, since the numerical notation employed the letters of the alphabet according to a Greek model: the first nine letters for units, the next nine for tens, and the rest for hundreds.[13] An age-old rule, protecting the sanctity of the letters of the Hebrew scroll, was applied to the codex.[14]

The earliest dated codices of the Hebrew Bible are from the 9th century (none of them, of course, dated according to the Christian era). These have the Tiberias notation. Some with the other two Hebrew notations are probably older; but being fragmentary, they have lost the final leaf with the dated colophon. To what extent the credit for the Tiberias notation (or any other) belongs to the Karaite sect, has been controversial ever since Heinrich Graetz, the eminent German Jewish historian, attributed it to certain Karaites around 780–800.[15] Beyond question, the Karaites were avid *users* of Bible codices. Graetz was sharply attacked by contemporary Jewish scholars, who were closer to rabbinical orthodoxy; but recently Paul Kahle, the foremost Christian authority on the notations of the Hebrew Bible, has brought out more detailed evidence that the Ben-Asher family—the

---

[13] For single occurrences, however, the regular note is not א "one" or "once" but ל, the abbreviation of the Aramaic word לית "nowhere [else]." (See the accompanying figure).

[14] The superseded Babylonian notation had indeed used—besides dots and nearly horizontal lines—some tiny letters for vowels and other phonetic purposes.

[15] See *Geschichte der Juden vom Abschlusz des Talmud (500) bis zum Aufblühen der jüdisch-spanischen Cultur (1027)*, (Magdeburg: Falckenberg, 1860), 207; in later editions this was treated as vol. 4 of Graetz's vast *Geschichte der Juden*, and the particular passage much revised. Though not a Karaite himself, he looked upon them with some sympathy; he had grown up in the Protestant part of Germany, where Luther's vindication of Holy Scripture as the supreme authority was generally esteemed to be a singular victory for the spirit of truth.

[עמודה ימנית]

אַחֲרִ֖ת לִֽירַחְמְאֵ֑ל וְשֵׁמָ֥ה
עֶזְרָ֖ה חָיָ֥א אֵ֥ם אוֹנָֽם׃
וַיִּהְי֥וּ בְנֵי־רֶ֖סֶם בְּכָ֣ר יי
וְרִחְמַ֑אֵל מַ֥עַן וּמִין וְעֵ֖קֶר
וַיִּהְי֥וּ בְּנֵי־אוֹנָ֖ם שַׁמַּ֣י וְיָדָ֑ע
וּבְנֵ֣י שַׁמַּ֔י נָדָ֖ב וַאֲבִישֽׁוּר׃
וְשֵׁ֣ם אֵ֤שֶׁת אֲבִישׁוּר֙ אֲבִיחַ֔יִל
וַתֵּ֤לֶד ל֙וֹ אֶת־אַחְבָּ֔ן וְאֶת־
מוֹלִ֑יד וּבְנֵ֥י נָדָ֖ב סֶ֥לֶד וְאַפָּ֑יִם
וַיָּ֧מָת סֶ֛לֶד לֹ֥א בָנִ֖ים ס
אַפַּ֥יִם יִשְׁעִ֖י וּבְנֵ֥י יִשְׁעִ֖י שֵׁשָׁ֑ן
וּבְנֵ֥י שֵׁשָׁ֖ן אַחְלָ֑י וּבְנֵ֥י יָדָ֖ע
אֲחִ֣י שַׁמַּ֔י יֶ֖תֶר וְיוֹנָתָ֑ן וַיָּ֛מָת
יֶ֖תֶר לֹ֥א בָנִֽים׃
וּבְנֵ֤י יוֹנָתָן֙ פֶּ֣לֶת וְזָזָ֔א אֵ֖לֶּה הָי֣וּ בְנֵ֥י
יְרַחְמְאֵֽל׃ וַֽיִּֽהִי֞ אַֽחֵ֤ר לַשָּׁ֑שָׁן
בֶּ֛גֶם כִּ֥י אִס־פָּתֽוֹ֙ וְל֣וֹ לַשָּׁ֔שָׁן יי
עֶ֥בֶד מִצְרִ֖י וּשְׁמ֥וֹ יַרְחָ֑ע
וַיִּתֵּ֨ן שֵׁשָׁ֤ן אֶת־בִּתּ֙וֹ לְיַרְחָ֔ע
עַבְדּ֖וֹ לְאִשָּׁ֑ה וַתֵּ֥לֶד ל֖וֹ אֶת־
עַתָּ֑י וְעַתַּ֖י הוֹלִ֥יד אֶת־נָתָ֑ן
וְנָתָ֖ן הוֹלִ֥יד אֶת־זָבָ֖ד וְזָבָ֛ד
הוֹלִ֥יד אֶת־אֶפְלָ֖ל וְאֶפְלָ֛ל
הוֹלִ֥יד אֶת־עוֹבֵ֖ד וְעוֹבֵֽד׃
הוֹלִ֥יד אֶת־יֵה֖וּא וְיֵה֛וּא
הוֹלִ֥יד אֶת־עֲזַרְיָ֖ה וַעֲזַרְיָ֛ה
הוֹלִ֥יד אֶת־חֶ֖לֶץ וְחֶ֖לֶץ הוֹלִ֥יד
אֶת־אֶלְעָשָׂ֖ה וְאֶלְעָשָׂ֛ה יי

[עמודה אמצעית]

חֹלִ֖יד אֶת־סִסְמָ֑י וְסִסְמַ֖י יי
הֹלִ֖יד אֶת־שַׁלּ֑וּם וְשַׁלּ֖וּם
הֹלִ֖יד אֶת־יְקַמְיָ֑ה וִיקַמְיָ֖ה
הֹלִ֖יד אֶת־אֱלִישָׁמָֽע׃
וּבְנֵ֥י כָלֵב֙ אֲחִ֣י יְרַחְמְאֵ֔ל
מֵשָׁ֥ע בְּכֹר֖וֹ ה֥וּא אֲבִי־זִ֑יף
וּבְנֵ֥י מָרֵשָׁ֖ה אֲבִ֥י חֶבְרֽוֹן׃
וּבְנֵ֥י חֶבְר֑וֹן קֹ֥רַח וְתַפֻּ֖חַ וְרֶ֖קֶם
וָשָׁ֑מַע וְשֶׁ֛מַע הוֹלִ֥יד אֶת־
רַ֖חַם אֲבִ֣י יָרְקֳעָ֑ם וְרֶ֖קֶם
הֹלִ֖יד אֶת־שַׁמָּֽי׃ וּבֶן־שַׁמַּ֖י
מָע֑וֹן וּמָע֖וֹן אֲבִ֥י בֵית־צֽוּר׃
וְעֵיפָ֞ה פִּילֶ֤גֶשׁ כָּלֵב֙ יָלְדָ֔ה
אֶת־חָרָ֥ן וְאֶת־מוֹצָ֖א וְאֶת־
גָּזֵ֑ז וְחָרָ֖ן הֹלִ֥יד אֶת־גָּזֵֽז׃
וּבְנֵ֣י יָהְדַּ֔י רֶ֖גֶם וְיוֹתָ֑ם
וְגֵישָׁ֖ן וָפֶ֛לֶט וְעֵיפָ֖ה וָשָֽׁעַף׃
פִּ֖לֶגֶשׁ כָּלֵ֖ב מַעֲכָ֑ה יָלַ֛ד
שֶׁ֥בֶר וְאֶת־תִּרְחֲנָֽה׃ וַתֵּ֙לֶד֙
שַׁ֖עַף אֲבִ֣י מַדְמַנָּ֔ה אֶת־
שְׁוָ֖א אֲבִ֣י מַכְבֵּנָ֔ה וַאֲבִ֖י
גִבְעָ֑א וּבַת־כָּלֵ֖ב עַכְסָֽה׃
אֵ֖לֶּה הָי֣וּ בְנֵ֣י כָלֵ֑ב
בְּֽחוּר־בְּכ֞וֹר אֶפְרָ֤תָה שׁוֹבָ֑ל
אֲבִ֖י קִרְיַ֣ת יְעָרִֽים׃ שׂוֹבָ֑ל
אֲבִ֖י בֵ֣ית־לָ֑חֶם חָרֵ֖ף אֲבִ֣י
בֵית־גָּדֵֽר׃ וַיִּֽהְי֥וּ בָנִ֖ים לְשׁוֹבָ֑ל
אֲבִ֖י קִרְיַ֣ת יְעָרִ֑ים הָרֹאֶֽה׃

[עמודה שמאלית]

חֲצִ֣י הַמְּנֻחֹ֑ת וּמִשְׁפְּח֖וֹת
קִרְיַ֣ת יְעָרִ֑ים הַיִּתְרִ֖י וְ
הַפּוּתִ֔י וְהַשֻּׁמָתִ֖י וְהַמִּשְׁרָ֑עִי
מֵאֵ֙לֶּה֙ יָצְא֣וּ הַצָּרְעָתִ֔י
וְהָאֶשְׁתָּאֻלִֽי׃
בְּנֵ֥י שַׁלְמָ֖א בֵּ֣ית
לֶ֔חֶם וּנְטוֹפָתִ֖י עַטְר֑וֹת
בֵּ֣ית יוֹאָ֔ב וַחֲצִ֥י הַמָּנַחְתִּ֖י
הַצָּרְעִֽי׃ וּמִשְׁפְּח֤וֹת סֹפְרִ֙ים֙
יֹשְׁבֵ֣י יַעְבֵּ֔ץ תִּרְעָתִ֥ים
שִׁמְעָתִ֖ים שׂוּכָתִ֑ים הֵ֣מָּה
הַקִּינִ֗ים הַבָּאִ֛ים מֵחַמַּ֖ת
אֲבִ֥י בֵית־רֵכָֽב׃
וְאֵ֤לֶּה הָיוּ֙ בְּנֵ֣י דָוִ֔יד
אֲשֶׁ֥ר נֽוֹלַד־ל֖וֹ בְּחֶבְר֑וֹן
הַבְּכ֣וֹר ׀ אַמְנֹ֗ן לַאֲחִינֹ֙עַם֙
הַיִּזְרְעֵאלִ֔ית שֵׁנִי֙ דָּ֣נִיֵּ֔אל
לַאֲבִיגַ֖יִל הַֽכַּרְמְלִֽית׃
הַשְּׁלִשִׁי֙ לְאַבְשָׁל֣וֹם בֶּן־
מַעֲכָ֔ה בַּת־תַּלְמַ֖י מֶ֣לֶךְ
גְּשׁ֑וּר הָרְבִיעִ֖י אֲדֹ֥נִיָּ֖ה בֶן־
חַגִּֽית׃ הַחֲמִישִׁ֥י שְׁפַטְיָ֖ה
לַאֲבִיטָ֑ל הַשִּׁשִּׁ֥י יִתְרְעָ֖ם
לְעֶגְלָ֣ה אִשְׁתּ֑וֹ שִׁשָּׁ֖ה
נֽוֹלַד־ל֣וֹ בְחֶבְר֑וֹן וַיִּ֣מְלָךְ
שָׁ֗ם שֶׁ֤בַע שָׁנִים֙ וְשִׁשָּׁ֣ה
חֳדָשִׁ֔ים וּשְׁלֹשִׁ֤ים וְשָׁלוֹשׁ֙
שָׁנָ֔ה מָלַ֖ךְ בִּירוּשָׁלָֽם׃

The letter-text of I Chronicles 2:26-40 (a genealogical passage), as it appeared in scrolls and as it was copied on a page before being marked with the Miqrå? and bound in the "Aleppo Codex" (as depicted in the adjacent column of the accompanying figure):

Transcription of I Chronicles 2:26-40

Only the consonantal letters in bold type (including ? for א and ʕ for ע) represent the ancient written text, as preserved in scrolls. Any diacritical mark above these transcribed letters, and everything in raised type between them stands for the little marks added by Ben-?åšer to show the Miqrå?.

אחרת לירדחמאל ושמה
עטרה היא אם אונם
ויהיו בני רם בכור
ירחמאל מעץ וימין ועקר
ויהיו בני אונם שמי וידע
ובני שמי נדב ואבישור
ושם אשת אבישיר אביחיל
ותלד לו את אחבן ואת
מוליד ובני נדב סלד ואפים
וימת סלד לא בנים ובני
אפים ישעי ובני ישעי ששן
ובני ששן אחלי ובני ידע
אחי שמי יתר ויונתן וימת
יתר לא בנים ובני
יונתן פלת וזזא אלה היו בני
ירחמאל ולא היה לששן
בנים כי אם בנות ולששן
עבד מצרי ושמו ירחע
ויתן ששן את בתו לירחע
עבדו לאשה ותלד לו את
עתי ועתי הליד את נתן
ונתן הוליד את זבד וזבד
הוליד את אפלל ואפלל
הוליד את עובד ועובד
הוליד את יהוא ויהוא
הליד את עזריה ועזריה
הליד את חלץ וחלץ הליד
את אלעשה ואלעשה

?aħᵉrēt liyrᵃħᵃmᵊ?ēl uwšᵊmᵃh·
ʕᵃᵗᵊrᵃh hiy? ?ēm ?ᵓwnᵃm·
wayyihyuw bᵊney-rᵃm bᵊkᵓwr
yᵊrᵃħᵃmᵊ?ēl mᵃʕac wᵊyᵃᵓmiyn wᵊʕēqᵉr·
wayyihyuw bᵊney-?ᵓwnᵃm šᵃmmᵃy wᵊyᵃᵈᵃʕ
uwbᵊney šᵃmmᵃy nᵃdᵃᵇ wᵃ?ᵃᵇiyšᵘwr·
wᵊšēm ?ēšēt ?ᵃᵇiyšᵘwr ?ᵃᵇiyħᵃyil
wattēlᵉd lᵓw ?ēt-?ᵃħbᵃn wᵊ?ēt-
mᵓwliyd uwbᵊney nᵃdᵃᵇ σᵉlᵉᵈ wᵊ?appᵃyim·
wayyᵃᵐᵃᵗ σᵉlᵉᵈ lᵓ bᵃniym· uwbᵊney
?appᵃyim yišʕiy uwbᵊney yišʕiy šēšᵃn
uwbᵊney šēšᵃn ?aħlᵃy· uwbᵊney yᵃᵈᵃʕ
?ᵃħiy šᵃmmᵃy yētᵉr wᵊyᵓwnᵃᵗᵃn wayyᵃᵐᵃᵗ
yētᵉr lᵓ bᵃniym·   uwbᵊney
yᵓwnᵃᵗᵃn pᵉlᵉᵗ wᵊzᵃzᵃ? ?ēllᵉh hᵃyuw bᵊney
yᵊrᵃħᵃmᵊ?ēl· wᵊlᵓ-hᵃyᵃh lᵊšēšᵃn
bᵃniym kᵊy ?im-bᵃnᵓwt uwlᵊšēšᵃn
ʕᵉᵇᵉᵈ micriy uwšᵊmᵓw yᵃrħᵃʕ·
wayyittēn šēšᵃn ?ēt-bittᵓw lᵊyᵃrħᵃʕ
ʕᵃᵇdᵓw lᵊ?iššᵃh wattēlᵉd lᵓw ?ēt-
ʕᵃttᵃy· wᵊʕᵃttᵃy hᵓwliyd ?ēt-nᵃᵗᵃn
wᵊnᵃᵗᵃn hᵓwliyd ?ēt-zᵃᵇᵃᵈ wᵊzᵃᵇᵃᵈ
hᵓwliyd ?ēt-?ᵃflᵃl wᵊ?ᵃflᵃl
hᵓwliyd ?ēt-ʕᵓwbēᵈ wᵊʕᵓwbēᵈ
hᵓwliyd ?ēt-yēhᵘw? wᵊyēhᵘw?
hᵓliyd ?ēt-ʕᵃzᵃryᵃh· wᵊʕᵃzᵃryᵃħ
hᵓliyd ?ēt-ħᵃlᵉc wᵊħᵃlᵉc hᵓliyd
?ēt-?ᵉlʕᵃśᵃh· wᵊ?ᵉlʕᵃśᵃh

preeminent Masoretes of Tiberias—were Karaites.[16] The documentation, however, is allusive rather than outright; and moreover the notation of Bible codices was never itself at issue between Karaites and their mainstream opponents, the Rabbanites, except for a few Biblical passages[17]—much as they disagreed in their inferences from the Bible. It seems to me that a man known mainly for the excellence of his traditional reading of the scriptures would scarcely have been bound to take sides between Karaism and rabbinical Judaism; and that if he did adhere to one side, both sides could still respect his expertise.

Neither Rabbanite nor Karaite Jews ever intended the codex to supplant the scroll. But it readily did that for all purposes of study, because it was so much simpler to read. Even for liturgical reading the synagogues began to put the scrolls aside—not indeed the scroll of the To^{w}rå^h, which was at the heart of the liturgy, being read from beginning to end in either an annual or a triennial cycle; but only scattered selections were read from the eight prophetic books: the former four—Joshua, Judges, Samuel, Kings—and the latter four—Isaiah, Jeremiah, Ezekiel, and the twelve "minor" prophets—so the advantage of the codex was overwhelming, and scrolls of these books went out of use altogether. To find the place to begin was far easier by flipping the pages of a codex than by unrolling a scroll. Also four of the five short scrolls that were read on a prescribed holiday—the Song of Songs on Passover, Ruth on Pentecost, Lamentations on the ninth of ʔå̄b̄, and Ecclesiastes on Tabernacles—were superseded by codices. The fifth scroll, however—Esther on the feast of Purim—remained indispensable; for, as the influential Yehuday (the head of the academy in Sura) pointed out around 760, the text itself refers to Esther's declaration establishing the holiday, "written in the scroll" (*bassep̄er*, 9:32), not codex.[18] The reading of Esther was rehearsed in private with a fully marked codex, but the public reading in the synagogue was (and is) still from a scroll with the bare letters.

One part of the oral heritage remained unwritten, at least in Tiber-

---

[16] *The Cairo Geniza*, 2d ed. (Oxford: Blackwell, 1959 = New York: Praeger, 1960), 77–109.

[17] Fred N. Reiner, "Masoretes, Rabbis, and Karaites," *1972 and 1973 Proceedings, I[nternational] O[rganization for] M[asoretic] S[tudies] (=Masoretic Studies)*, 1:137–47.

[18] Quoted by Eliezer Ben Judah, *Thesaurus totius Hebraitatis, et ueteris et recentioris*, s.v. מצחף:

ומגלה כתובה במצחף אין אדם יוצא בה ידי חובתו שכתוב ונכתב
בספר ומצחף אינו ספר

("And with an [Esther-]roll written in a codex no one fulfills his obligation [to hear the reading of the story]; according to Scripture [Esther 9:32], 'And it is written in the scroll,' and a codex is no scroll.")

ias: the Targu^{w}m or Aramaic translation, sometimes rigidly literal, sometimes expansive. As early as the pre-Christian era, when knowledge of Hebrew was already declining, the custom began for the synagogue reader of any Hebrew scripture to pause after each verse and for an able bilingual to interpret it in Aramaic. At first, presumably, the translation was quite spontaneous; but as the scripture readings recurred from year to year, in time the oral translation tended to become standardized—not much less so than the Hebrew Miqrå' itself. By the time of the Arab conquest, one Aramaic version or Targu^{w}m of the To^{w}rå^h—attributed to an unknown man named Onqelos—had been generally accepted; then another Targu^{w}m of the prophetic books, and so on.

In Tiberias, during the centuries of Muslim rule before this center of Jewish learning was ruined in the crusaders' wars, no codex was made that included the Targu^{w}m (to judge from the surviving codices).[19] We cannot suppose that the synagogue liturgy there dispensed with an oral Aramaic version, and that therefore the tradition of learning it, in that particular place, had failed. Rather the scribes of Tiberias would not write down an Aramaic translation to come right after each verse of the Hebrew; for the two languages were written in the very same alphabet, and it would have amounted to alternating a stretch of holy writ and something much less sacred, as symbolized by the fact that the Targu^{w}m (unlike some ancient examples of the Septuagint) never dared to reproduce the divine Tetragrammaton.

Outside of Tiberias, however, not all Jews were willing to leave the Targu^{w}m unwritten. Wherever they used the so-called Babylonian notation of the Miqrå', most of the surviving fragments from Bible codices show that each Hebrew verse was followed by the Aramaic rendering of it, the latter being also marked with the Babylonian notation.[20] In the long run the Tiberias notation for the scriptures in the original language won out everywhere because it was more accurate, more complete, more prestigious; the men of Tiberias were admired as "the priests of the Hebrew language."[21] But many who adopted it wanted the written Targu^{w}m too, even though there was

[19] See Paul Kahle, *Masoreten des Westens* (Stuttgart: W. Kohlhammer, 1927; repr., Hildesheim: Georg Olms, 1967), 1:56–77. Some of the later codices described by him were copied in Egypt from Tiberias exemplars.

[20] Kahle, *Masoreten des Ostens: Die ältesten punktierten Handschriften des Alten Testaments und der Targume* (Leipzig: J. C. Hinrichs, 1913; repr., Hildesheim: Georg Olms, 1966).

[21] העברית הלשון כהני, as the physician and polymath Isaac Israeli (c. 855–955) called them.

no Tiberias notation for the Targu^{w}m. The Jews of Yemen, in southern Arabia, where the rabbinical schools of Mesopotamia had the most enduring influence, simply alternated in their codices the Tiberias notation for the Hebrew and the Babylonian notation for the Targu^{w}m.[22] Their actual pronunciation of both languages was more in accord with their Mesopotamian teachers, with six distinct vowels rather than the seven required by the Tiberias system. Elsewhere, even in Mesopotamia itself, the Babylonian notation was abandoned on account of the obvious inconvenience of maintaining it for the Targu^{w}m in contrast—and, to some extent, in conflict—with the Tiberias notation for the Hebrew. But the Babylonian *reading* of the Targu^{w}m was indirectly perpetuated by substituting for each Babylonian sign the Tiberias sign most like it functionally, if not graphically.

This Targu^{w}m text was a makeshift, with a reduced Tiberias notation but not based on a real Tiberias tradition. On the contrary, the Aramaic in it was at odds with the authentic biblical Aramaic in the Miqrå$^?$ of Daniel 2:4–7:28 and Ezra 4:8–6:18, 7:12–26. In the subsequent centuries, down to the age of printing, the Targu^{w}m text deteriorated as the Aramaic language receded in the Jewish communities.[23]

On the other hand, the Tiberias text of the scriptures in the original language kept on being copied in codices with virtually no deterioration throughout the Jewish world, notwithstanding the eventual extinction of the great school in Tiberias itself. The pronunciation that properly went with it was not learned perfectly, and did suffer from the influence of the Jews' vernacular languages. But this was counterbalanced by the improved knowledge of Hebrew in other respects, thanks to the belated application of grammatical analysis to this language.

The Jews, especially those whose vernacular was Aramaic, had kept up Hebrew without grammar, by a sort of bilingual education. A boy was to begin learning the Miqrå$^?$ at the age of five;[24] the meaning of each verse was conveyed in Aramaic through the Targu^{w}m. Hebrew was, besides, spoken a great deal in school, although this Hebrew—unlike that of the Miqrå$^?$—was heavily contaminated with Aramaic. In the centuries when Greek was the dominant interna-

---

[22] Long after the printing of Hebrew Bibles—with or without the Targu^{w}m—in Europe, Yemen remained beyond the orbit of the international book trade. As late as the nineteenth century the Yemenite Jews were still copying their codices with the same old combination.

[23] Kahle, *Cairo Geniza*, 1st ed. (1947), 127–28; this passage was omitted when he revised the chapter extensively for the second edition.

[24] בֶּן חָמֵשׁ שָׁנִים לַמִּקְרָא ("A child of five [is ready] for the Miqrå$^?$"); attributed to Judah, son of Tema (?åbo^{w}ṯ 5:21).

tional language and grammarians flourished to make it more accessible, the grammatical method was applied to Aramaic by Christians, but the Jews did not follow suit. A vowel-notation was a precondition for grammar in a Semitic language, and the Jews were unreceptive until they had an Arabic model. The Hebrew notation was perfected in the ninth century (to judge from the extant codices), and Hebrew grammar began in the tenth with the great Saʿadyah.[25] He and his successors were Arabic-speaking Jews. To adapt the principles and the terminology of Arabic to a kindred language was not very difficult; but those Jewish grammarians deserve special credit for being the forerunners of modern comparative grammar, as they set forth the recurrent correspondences between Hebrew, Aramaic, and Arabic, at least in the consonants. Their motive, however, for bringing in the other two Semitic languages was to clarify difficulties in Hebrew, the holy tongue, rather than to explore its prehistoric relationship to cognate languages.

A literary renaissance of Hebrew followed, whether or not grammar deserves much of the credit for making it possible. Grammar never became so fundamental in Hebrew education as it already was and remained in Greek or Latin education; but it does appear to have given the talented ones more confidence in their ability to write Hebrew, adhering pretty closely to biblical models. The Jews whose vernacular was neither Aramaic nor Arabic—i.e., the great bulk of European Jews—were at a disadvantage until the twelfth century or so; but codices with the Miqrå' made the Hebrew language more accessible to them too, especially to those who also got some instruction in grammar.

The advances due to Jews in Muslim countries redounded secondarily to the benefit of the Christians. It had previously taken rare luminaries of Christian scholarship—Origen or Jerome—to penetrate the outer edge, at least, of Jewish learning; and the study of Hebrew had not endured among their disciples. But when there were Hebrew Bible codices in Europe, it was no longer hard for an interested Christian to learn this language. To be sure, only a sprinkling of Christians availed themselves of the possibility until well into the fifteenth century, by engaging Jewish teachers. The study was unorganized, liable to be unsteady, hit-or-miss;[26] so an individual misap-

---

[25] See W. Bacher, *Die Anfänge der hebräischen Grammatik* (Leipzig: F. A. Brockhaus, 1895; repr., Amsterdam: John Benjamins, 1974), 38 ff.

[26] The Council of Vienne in 1311 urged the universities to establish chairs of Hebrew, but for nearly two hundred years little was done; Jerome Friedman, *The Most Ancient Testimony: Sixteenth-century Christian-Hebraica in the Age of Renaissance Nostalgia* (Athens, Ohio: Ohio Univ. Press, 1983), 28.

prehension could readily go on uncorrected. The most startling defect was the misreading of the holy Tetragrammaton by Christians, who learned how to pronounce each Hebrew sound more or less correctly—as this bore a pretty close analogy to a language written in the Latin alphabet—but could not grasp the Biblical Hebrew peculiarity of certain words being written but something else being pronounced instead (see above, p. 166). Hence the hybrid transcribed *Iehoua*, which was ultimately rendered *Jehovah*.[27]

A few Hebrew Bible codices gained something from the dealings between Jews and Christians—i.e., chapters marked by numbering. This had been devised for the Latin Bible around 1200 and attributed to Stephen Langton[28] (who was later archbishop of Canterbury and a leader of the movement that won the Magna Charta from King John). For reference it was so handy that it soon became a common feature of Christian Bibles, either in Latin or in vernacular languages. Jews got acquainted with this innovation later, in the course of arguments with Christians, and first brought it into the Hebrew Bible for the purpose of locating the controversial passages.[29] But in time they grasped the convenience of the numbered chapters quite apart from that, and used the Christian system more and more in preference to their traditional way, which instead relied on remembering some prominent word or words from the context. The numbers were of course restricted to the margin of a Hebrew codex, where they would not be mistaken for letters of the sacred text.[30] An intrinsically better division of the text is conveyed by the paragraphs and sub-paragraphs, which go back to the ancient scrolls; but these were never numbered and therefore could not serve so well for reference.[31]

What finally gave many more Christians access to the language was the printing of Hebrew Bibles and the translation into Latin of

---

[27] See Beryl Smalley, *The Study of the Bible in the Middle Ages*, 2d ed. (Oxford: Blackwell, 1952; repr., Univ. of Notre Dame Press, 1978), 329–55.

[28] Smalley, 223–24.

[29] Christian D. Ginsburg, *Introduction to the Massoretico-critical Edition of the Hebrew Bible* (London: Trinitarian Bible Society, 1897; repr., [New York]: Ktav, 1966), 25–26.

[30] Many small but annoying discrepancies as to the starting point of a chapter arose between the Hebrew and any Christian Bible, through inexact placement of the Hebrew numerical letters (see above, pp. 169) in the margin. The verses within a chapter were never numbered in a Hebrew codex, but this subsidiary numbering was gradually adopted after printed books came in.

[31] These precious paragraph and sub-paragraph divisions, except within the To\u02b7râ\u02b0, came to be suppressed by most editors, Jewish as well as Christian, as though the chapters had made them unnecessary.

Hebrew grammars written in Hebrew. The most voluminous translator and adapter was Sebastian Münster (1488–1553), who relied on the Jewish grammarians—above all, on his contemporary Elias Levita.[32] But soon the Christian Hebraists grew virtually independent of any Jewish contemporaries; and finally, by the eighteenth century, they were even able to improve upon the primary Jewish grammarians. For then the most learned Christians had the advantage over the European Jews when it came to Arabic—not to mention still other Semitic languages beyond the ken of those Jews, handicapped as they were by the prevalence of a tradition, especially among the Ashkenazim of Germany and the East, that treated grammar as marginal rather than fundamental.[33]

The Christian Hebraists put their knowledge to use for the laity as a whole when they translated the Old Testament into German, English, and other modern languages. Whereas Jerome had been a lonely linguistic genius, able in his day to take a Hebrew scroll and turn the text into Latin, more than a few Protestant scholars—beginning with Luther—participated in the movement to bring the exact sense of the ancient scriptures to the common people.

Hebrew was, after Greek, the second great conquest of the occidental intellect, around the time that the European exploration and colonization of the rest of the world was getting under way. The curiosity to learn Greek, Hebrew, and then more exotic languages was the intellectual counterpart to the physical activity of mariners and settlers in distant lands. The Christian scholars of Europe got access to Hebrew through what the Jews had written down for their own use but could not restrict from spreading, even had they wanted to keep it to themselves. As long as an essential part of the Hebrew language depended on oral memory, it was practically closed to outsiders as it had been since ancient times. But once it was in writing, the main barrier was gone, and any determined person could master this language and its unique literature.

One major reservation has to be mentioned: the Talmud, that vast commentary—mainly in Aramaic—upon the Mišnåʰ. While a number

---

[32] Friedman, *Most Ancient Testimony*, 44–48; Louis Kukenheim, *Contributions à l'histoire de la grammaire grecque, latine et hébraïque à l'époque de la Renaissance* (Leiden: E. J. Brill, 1951), 119 ff.

[33] My uncle Jacob Levin, who as the eldest of a large family in Mozir (White Russia) had received the best traditional education, told me toward the end of his long life that the method of his teachers had lacked one thing above all: they taught every subject—from the alphabet (*alef-beys*) to Talmud—without grammar (*diqduq*; he used both the English and the Yiddish word).

of codices of the Mišnå[h] itself were equipped with either the Babylo-nian or the Tiberias vowel-notation,[34] the great majority were not, and the Talmud was never marked thus. Therefore the Talmud was no easier to read in a codex—nor, for that matter, in a printed copy—than the Hebrew scriptures had been in a scroll. Or rather, it was much harder; for the phrasing of the Talmud is very elliptical and al-lusive, and many of the words, besides, are written in a highly abbre-viated fashion, whereas the Hebrew Bible has been protected by an absolute rule against abbreviations. Therefore prolonged oral instruc-tion by Jewish teachers was still necessary. Interested Christians, who could not or would not study the Talmud in a Jewish setting, had to depend mostly on what they could learn about it from an occasional convert that had previously gotten a thorough rabbinical education.

Book-bound as the Jewish schools were by this time and accus-tomed to reading the Talmud—not reciting it from memory as be-fore—still they could not put it into a readily legible and comprehen-sible form. They had done that earlier with the Hebrew Bible for their own benefit, and in so doing they inevitably opened it up to the Christians too. Thereby they somewhat lessened the separation be-tween Judaism and Christianity, which was paradoxically embodied even in the Scriptures that the two religions shared; for only the Jews had preserved the original Hebrew text,[35] and only the Orthodox Christians had preserved the Greek translation made by the Jews in the pre-Christian era. The *rapprochement* in regard to the Hebrew Bible, especially in the sixteenth century, had a noteworthy effect on the development of Protestantism. Yet otherwise the Jews' heritage remained peculiarly theirs and alien to the Christians at large.[36]

---

[34] The finest of these has been published: Georg Beer, *Faksimile-Ausgabe des Mischnacodex Kaufmann A 50* (The Hague: N. V. M. Nijhoff, 1929; repr., Jerusalem [1968]). In recent years many facsimiles of Bible codices have also been published; some of them, unfortunately, appear to have been taken from microfilms and are very hard to make out.

[35] The shrinking and secluded community of Samaritans in Nablus, quite separ-ate from the Jews, also preserved the Hebrew of the To[w]rå[h]—the only scripture rec-ognized by them. Their Hebrew lettering harks back to the most ancient models, but otherwise their text is less conservative than the Hebrew text of the Jews.

[36] Right after the session on October 21, 1988, when I read this paper, my col-league, Professor Norman Stillman, pointed out to me that the Siddur or synagogue service is still another important text that remained unwritten until the Jews adopted the codex. We know of no earlier rule against writing it down; indeed much of the liturgy consists of Psalms and passages from other Scriptures, which could of course have been looked up in scrolls but were familiar to religious people through frequent—even daily—repetition.

JOHN LINDOW

Þættir and Oral Performance

Since Andreas Heusler coined the terms *Buchprosa* and *Frei-prosa*,[1] oral tradition has never been far from the center of the debate about Old Norse-Icelandic prose. Concerns about the orality of Old Norse-Icelandic verse may be more recent, but the Parry-Lord theory had an impact in this field, too, and its continuing influence has recently been manifested in the publication, some thirty years after its completion, of Robert Kellogg's Harvard dissertation, a concordance to Eddic poetry inspired precisely by the Parry-Lord theory.[2] The debate goes on: "oral theory" and "oral performance" together received more index entries in Carol Clover's and my *Old Norse-Icelandic Literature* than any subject other than "foreign influences and parallels"—more than such central topics as "authorship,"

[1] Andreas Heusler, *Die Anfänge der isländischen Saga*, Abhandlungen der Königlichen Preussischen Akademie der Wissenschaften, philosophisch-historische Classe 1913, no. 9 (Berlin: Verlag der Königlichen Akademie der Wissenschaften).
[2] Robert Kellogg, *A Concordance to Eddic Poetry* (East Lansing, Mich.: Colleagues Press, 1988).

"Christianity," and "style."[3] In keeping with the established terms of the debate, we and our co-authors paid more attention to the fabric of tradition than the details of performance, and the *þættir* were among the genres we were unable to treat at all. I therefore hope to fill two tiny lacunae by discussing what the *þættir* have to say about performance and what, ultimately, performance has to say about the *þættir*.[4]

Þáttr (plural *þættir*), which originally meant "strand of a rope," whence "part of a manuscript or text," has been applied since the late Middle Ages as a literary term for texts with more or less independent status.[5] Length is in fact about all that separates *þættir* reliably from sagas, and a general distinction is therefore quite difficult to maintain.[6] One group of *þættir*, however, is recognized for considerable generic unity: the so-called *Íslendinga þættir*. Texts in this group detail an encounter between a person of low status, most often an Icelander, and a person of high status, most often the king of Norway. The hero performs successfully in this encounter and is rewarded by the figure of authority; often, too, the hero gains in social status. Joseph Harris, whose work continues to dominate discussion of the genre, saw the encounter as a move from alienation to reconciliation that stood at the core of a more complex chiastic structure,[7] although it might be equally identified as the core of an exchange testing the loyalty of the hero and the generosity of the king.[8] In any case, the hero effects reconciliation through several means, such as offering a gift or carrying out a difficult task; in a great many cases, the hero is an Icelandic poet who offers verse to the king. For that reason, the *Íslendinga þættir* are a good place to look for oral performance, the more so because the skaldic craft quickly became something of an Ice-

---

[3] Carol J. Clover and John Lindow, eds., *Old Norse-Icelandic Literature: A Critical Guide*, Islandica, vol. 45 (Ithaca, NY: Cornell Univ. Press, 1985).

[4] Quotations from the *þættir* are from Bragi Halldórsson, Jón Torfason, Sverrir Tómasson, and Örnólfur Thorsson, eds., *Íslendinga sögur og þættir* (Reykjavík: Svart á Hvítu, 1986).

[5] John Lindow, "Old Icelandic *þáttr* : Early Usage and Semantic History," *Scripta Islandica* 29 (1978): 3–44; Lars Lönnroth, "Tesen om de två kulturerna: Kritiska studier i den isländska sagans sociala förutsättningar," *Scripta Islandica* 15 (1964): 1–97.

[6] Rodney Maack, "Þáttr and Saga: The Relation of Short and Long Narrative in Medieval Iceland" (Ph.D. diss., Univ. of California at Berkeley, 1987).

[7] Joseph Harris, "Genre and Narrative Structure in Some *Íslendinga þættir*," *Scandinavian Studies* 44 (1972): 1–27; idem, "Theme and Genre in Some *Íslendinga þættir*," *Scandinavian Studies* 48 (1976): 1–27.

[8] Vésteinn Ólason, "Íslendingaþættir," *Tímarit máls og menningar* 46 (1985): 60–73.

landic monopoly, and much surviving verse describes the exploits of Norwegian kings. In general, Icelanders seem to have been regarded (or to have regarded themselves) as particularly good scholars, at a time when scholarship meant being an active bearer of oral tradition.

Þættir offer scenes in which both prose narrative and verse are performed. One of the most oft-cited of them is *Íslendings þáttr sǫgufróða*, also known as Þorsteins þáttr sǫgufróða after a version in which the hero is named.[9] In either version, this text is perhaps second only to Þorgils saga ok Hafliða for the speculation it has inspired on oral sagas.[10] When the Icelander arrives at the court of King Haraldr harðráði (Harald Hardrule) and is asked whether he has any talents, he replies that he knows sagas. The exchange gives information on the vocabulary of oral tradition: in one text, Haraldr asks the Icelander if he can amuse in any way (*Kanntu nokkuru að skemmta*), in the other if he possesses any learning (*ef hann kynni nokkverja frœði*). In both the Icelander responds that he "knows" sagas; he uses the verb *kunna*, which denotes skill or understanding of some art. The king instructs him to recite for anyone who asks him to, and the Icelander becomes popular with the retainers, who reward his oral performances with clothing; the king gives him weapons. Toward Christmas the Icelander seems downcast, and the king rightly guesses that the Icelander has run out of materials. He has, it turns out, only one saga left, and he is afraid to tell it, for it is Haraldr's own *útfararsaga* (lit. "account of a journey abroad"), the story of his journey to Byzantium. The king announces that he would like to hear it and instructs the Icelander to begin reciting it on the first day of Christmas, and he will see to it that the performance lasts all the days of Christmas. It does, and the king is pleased with the saga. The Icelander receives appropriate rewards. One interesting aspect of the text is the Icelander's response to the king's question of how he learned the text. At the Icelandic *alþingi* (national assembly), the Icelander replies, he learned it seriatim from Halldórr Snorrason over the course of several years.

Íslendings þáttr sǫgufróða provides evidence relating to several aspects of the performance of oral sagas: serial performances (a phenomenon also indicated by *Norna-Gests þáttr*) of varying length—obviously the point of the Icelander's performances is that they were unusually short; some kind of shorthand that substituted for titles (one version calls the last saga Haraldr's *útfararsaga* and the other

[9] Texts in Bragi Halldórsson et al., 2179–80, 2299–2300.
[10] Hermann Pálsson, *Sagnaskemmtun Íslendinga* (Reykjavík: Mál og Menning, 1962).

uses the synonym *útferðarsaga)*; the possibility that performance could
be initiated by audience request. Here the audience is the royal court
(as it was understood in Iceland in the late Middle Ages), and many
of its members seem to have rewarded the performer, some perhaps
after they had requested his performances.

Several other medieval Icelandic sources mention Halldórr, the
Icelander's putative source, including *Heiðarvíga saga, Laxdœla saga,
Heimskringla*, and *Hemings þáttr Áslákssonar*. *Halldórs þáttr Snorrasonar
I* mentions his saga about King Haraldr and generally presents him
as a gifted raconteur. Since scholars have linked *Halldórs þáttr Snorrasonar I* with the clerical authors at Þingeyrar in northwest Iceland in
the later twelfth century, the traditions about him appear relatively
old. The historical Halldórr may well have been an important link in
early Icelandic oral tradition.

Indeed, *Halldórs þáttr Snorrasonar I* itself centers on an oral performance.[11] According to this text, which is retained in manuscripts associated with King Óláfr Tryggvason, Halldórr was at odds with
King Haraldr harðráði and sought out the Norwegian noble Einarr
þambarskelfir (bow-string shaker) for protection. Halldórr is then in-
sulted by one of Einarr's retainers, kills him, and appeals to Einarr's
wife Bergljót for help. She advises Halldórr to throw himself on
Einarr's mercy, and Einarr recounts this story: he was once released
from slavery by a masked man who turned out to be Óláfr Tryggvason and bade him apply the same mercy to someone later. That
someone is Halldórr.

Einarr's performance occurs at a crowded *þing* (assembly) which
he himself has summoned. "He stood up at the *þing* and said this: 'I
wish to entertain you now and tell you what happened long ago
when I was aboard the Long Serpent with King Óláfr Tryggvason.'"
The story itself is then told in its entirety. It uses the first person
when necessary but otherwise is more or less in saga style, and when
it is over, the narrator of *Halldórs þáttr* refers to it as a saga.[12] The request for permission to perform also typifies *þættir* in which poets re-

---

[11] Text in Bragi Halldórsson et al., 2144–49.

[12] In this context may be mentioned the speech by Jón Ǫgmundarson, later the
Holy Bishop Jón of Hólar, to King Magnús berfœttr (Magnus Bareleg) in *Gísls þáttr
Illugasonar* (text in Bragi Halldórsson et al., 2116–28). Jón speaks on behalf of Gísl
and other Icelanders imprisoned by the king, and the speech is given in full in two
versions of the *þáttr*. Analysis of the speech itself belongs properly to the study of
Norse rhetoric, but it is worth pointing out that the circumstances mirror those of
Einarr's performance in *Halldórs þáttr Snorrasonar I*. Jón speaks at a crowded *þing*
after identifying himself and obtaining the king's leave.

cite longer poems. *Gull-Ásu-Þórðar þáttr, Hrafns þáttr Guðrúnarsonar, Hreiðars þáttr heimska, Sneglu-Halla þáttr,* and *Stúfs þáttr* all contain this motif. It is most elaborated in *Stúfs þáttr.*

Two versions are found, a shorter one in manuscripts of the kings' sagas, including *Morkinskinna, Flateyjarbók,* and *Hulda-Hrokkinskinna,* and a longer one in three fifteenth-century paper manuscripts in which the text is recorded independently.[13] The versions differ in style and in some details (e.g., Stúfr is explicitly said to be blind only in the shorter version), but they tell essentially the same story. Stúfr has arrived in Norway and is staying with an unidentified farmer when King Haraldr harðráði arrives unexpectedly. The king takes a liking to the independent-minded Icelander and asks him for entertainment late into the night. Stúfr recites *flokkar* (ordinary poems), which the king later counts at from twenty to sixty (depending on the version), but none of the more elaborate *drápur* (poems equipped with introductory and closing sections and an internal refrain). These he promises to recite when next they meet. Later Stúfr asks the king for three boons, to be granted without knowing what they are; one turns out to be permission to compose a *drápa* for the king. After some discussion about Stúfr's skaldic ancestry—Glúmr Geirason was Stúfr's paternal grandfather and many other good skalds are related to him—the king allows him to compose the *drápa,* and after hearing it the king admits Stúfr to his retinue.

The text offers obvious insight into medieval oral tradition. Stúfr is a *fræðimaðr* (man of learning) because he knows many of the works of other poets; in the *þáttr* he obtains permission to compose his own *drápa* and thus become a skald (i.e., one who composes verse as well as performs orally)[14] only after the king is satisfied that Stúfr comes from a skaldic family. The *þáttr* shows the context of a performance situation: a royal audience, late at night, a distinction between *flokkar* and *drápur* suggesting that both might ordinarily have been performed.

Kings' invitations to Icelanders to perform are not uncommon. One of the *Íslendinga þættir,* however, converts the invitation into an order. *Óttars þáttr svarta* is connected with the saga tradition of Óláfr Haraldsson the Saint and therefore exists in a number of slightly differing versions.[15] They agree that Óttarr composed erotic verse

---

[13] Texts in Bragi Halldórsson et al., 2243–49.

[14] Cf. Klaus von See, "Skop und Skald: Zur Auffassung des Dichters bei den Germanen," *Germanisch–romanische Monatsschrift* 45, new ser. 14 (1964): 1–14.

[15] Texts in Bragi Halldórsson et al., 2201–06.

about Ástríðr, the daughter of the Swedish king Óláfr and later the
wife of St. Olaf, and that St. Olaf therefore incarcerated Óttarr when
he came to Norway. The skald Sighvatr Þórðarson, Óttarr's friend,
advises Óttarr to revise the erotic verse and to compose a paean to St.
Olaf, which Óttarr does in three nights. Summoned before the king
and queen, he is commanded to recite the erotic verse, so that Ástríðr
may hear how he has praised her. Óttarr sits at the king's feet and recites the edited version of the love poetry, at which the king blushes,
but he does not interrupt. Óttarr then goes directly into the *drápa* for
Olaf, and when the retainers try to shout him down, Sighvatr inter-
cedes, and Óttarr finishes the poem. Again Sighvatr puts in a word
for Óttarr, and the king pardons him.

This text adds a few additional pieces to the puzzle. The retainers
try to stop Óttarr, and his continuation directly into a second poem
without pause is unusual enough for the author to take explicit note
of it. If we regard the retainers' shouts as a form of audience interaction, we can locate parallel passages in the *þættir* suggesting that
audience interaction might have been common during the performance of longer poems. *Stúfs þáttr* offers such a suggestion, but the
best example is *Arnórs þáttr jarlaskálds*.[16] Retained in *Morkinskinna*
and *Flateyjarbók*, its extreme brevity and exclusive focus on a single
incident almost remove it from the *Íslendinga þættir* and other generically defined groups of texts; we might simply refer to it as an anecdote. Arnórr Þórðarson, who is called *jarlaskáld* because of his connection with the Orkneyan jarls Rǫgnvaldr and Þorfinnr, is suddenly
summoned from preparing his ship by the Norwegian joint kings
Magnús inn góði (Magnus the good) and Haraldr harðráði; he has
composed a poem about each. Without washing the tar from himself,
Arnórr rushes to court and boldly orders people to make room for
the kings' skald. The older, rather touchy Haraldr asks whose poem
he will recite first, and Arnórr replies that impatience accompanies
youth, meaning that he will recite first the poem to Magnús. Haraldr,
who was himself a skald and was noted for his poetic taste, interrupts occasionally with remarks and questions, one of which Magnús
answers. Four stanzas of the poem are quoted. Immediately after the
last of these, Arnórr begins reciting his poem to Haraldr; none of
these stanzas is recorded. Afterwards Haraldr remarks that the poem
to himself will be wholly forgotten, whereas the one to Magnús will
be remembered as long as the northern lands are settled. He was

---

[16] Ibid., 2080–82.

mostly correct: we may not have all of the *Magnúsdrápa hrynhent*, but we certainly have nothing whatever of the *Bagdrápa*. Haraldr rewards the skald with a spear chased with gold, and Magnús gives him a ring. Arnórr puts the ring on the spear blade and leaves the hall declaring that the gifts of kings should be held high.

This episode is not really about the recitation of poetry. It is about another kind of performance: the witty Icelander managing to extricate himself from a potentially ugly situation with speech and gesture. There we have a key to the essence of the *Íslendinga þættir*. The lower-stationed Icelander seeks to gain status from the higher-stationed king. One means of doing so is to perform orally. Indeed, there are *þættir* in which the king sets a skaldic hoop for the Icelander to jump through, involving the speed or complexity of composition (e.g., *Einars þáttr Skúlasonar, Mána þáttr skálds, Sneglu-Halla þáttr, Þórarins þáttr stuttfeldar*).

To conclude: the *Íslendinga þættir* offer pictures of the performance of prose narrative, individual stanzas, and longer poems. Many individual details of context are variables from text to text: the performance occurs sometimes at night, sometimes during the day; before an audience of one or an audience of many; the skald sits at the king's feet, stands on a mound, or simply declaims in a crowded place. Skalds recite verses as tiny infants and as dying adults, before battles and after them. The constants of all these pictures are few: the requests for performance, occasional commentary during the performance, and the judgment of the performance, followed frequently by tangible and intangible rewards. In other words, the *Íslendinga þættir* do not offer a rich array of unassailable ethnographic detail about oral performance. They do, however, in all certainty portray oral performance as an interactive phenomenon with real results at stake. This interaction has already been highlighted in the contemporary sagas by Richard Bauman, who found that "artistic verbal art was a means of gaining honor in thirteenth-century Iceland." He added: "honor and verbal art constituted an integrated semiotic system organized around performance as the communicative mode by which moral values were enacted."[17] Given the anchoring of that semiotic system in contemporary sagas, we are justified in regarding as plausible at least some of the variables the *þættir* have to offer about performance, and we are equally justified in regarding the *Íslendinga þættir*

---

[17] Richard Bauman, "Performance and Honor in 13th-century Iceland," *Journal of American Folklore* 99 (1986): 131–50, esp. 146.

as a performance-centered genre. To justify this last point, I would
submit the evidence of *Brands þáttr ǫrva*.

This text, which is very short, is found in *Morkinskinna* and *Hulda-
Hrokkinskinna*, in versions that differ only slightly.[18] It tells of the
Icelander Brandr the Generous, who has arrived in Niðaróss on a
trading voyage. His friend Þjóðólfr the poet has boasted to King Haraldr harðráði of Brandr's generosity and has even gone so far as to
suggest that no man would be more fitting a choice if Iceland were to
have a king. Haraldr sends Þjóðólfr to ask Brandr to give him first his
cloak, then his ax chased with gold, and finally his precious tunic.
Brandr complies wordlessly with all three requests but tears an arm
from the tunic. At this the king responds: "This man is both wise and
noble. It is clear to me why he has torn off the arm; it seems to him
that I have only one arm, and that one only to receive, but never to
give. Bring him to me." The king rewards Brandr, "and this was
done," the text ends, "to test him."[19]

Brandr's performance is silent, but it shares everything with the
oral performances of the other Icelanders who perform before kings.
In this light, we may have to rethink our definition of the genre and
assign performance to its very core.

---

[18] Text in Bragi Halldórsson et al., 2105–06.
[19] Ibid., 2106.

MARY LYNN RAMPOLLA

"A Pious Legend": St. Oswald and the Foundation of Worcester Cathedral Priory

I n the century following the Norman Conquest, the monks of Worcester cathedral priory set about rediscovering their past. Under the guidance of Wulfstan, the last Anglo-Saxon bishop of Worcester (1062–1095), they undertook a detailed examination of their archives; compiled a cartulary; transcribed old saints' lives and composed new ones; and began an ambitious chronicle designed to integrate local and universal history. It is likely that these efforts were initially a response to the Norman Conquest;[1] believing their traditions

---

[1] For this view of historical writing in England in the late eleventh and early twelfth centuries, see esp. R. W. Southern, "Aspects of the European Tradition of Historical Writing: 4. The Sense of the Past," *Transactions of the Royal Historical Society*, 5th ser., 23 (1973): 243–63. See also three works by Antonia Gransden: *Historical Writing in England c. 550 to c. 1307*, (Ithaca, NY, 1974), chap. 6–8, passim; "Cultural Transition at Worcester in the Anglo-Norman Period," *British Archaeological Association Conference Transactions: Medieval Art and Architecture at Worcester Cathedral* 1 (1978): 1–14; and "Traditionalism and Continuity during the Last Century of Anglo-Saxon Monasticism," *Journal of Ecclesiastical History* 40 (1989): 159–207, passim. For a recent examination of the impact of the Norman conquest on Worcester, see Emma Mason, "Change and Continuity in Eleventh-Century Mercia: The Experience of St. Wulfstan of Worcester," in *Anglo-Norman Studies VIII: Proceedings*

to be threatened, and fearing, as the cartulary says, that important events would be "lost from sight in clouds of ignorance and completely obliterated from memory,"[2] the monks decided to create a written record of their past. Preserving the past in writing did not, however, immediately divest the practice of history of its oral characteristics. As in orally transmitted histories,[3] the past as it was described in the records of the late eleventh and early twelfth centuries was adjusted to accomodate the needs of the present. This flexibility is particularly evident in the Worcester monks' accounts of the event that stood at the beginning of their corporate life: the conversion of the cathedral from the secular to the monastic life. The story told of this event, which defined their identity as a group, was altered rapidly in the late eleventh and early twelfth centuries to reflect their changing views of themselves and their role in society.

Sometime during the pontificate of Oswald (961–992), the cathedral church of Worcester was transformed from a secular institution, dedicated to St. Peter, into a monastic one, dedicated to the Virgin. No contemporary accounts of Oswald's actions at Worcester survive: the first detailed written records of this pivotal event, which occurred sometime in the 960s or 970s, did not appear until over a century later. Even more striking than the absence of contemporary records is the abundance of written accounts composed between 1092 and c.1140, when the history of Worcester's conversion was written down at least eight times. All but one of these accounts originated at Worcester cathedral priory. It would seem, then, that for the first century or more of the priory's existence, the monks of Worcester cathedral were content to rely on memory as the sole repository of their early history, and that it was not until the closing years of the eleventh century that they became concerned with preserving this portion of their past in writing.

While all the sources are agreed about the *fact* of Worcester's transformation, they offer two radically different descriptions of how

---

of the Battle Conference (Suffolk, England, 1986), 154–76, and idem, St. Wulfstan of Worcester, c. 1008–1095 (Oxford, 1990), 108–155.

[2] Hemming, Chartularium Ecclesiae Wigornensis, ed. Thomas Hearne, 2 vols. (Oxford, 1723), 2:283.

[3] For the flexibility of the past in orally transmitted history, see Jack Goody and Ian Watt, "The Consequences of Literacy," in Literacy in Traditional Societies, ed. Jack Goody, (Cambridge, 1968). Goody and Watt argue that in oral societies, the past is "transmuted in the course of being transmitted," being "automatically adjusted to existing social relations as they are passed by word of mouth from one member of the society to another" (33).

that transition came about. In the first, advanced by Eadmer in his life of St. Oswald and also found in a contemporary record of the diocesan synod held at Worcester in 1092, Oswald's reform is described as a slow process, in which the secular priests of the cathedral were gradually converted to the monastic life. The alternative description of Worcester's conversion, found in the Worcester chronicle, its abbreviation, and the rather problematic *Altitonantis* charter, suggests that Oswald forcibly expelled the secular clerks in order to install a monastic community at Worcester cathedral.

What Oswald "really did" to reform Worcester cannot be ascertained conclusively from the written accounts of the eleventh and twelfth centuries.[4] More important, however, is what these sources *can* tell us about the monks of Worcester cathedral priory in the late eleventh and early twelfth centuries: How, from the scanty records available to them, did they reconstruct their past? And how, over the course of some fifty years, was that past transformed to reflect the monks' changing interests and concerns?

The Synod of 1092

It was during the episcopate of Wulfstan that the monks of Worcester first became interested in committing the history of the priory's foundation to writing. Wulfstan had entered the curia of Bishop Brihtheah of Worcester as a young man and was ordained as a secular priest. He soon felt the call to the monastic life and entered the cathedral priory, where he rapidly rose through the ranks, holding the offices of schoolmaster, precentor, sacristan and ultimately prior. To the

---

[4] For the debate over the nature of Oswald's reforms at Worcester, see J. Armitage Robinson, "St. Oswald and the Church of Worcester," *British Academy Supplemental Papers* 5 (1919): 3–51, who supports the theory of a gradual change, and Eric John, "St. Oswald and the Church of Worcester," in *Orbis Brittaniae and Other Studies*, vol. 4 in Studies in Early English History, gen. ed. H. P. R. Finberg (Leicester, 1966): 234–48, who argues that change was sudden and drastic. The debate has not been entirely settled by appealing—as proponents on both sides of the issue have done—to the evidence supplied by the witness lists of Oswald's leases. P. H. Sawyer has argued that "the development of the community during Oswald's episcopate as revealed by the witness lists is best described as a process of gradual change with much continuity through the whole period, with no dramatic losses at any time." See his "Charters of the Reform Movement: The Worcester Archive," in *Tenth-Century Studies: Commemoration of the Millenium of the Council of Winchester and Regularis Concordia*, ed. with an introduction by David Parsons (London and Chichester, 1975), 89–92. Most recently, the issue has been addressed by Antonia Gransden, "Traditionalism," 172–73, and by Mason, *St. Wulfstan of Worcester*, 13–16, both of whom support Robinson's conclusions.

monks of Worcester, then, Wulfstan's election to the episcopacy in 1062 was the elevation of one of their own.[5]

As prior, Wulfstan had undertaken an energetic campaign to restore the fortunes of the priory: he recovered several of the monastery's estates; attracted new gifts from pious patrons; began a building project; and initiated a program of spiritual reform among the monks.[6] His efforts as bishop followed the same pattern. When William the Conqueror vanquished Harold and his forces in the fourth year of Wulfstan's episcopacy, his presence at Worcester eased the transition from English to Norman rule. Wulfstan quickly made his peace with both the Conqueror and Lanfranc,[7] and although his reign was not entirely untroubled,[8] his working relations with the Norman secular and ecclesiastical hierarchy were, on the whole, cordial. It was thus largely because of Wulfstan that Worcester cathedral priory was able to retain its Anglo-Saxon culture and traditions well into the third decade of Norman rule.

The only version of the priory's foundation which can be ascribed with certainty to the pontificate of Wulfstan is contained in a document drawn up by Wulfstan himself, which records the findings of a diocesan synod held in 1092 in the crypt of the new cathedral.[9] The synod was ostensibly called to settle a dispute between the priests of

---

[5] For Wulfstan's early career, see *The Vita Wulfstani of William of Malmesbury*, ed. R. R. Darlington, Camden Society, 3d ser., 40 (London, 1928), 7–9. The *Vita* has been translated by J. H. F. Peile, *William of Malmesbury's Life of St. Wulfstan* (Oxford, 1934) and by Michael Swanton, *Three Lives of the Last Englishmen*, vol. 10 of The Garland Library of Medieval Literature (New York, 1984), 89–148. For a modern biography, see Mason, *St. Wulfstan*.

[6] For Wulfstan's career as prior, see Darlington, *Vita*, 11–15. For estates that he restored to the priory, see Hemming, *Chartularium*, 2:249–50, 406, 408–10.

[7] Wulfstan was among the first bishops to submit to the Conqueror in 1066 (see Florence of Worcester, *Chronicon ex Chronicis*, ed. Benjamin Thorpe, English Historical Society [London, 1848], 1:228–29); in 1067, he received a grant of land from William (printed in Hemming, *Chartularium*, 2:413). His early relationship with Lanfranc also seems to have been good: in c. 1072 Wulfstan swore obedience to Lanfranc as "metropolitan of the holy church of Canterbury" (printed in Darlington, *Vita*, 190), and he sent his favorite, Nicholas, to study under Lanfranc at Canterbury (Darlington, *Vita*, 57).

[8] Worcester lost the revenues of several estates to Urse, the new Norman sheriff (see Hemming, *Chartularium*, 2:248–70, passim); and Thomas, the Norman archbishop of York, not only held land which had been alienated from Worcester, but even claimed the right to rule the see (Darlington, *Vita*, 24–26).

[9] Printed in R. R. Darlington, *The Cartulary of Worcester Cathedral Priory (Register I)*, Publications of the Pipe Roll Society, n.s., 38 (London, 1968), 31–32. An English translation can be found in Sir Ivor Atkins, "The Church of Worcester from the Eighth to the Twelfth Century," *The Antiquaries Journal* 20 (1940): 204–206. For a description of the synod, see Mason, *St. Wulfstan*, 213–14.

St. Alban and St. Helen over the rights and customs of their respective churches. The monks claimed that this altercation was also damaging the priory, causing them to lose their income from the church of St. Helen. In order to settle these issues, Wulfstan assembled a prestigious group of monastic and ecclesiastic officials to determine the rights of St. Mary's vis-à-vis the city churches. It was in this context that an investigation into the history of the priory's foundation was undertaken.

The record of the synod preserves not only the foundation story itself, but a description of how Wulfstan's committee went about reconstructing an event which had occurred nearly one hundred years previously. Although no mention is made of the fact, written sources were certainly consulted. The date of Worcester's conversion, for example, was derived either from a charter or from the Worcester chronicle or its source.[10] The committee probably also had access to an early eleventh century Life of St. Oswald by Byrhtferth of Ramsey,[11] which records the bare facts about the foundation of the priory: that Oswald "made a monastery" at Worcester; that he appointed Wynsius, a priest who had been educated at Ramsey, as prior of the new foundation; and that Wynsius brought other Ramsey monks with him to his new post.[12] It is clear, however, that local oral tradition was of paramount importance; Wulfstan's committee, as he describes it, was comprised of "old men, and others who were most familiar with the ancient customs of the churches and parishes of Worcester."[13] Moreover, in "declaring the truth"[14] about these cus-

---

[10] The record of the synod of 1092, like the Worcester chronicle, advances exact dates for Worcester's conversion (969) and for the foundation of the see under bishop Bosel (680). Since dates rarely survive oral transmission, it is likely that these were derived from some written source, such as the hypothetical annals, no longer extant, which are presumed to have been the source used by the compiler of the early section of the Worcester chronicle. For this suggestion, see Darlington, *Cartulary*, xvii. Alternatively, the date of the cathedral's conversion may have been derived from a Worcester charter, dated 969, found in an early eleventh century Worcester cartulary. For this suggestion, see Robinson, 33. The charter is listed as no. 1321 in P. H. Sawyer, *Anglo-Saxon Charters: An Annotated List and Bibliography*, Royal Historical Society Guides and Handbooks, no. 8 (London, 1968).

[11] *Vita Sancti Oswaldi auctore anonymo*, in vol. 1 of *Historians of the Church of York*, James Raine, ed., Rolls Series, 71 (London, 1879), 399–475. For the attribution of this life to Byrhtferth, see Michael Lapidge, "Byrhtferth and the *Vita S. Ecgwini*," *Medieval Studies* 41 (1979): 331–53. This *Vita* was copied into one of the priory's collections of saints' lives in the late eleventh or early twelfth century, and is now BM MS. Cotton Nero E. i., fols. 3–23v. It was clearly read aloud: it is accented for reading, and corrected in several places.

[12] *Vita Sancti Oswaldi*, 435.

[13] Darlington, *Cartulary*, 31.

toms, the members of the commission do not describe themselves as
"historians" who have undertaken archival research, but as "witnesses": aural witnesses to information that has been handed down
"from our predecessors," and physical witnesses to the customs
observed at Worcester "in our own time; both under Aldred, your
predecessor, and yourself [Wulfstan]."[15]

The story of the priory's foundation as recounted by Wulfstan's
committee is much more detailed than the version found in Byrhtferth's life. Worcester, we are told, had been served by clerks from its
foundation in 680 until the time of Oswald who, with the help of
King Edgar and the authority of Archbishop Dunstan, "transformed
and changed" (*transtulit et mutauit*) the church of Worcester from
"the irregular (*irregulari*) way of life of the clerks to the regular
(*regularum*) society of monks" in 969.[16] At that time, Wynsius was
the vicar of the church of St. Helen, acting on behalf of the Mother
Church. Along with the other secular clergy who served the cathedral, he was persuaded by Oswald to become a monk, whereupon he
surrendered the keys of St. Helen, along with its income, to the
monks. The monks also acquired the other churches, lands, tithes and
rights which had belonged to the clerks. Three years after his conversion, Wynsius was made Worcester's first prior and appointed as
dean (*decanus*) over all the monks' churches, a right also granted to
all his successors.

What should we make of this account, and to what extent can we
trust it? Orally transmitted history, as noted above, is continuously
adjusted to accommodate contemporary problems and circumstances.
We should therefore expect the foundation story to reflect both the
experiences of the community, as embodied in its structures, and its
current interests and concerns. Our understanding of the foundation
story will thus depend largely on our overall interpretation of the
purposes for which the synod was called.

It is clear that far more was at stake than the respective rights of
two parish priests. As previously noted, the priests' quarrel was
having an adverse economic impact on the priory. In addition, the
monks clearly desired to limit the growing power of a relatively new
official, the archdeacon.[17] More important, however, is the fact that

---

[14] Ibid.

[15] Ibid., 32.

[16] Ibid., 31.

[17] For the role of the archdeacon in England in this period, see Christopher
Brooke, "The Archdeacon and the Norman Conquest" in *Tradition and Change:*

underlying the quarrel between the two priests was the perennial controversy between Worcester and Evesham. Evesham claimed the right to revenues from St. Alban, a church lying within one hundred and eighty meters of the cathedral which, according to an Evesham charter, had been given to the abbey by Ethelbald of Mercia in 721.[18] If the priest of St. Alban was challenging the rights and customs of St. Helen, Evesham was in effect threatening Worcester, and it is likely that the synod was called partially from a desire to exclude Evesham from influence in the city of Worcester.[19]

The foundation story as related in the records of the synod clearly reflects these concerns. In the first place, by affirming, anachronistically, that no dean or archdeacon would be admitted to the monks' churches without the permission of the prior,[20] the foundation story provides a justification for severely restricting the archdeacon's sphere of influence. The story of the priory's conversion also bolstered the monks' claim to the incomes of the city churches. Wynsius' connection with Ramsey is not mentioned; instead, he is described as a priest of Worcester, and emphasis is placed on the fact that he, and the other priests who converted with him, surrendered their churches and incomes to the monastery. Finally, the end result of the synod's deliberations was to increase and strengthen the control of the cathedral priory over the churches of the city. The committee concluded that there was only one parish in the city of Worcester, that of St. Mary; *both* St. Helen and St. Alban were, in fact, vicarages of the mother church. The decision of the synod thus effectively locked Evesham out of the city's pastoral life and incomes.

That the synod's account of the priory's foundation, "remembered" by the older members of the community, would provide solutions to the monks' most pressing problems is precisely what we should expect. But even if we treat these "self-serving" aspects of story with some caution, there is no reason to doubt that the record

---

Essays in Honor of Marjorie Chibnall, ed. Diana Greenway, Christopher Holdsworth and Jane Sayers, (Cambridge, 1985), 1–19. According to Brooke, "no single archdeacon can be securely named between 900 and 1066. By the death of Lanfranc in 1089 we have some evidence of an archdeacon in almost every diocese" (2).

[18] Printed in *Chronicon Abbatiae de Evesham*, ed. W. D. Macray, Rolls Series 29 (London, 1863), 73.

[19] For this suggestion, see Atkins, "The Church of Worcester," 206. For an alternate interpretation of this synod, see Eric John, "An Alleged Charter of the Reign of Edgar," *Bulletin of the John Rylands Library* 41 (1958–59): 54–80 and *Land Tenure in Early England: A Discussion of Some Problems* (Leicester, 1960), 109–12. Darlington takes issue with John's views in *Cartulary*, xliv–xlvi.

[20] Darlington, *Cartulary*, 31.

of the synod does indeed preserve the genuine tradition of the monastery in 1092.

The method Oswald employed in effecting his reforms at Worcester, and the speed with which those reforms were carried out, were irrelevant to the synod's concerns; there is no reason, therefore, to distrust the committee's description of the cathedral's conversion, which suggests a gradual transition from a secular to a monastic life. Wynsius and the other priests of Worcester, we are told, were moved by Oswald's persuasions and chose to convert "of their own accord" (*sponte*).[21] The statement that Wynsius did not become Worcester's first prior until three years after his conversion suggests that the transformation of the cathedral into a monastic house was achieved slowly. There is no indication that any of the secular clergy of the cathedral refused to convert. Most importantly, whether all converted or not, Worcester tradition in 1092 did not include a conflict between the monks and the secular clerks.

The Evidence of Hemming's Cartulary

Sometime between c. 1089 and 1112, Hemming, the subprior of St. Mary's Worcester, completed the cartulary that he had begun at Wulfstan's request.[22] For Hemming, the cartulary was more than just a collection of documents; moved by Wulfstan's lament that the monks of Worcester were not sufficiently interested in their own past,[23] Hemming set out to compose a work of history. To this end, the charters which he assembled and copied into his cartulary were set in a narrative framework.

Hemming discusses the priory's early history as a gloss on an eighth century charter of two local notables named Wiferd and Alta.[24] His account incorporates a tradition that is completely independent from that of the synod of 1092; neither narrative confirms— nor contradicts—the other, and they should be seen as complementary, or supplementary, versions of the story.

After the deaths of Wiferd and Alta, Hemming tells us, a stone structure with a cross was erected over their grave in their memory. This structure apparently became a local landmark, for it was by this

---

[21] Ibid.

[22] See Hemming, *Chartularium*, 2:282–84. Hemming is identified as subprior of the monastery in Darlington, *Vita*, 7.

[23] Hemming, *Chartularium*, 2:284.

[24] Ibid., 342–43. The charter is listed in Sawyer, *Anglo-Saxon Charters*, no. 1185.

cross that St. Oswald used to preach; the church of St. Peter had become too small to accommodate the crowds that came to hear him, and St. Mary's had not yet been constructed. The monument, Hemming tells us, survived until the reign of King Edward, when Alric, the brother of Bishop Brihtheah (1033–1038) pulled it down, and used the stone to expand the church of St. Peter.

Armitage Robinson sees this description as a "parable" of the tenth century reform movement: "A great spiritual movement was in progress: the old limits were too narrow for the new enthusiasm."[25] It is not clear that Hemming saw his account in this light. For Hemming, the priory's identity was tied to the concrete; his chief preoccupation was with questions of land tenure. It is therefore appropriate that his discussion of Worcester's early history focuses on monuments and buildings. What Hemming is concerned with is the physical history of the cathedral: the fact that St. Peter had become too small; that the church of St. Mary was begun by Oswald as his new episcopal see; that the old monument survived until the eleventh century; that St. Peter was expanded with stone taken from that same monument. He even notes that stone from the monument was used as a milestone until the time of William the Conqueror, when it was incorporated into the monks' lavatory. He is not, however, particularly interested in why the cathedral came to be staffed by monks, nor does he tell us how this happened; in fact, his account does not even mention the conversion of the cathedral's personnel from the secular to the regular life. We can only surmise from his description that the construction of St. Mary may have taken some time, which suggests that the transition from one building to the other was gradual.

Worcester and the Norman Episcopate

The sources closest to Wulfstan's pontificate, then, relate a version of Worcester's early history in which the transformation of the cathedral from a secular into a monastic institution was slow, effected, perhaps, by the gradual conversion of the priests of the cathedral to the monastic life. A rather different picture begins to emerge, however, from the sources dating from the first three decades of the twelfth century.

Wulfstan had been an Englishman and a monk; his death, however, brought a less congenial kind of bishop to Worcester. Samson had been a canon of Bayeux and was in minor orders at the time of his

---

[25] Robinson, "St. Oswald," 5.

election in 1096.[26] He had been married, and came from an important clerical family. His brother, archbishop Thomas of York,[27] had
attempted to gain control of the see of Worcester during Wulfstan's
pontificate; his son, Thomas, would later be elected to the northern
archbishopic.[28] Samson's successor, Theulf, had also been a canon of
Bayeux.

On the surface, the monks seem to have gotten along well enough
with their new bishops. Samson was apparently a capable admini-
strator,[29] and granted several estates to the priory.[30] Despite his
generosity, however, he displayed a rather dismaying lack of sensitivity towards his chapter. Sometime during his rule, he disbanded the
priory of Westbury-on-Trym, which Wulfstan had established in 1093
as a daughter house of the cathedral priory.[31] It seems likely that he
intended to use the church and its income to support the secular
priests of his *familia*, and his gift of Wolverhampton may have been
offered to the monks in compensation.[32] Even if reimbursement
were offered, however, the loss of Westbury was a serious blow.
Westbury had been Oswald's original monastic foundation in Worcestershire, the cradle of his greater foundation, Ramsey, from which,
in turn, the monastic chapter of Worcester had sprung. In his original
grant of Westbury to the monks, Wulfstan draws attention to its
foundation by Oswald, and deplores the decline of the priory after
the Danish invasions.[33] The restoration of Westbury, then, was as
important symbolically as it was economically; it created a living link
with Worcester's glorious past and its greatest bishop, Oswald.
Samson's disruption of the new foundation so soon after its revival
must have been deeply shocking to the monks of Worcester, and an
insult to both Wulfstan and Oswald.

---

[26] For Samson's character and career, see V. H. Galbraith, "Notes on the Career
of Samson, Bishop of Worcester (1096–1112)," *English Historical Review* 82 (1967):
86–101, and Frank Barlow, *The English Church 1066–1154*, (London, 1979), 71–72.

[27] Thomas I ruled the see of York from 1070 to 1100. See Sir F. Maurice Powicke
and E. B. Fryde, *A Handbook of British Chronology*, 2d ed. (London, 1961), 264.

[28] Thomas II was nominated in May of 1108 and consecrated in 1109. He died
in 1114. See Powicke and Fryde, *Handbook*, 264.

[29] See Galbraith, "Career of Samson," passim.

[30] See, for example, the charter granting Hartlebury to the monks, printed in
Hemming, *Chartularium*, 2:426–27.

[31] This action was much deplored by William of Malmesbury, and, presumably,
by the monks of Worcester. William of Malmesbury, *De Gestis Pontificum Anglorum*,
ed. N. E. S. A. Hamilton, Rolls Series 90 (London, 1870), 290.

[32] Darlington, *Cartulary*, xlvii–xlviii.

[33] Printed in Hemming, *Chartularium*, 2:421–24.

Of Theulf's reputation with the monks we know even less, but the rather unflattering epitaph on him, written in the hand of the chronicler John, is suggestive.[34] William of Malmesbury accused him of having bought his office, and he may have attempted to depose Nicholas, who was a favorite of Wulfstan and had become prior of Worcester in c.1116.[35] The main evidence of tension between the new bishops and their chapter, however, is that in the vacancy following Theulf's death, the prior, Nicholas, wrote to the archbishop of Canterbury and the bishop of Winchester expressing his fear that the church of Worcester might be handed over to "an alien and tyrant,"[36] and requesting a "canonical" election of the new bishop by the chapter.[37] His efforts were in vain; Simon, one of the Queen's chaplains, and still in minor orders at the time, was appointed in 1125.

At the same time as the monks of Worcester were coming to grips with their new bishops, they were also struggling with some of the issues raised by the Gregorian reform movement, which called into question the role of both monk and priest in society. On the one hand, the reform movement subjected the monks to attack from members of the secular clergy who challenged the propriety of monastic involvement in pastoral care.[38] Preaching and other pastor-

---

[34] Theulf's epitaph appears on the front flyleaf of Worc. Cath. Lib., MS. Q66. It is printed by J. K. Floyer and S. G. Hamilton, *Catalogue of MSS Preserved in the Chapter Library of Worcester Cathedral*, (Oxford, 1906), 143–44; by Elizabeth E. A. McIntyre, "Early-Twelfth-Century Worcester Cathedral Priory, with special reference to the manuscripts written there" (D. Phil. thesis, Oxford University, 1978), 248; and by Dorothy Bethell, "English Black Monks and Episcopal Elections in the 1120's," *English Historical Review* 84 (1969): 682, n. 2.

[35] William of Malmesbury, *De Gestis Pontificum*, 290–91.

[36] Nicholas' letter has been printed by Bethell, "English Black Monks," 696; and McIntyre, "Early-Twelfth-Century Worcester," 243–44.

[37] On this incident, see Bethell, "English Black Monks," 681–84. According to Bethell, the monks had never had the rights they were claiming.

[38] On the question of monastic involvement in pastoral care, see Thomas L. Amos, "Monks and Pastoral Care in the Early Middle Ages," in *Religion, Culture, and Society in the Early Middle Ages: Studies in Honor of Richard E. Sullivan*, (Michigan, 1987), 165–180; Ursmer Berlière, "L'exercise du ministère paroissial par les moines dans le haut moyen-âge," *Revue Bénédictine* 39 (1927): 227–50 and "L'Exercise du ministère paroissial par les moines du xiie au xviiie siecle," *Revue Bénédictine* 39 (1927): 340–64; Marjorie Chibnall, "Monks and Pastoral Work: A Problem in Anglo-Norman History," *Journal of Ecclesiastical History* 18 (1967): 165–72; Giles Constable, *Monastic Tithes*, (Cambridge, 1964); Sarah Foot, "Parochial Ministry in Early Anglo-Saxon England: The Role of Monastic Communities," in *The Ministry: Clerical and Lay*, W. J. Sheils and D. Wood, eds., *Studies in Church History* 26 (Oxford, 1989): 43–54; B. R. Kemp, "Monastic Possession of Parish Churches in England in the Twelfth Century," *Journal of Ecclesiastical History* 31 (1980): 144–45; Dom Jean

al activities had long been the province of monks in England, and English Benedictines mounted a spirited defense of their role in such matters. On the other hand, the Gregorian reform movement supported the monks in their increasingly outspoken condemnation of clerical marriage. While the Gregorian emphasis on clerical celibacy may have appeared novel to many 12th century observers, it would have been obvious to any English monk that the papacy had embarked on a course already charted by Oswald, Dunstan and Ethelwold, who had attempted to impose celibacy upon clerics in higher orders in the tenth century.[39] Seeing it as a heritage from their illustrious past, English monks enthusiastically supported the papacy on this issue. While Wulfstan had remained alive, the monks of Worcester had been ruled by a bishop who shared their values and defended their practices. Under the new regime, however, they could not be so sure of a sympathetic hearing. In any case, in the sources dating from the pontificates of Samson and Theulf, a new theme appears in the story of Worcester's conversion: a growing aversion towards the secular clergy.

Coleman and the *Vita Wulfstani*

Sometime during the pontificate of Samson (1096–1112), Coleman, a monk of Worcester and Wulfstan's chancellor, wrote his *Vita Wulfstani*.[40] Coleman had been Wulfstan's chaplain for fifteen years[41] and his name appears on the witness lists of several important Worcester charters.[42] His interest in the issues raised by the Gregorian reform movement is evident. Himself an object of criticism for preaching to the laity, Coleman was outspoken in his support of

---

Leclercq, "Prédicateurs bénédictins aux xie et xiie siècles, *Revue Mabillon* 33 (1943): 48–73; D. J. A. Matthew, *The Norman Monasteries and Their English Possessions* (Oxford, 1962), 59–61; and T. P. McLaughlin, "Le très ancien droit monastique de l'occident," *Archives de la France monastique*, 38 (Paris, 1935).

[39] For the ideal of celibacy in the tenth century reform movement, see esp. C. N. L. Brooke, "Gregorian Reform in Action: Clerical Marriage in England, 1050–1200," *Cambridge Historical Journal* 12 (1956): 1–21; R. R. Darlington, "Eccleciastical Reform in the Late Old English Period," *English Historical Review* 51 (1936): 385–428; W. A. C. Sandford, "Medieval Clerical Celibacy in England," *The Genealogists' Magazine* 12 (1957): 371–73.

[40] The *Vita* was written between Wulfstan's death in 1095 and Coleman's in 1113; Samson died in 1112.

[41] Darlington, *Vita*, 2.

[42] See, for example, the Alveston charter of 1089, printed in Hemming, *Chartularium*, 2:420.

monastic involvement in pastoral care, and included in the *Vita* two stories defending the practice.[43] Wulfstan had entrusted him with the office of preaching during his absence;[44] and his hand appears in several homily books and penitentials.[45] Despite his new bishop's marital status, Coleman was also a staunch proponent of clerical celibacy, and the *Vita* includes an enthusiastic (and probably exaggerated) description of Wulfstan's expulsion of married clergy from their benefices.[46] Coleman is, in fact, highly critical of the secular clergy throughout the *Vita Wulfstani*. Moreover, he had a personal ax to grind; he had been prior of the newly refounded Westbury-on-Trym, which Samson disbanded.[47]

Although the only extant version of the *Vita* is William of Malmesbury's Latin translation of the Old English original, the story of the priory's conversion is so different from William's own account of the same event in his *Life of St. Dunstan* that it is probably safe to assume that the translation accurately reflects Coleman's intent.[48] Coleman's comments on Oswald's reforms are brief, consisting of only one sentence in the Latin text. In the course of a story about Wulfstan's piety, Coleman simply notes that St. Oswald freed the cathedral from the "irreligious clerks" (*clericis irreligiosis vacuauerat*), and gave the honor of the episcopal chair to St. Mary, as was fitting.[49]

Brief as this account is, Coleman's description introduces important changes. First of all, the verb he used to describe Oswald's actions is ambiguous. *Vacuare*, meaning "to empty," "to clear," or "to free," is a stronger word than the more neutral *transferre* and *mutare* ("to transform," "to change") of the 1092 synod, implying that the secular clerks are a group from which the church should be "freed" or "emptied." The verb might also suggest that the secular priests were not converted, as the synod's account states, but replaced. This

---

[43] Darlington, *Vita*, 14, 39–40. In the second story, criticism is levelled against Coleman himself for preaching.

[44] Ibid., 40. For the importance of the role of designated preacher, see Milton McC. Gatch, *Preaching and Theology in Anglo-Saxon England: Aelfric and Wulfstan*, (Toronto, 1977), 56–57.

[45] See N. R. Ker, "Old English Notes Signed 'Coleman,' " *Medium Aevum* 18 (1949): 29–31.

[46] Darlington, *Vita*, 53–54.

[47] Ibid., 52.

[48] William of Malmesbury translated the original *Life* into Latin at the request of the Worcester monks. His own version of Worcester's conversion can be found in his *Vita Sancti Dunstani* (in *Memorials of St. Dunstan*, ed. W. Stubbs, Rolls Series 63 [London, 1874], 250–324).

[49] Darlington, *Vita*, 9–10.

rather negative view of secular priests is reinforced by a change in adjectives: the "irregular" clerks of 1092 (i.e., priests who do not live under a monastic rule, or *regula*) have become "irreligious" or "impious" clerks (*clericis irreligiosis*).

Eadmer's *Vita Oswaldi*

Dating from the early years of Theulf's episcopacy is Eadmer's *Vita Sancti Oswaldi*, written between 1113 and 1117 at the request of the Worcester monks.[50] Eadmer provides a more detailed account of Oswald's actions in Worcester than any of the earlier sources. Oswald, we are told, tried to reform the clergy of the cathedral, but they "shut their hearts" (*sui cordis occluserunt*).[51] He therefore began to build a new church for his monks next to the episcopal church of St. Peter. There is no indication that the secular priests, however recalcitrant, were expelled from the diocese of Worcester; in fact, Eadmer specifically asserts that they remained at St. Peter after the monks began serving the new church, St. Mary.[52] Originally, the people attended each church in turn; the old church was gradually eclipsed, however, as popular admiration for the monks grew. Ultimately, St. Mary "became richer from what the other lost."[53] In the meantime, Wynsius, a secular priest of the cathedral, was converted to monasticism. He was sent to Ramsey to study, and subsequently returned as prior of the monastery. Ultimately, *all* of the clerks, although they had previously despised the monks, were converted to monasticism. In this manner, Eadmer says, the pontifical see was translated from St. Peter to the Blessed Virgin, and given from clerks to monks.

Eadmer's version can best be seen as a skillful blending of the Ramsey and Worcester traditions. Although Byrhtferth's *Life* of Oswald provides the basis of his work,[54] Eadmer enlarged upon this account by incorporating aspects of the foundation story as it was known at Worcester. Like Hemming, Eadmer maintains that the

---

[50] Eadmer, *Vita Sancti Oswaldi* in vol. 2 of *Historians of the Church of York*, ed. James Raine, Rolls Series 71, (London, 1886), 1–40. The *Vita* was written at the request of the Worcester monks, as Eadmer himself asserts (p. 59), probably at the request of his friend Nicholas, who became Worcester's prior in c. 1113. For this suggestion, see R. W. Southern, *Saint Anselm and his Biographer: A Study of Monastic Life and Thought, 1059–c.1130*, (Cambridge, 1963), 283, n. 2.

[51] Eadmer, *Vita*, 23.

[52] Ibid., 24.

[53] Ibid., 25.

[54] Robinson, "St. Oswald," 16.

monastery and the cathedral existed for a time side-by-side, until St. Mary's eclipsed the old church. Like Byrtferth, he records that Wynsius studied at Ramsey before being appointed prior of the new monastic foundation. Nevertheless, Eadmer agrees with the synod of 1092 in asserting that Wynsius served the cathedral as a secular priest prior to his conversion; that some time elapsed after his conversion before Oswald appointed him prior; that eventually the other priests of St. Peter converted to the monastic life; and that they did this without coercion. Like the earlier sources, he records neither direct conflict between the monks and the secular priests, nor sudden change. Eadmer's only significant addition to the story, in fact, corresponds with Coleman's modifications. Like Coleman, Eadmer paints a negative picture of the secular clergy, who are recalcitrant, hardening their hearts against Oswald's pleas for reform, and who initially "despised" the monks.[55]

Eadmer shared Coleman's devotion to the aims of the Gregorian reform movement and his distrust of the secular clergy. His commitment to the ideal of clerical celibacy is documented in several of his writings,[56] as is his belief that English monasticism was under attack.[57] Though not a monk of Worcester, Eadmer was a close friend of Prior Nicholas, and clearly deplored recent developments there; after Theulf's death in 1125, he wrote to Nicholas, urging that the monks unite to resist the "evil men" who "envied the monastic order," and plotted to remove it from all bishoprics.[58]

The Worcester Chronicle and its Abbreviation

While Coleman's *Vita Wulfstani* might hint that the secular clergy of the cathedral was replaced, the Worcester chronicle is the first source to explicitly state that the clerks were expelled, affirming that some of the secular priests of Worcester refused to convert and were forcibly removed. The annal for 969 records that King Edgar ordered

---

[55] Eadmer, *Vita*, 25.

[56] See, for example, his account of the Council of London of 1108 in his *Historia Novorum in Anglia*, ed. M. Rule, Rolls Series 81 (London, 1884), 193.

[57] For example, Eadmer records that bishop Walkelin attempted to replace the monks of Winchester with secular canons, a scheme that was thwarted by Lanfranc. He also describes how Lanfranc foiled a similar attack on the monks of Canterbury. See ibid., 18–19.

[58] Eadmer's letter has been printed in Bethell, "English Black Monks," 697–98; McIntyre, "Early-Twelfth-Century," 246–47; and Migne, *Patrologia Latina* 159, col. 807.

Dunstan, Oswald and Ethelwold to expel the clerks from the great monasteries of Mercia and settle monks in their place. In compliance with these orders, we are told, St. Oswald ejected the priests who refused to become monks, accepted the vows of the others, and appointed Wynsius, a monk of Ramsey, as prior.[59]

The early sections of the chronicle have traditionally been ascribed to a monk named Florence; however, it is possible that the entire chronicle was compiled by a monk named John, who is known to have composed the chronicle's "continuation."[60] Work on the chronicle could have begun at Worcester as early as c. 1087;[61] thus, the dating of this entry is crucial: does it represent an early version of the legend, which was replaced by the story of gradual change? or does it represent a departure from Worcester tradition? Paleographic evidence suggests the latter: although the chronicle was begun during the episcopacy of Wulfstan, it is clear that the account of the priory's foundation is a later addition to the main text. In the earliest extant manuscript of the chronicle, which dates from c.1108–1110,[62] the entry for 969 is a palimpsest: it is written in a small, cramped hand and even so cannot fit into the space provided, but spills over into the margin. The physical appearance of the annal suggests that the Worcester chronicler was dissatisfied with the account of his monastery's founda-

---

[59] Florence of Worcester, *Chronicon* 1: 141.

[60] For John's contribution to the chronicle, see R. R. Darlington, "Anglo-Norman Historians" (Inaugural Lecture: Birkbeck College, London University, 1947), 14–15; Darlington, *Vita*, x–xviii; R. W. Southern, "The Place of England in the Twelfth Century Renaissance," *History* 45 (1960): 209–10; Martin Brett, "John of Worcester and his Contemporaries," in *The Writing of History in the Middle Ages: Essays Presented to Richard William Southern*, ed. R. H. C. Davis and J. M. Wallace-Hadrill (Oxford, 1981); McIntyre, "Early-Twelfth-Century," 173–75; Antonia Gransden, *Historical Writing*, 143–44. A lesser role is ascribed to John by Valerie I. J. Flint, "The Date of the Chronicle of 'Florence' of Worcester," *Revue Bénédictine* 91 (1976): 115–19.

[61] The chronicle is based on that of Marianus Scottus, which Wulfstan probably acquired from his friend Robert of Hereford, and uses Robert's short continuation of Marianus in its description of the Domesday survey, which suggests that it was begun no earlier than c. 1087. See W. H. Stevenson, "A Contemporary Description of the Domesday Survey," *English Historical Review* 22 (1907): 72–84.

[62] For a date of c. 1108, see *The New Paleographic Society, Facsimiles of Ancient MSS*, ser. II, photographed and printed by H. Hart, F. Hall, and J. Johnson, (London, 1913–30), pl. 86–87. J. R. H. Weaver and Antonia Gransden suggest a date of 1110. See John of Worcester, *The Chronicle of John of Worcester 1118–1140*, ed. J. R. H. Weaver, vol. 13 of *Analecta Oxoniensia*, Medieval and Modern Series, (Oxford, 1908), 8; and Gransden, *Historical Writing*, 146. The earliest extant manuscript, Oxford, Bodleian Library MS. C. C. C. 157, is written in a uniform hand up to the entry for 1110.

tion contained in his source[63] and emended it.[64] It is clearly an early correction; it is written in the main text hand and was added to the manuscript before 1129, when it was copied by Simeon of Durham.[65]

The Worcester chronicler's story of the expulsion of the clergy represents a significant change in the priory's view of its origins, and it would be useful to know how and why that change was introduced. It seems most likely that the chronicler, having erased the original entry for 969, and faced with a limited amount of space in which to describe Worcester's conversion, either conflated Oswald's behavior with that of other tenth century reformers or combined several disparate events in Oswald's own career. It was well-known that the reformers of the tenth century had sometimes forcibly expelled the secular clergy of a church in order to install monks; the behavior of St. Ethelwold at the Old Minster is an especially striking example, one known to the Worcester chronicler.[66] Moreover, according to Eadmer, Oswald's attempt to reform Worcester cathedral by the gradual conversion of the priests was an exception to his usual method.[67] The Worcester chronicler, drawing on the same traditions as Eadmer, may have simply overlooked the fine distinctions between Oswald's behavior at Worcester and elsewhere.

In any case, the assertion that Oswald expelled the secular priests of Worcester was clearly acceptable—and accepted—by c.1131, when John compiled an abbreviated version of the chronicle in which the entry for 969 is given prominence. Many entries of the chronicle are drastically shortened or eliminated entirely in the *chronicula*; the account of Oswald's expulsion of the clerks, however, is written out in full, taking

---

[63] The chronicler's source was most probably a set of annals compiled at Ramsey. See Cyril Hart, "The Early Section of the *Worcester Chronicle*," *Journal of Medieval History* 9 (1983): 251–315. The entry for 969 bears the stamp of its Ramsey origins: nothing is said about Wynsige's early career as a secular priest at Worcester, nor is any mention made of his conversion and years of study before his appointment as prior; he is simply described, as in Byrtferth's life, as a monk of Ramsey.

[64] An alternate, though less likely, explanation for the appearance of the annal is that the scribe may have entered the years first, leaving space for the annals, and miscalculated the amount of space needed for these two entries. See Hart, "The Early Section," 255.

[65] For Simeon's use of the Worcester chronicle, see Brett, "John of Worcester," 119–22.

[66] Florence of Worcester, *Chronicon*, 1: 140.

[67] According to Eadmer, Oswald "established the discipline of the Rule in seven monasteries in his diocese" by ejecting the wealthy clerks, who were consorting with women. See Eadmer, *Vita*, 20.

up 10 of the 28 lines on folio 72v. To emphasize its importance, John, who was scribe as well as author, wrote the entire entry in red.[68]

Although the interests of the chronicler are hard to discern in the early sections of the chronicle,[69] it is clear that John, like Coleman and Eadmer, was committed to the ideals of the Gregorian reform movement, especially clerical celibacy. The chronicle includes the canons of three synods which address the issue of clerical celibacy,[70] and a cautionary tale, added in a margin, illustrates the potentially terrifying results of clerical unchastity.[71] Moreover, although no negative comments about the new Norman bishops are recorded in the chronicle, the unflattering epitaph on Theulf, mentioned above, was written in John's hand.

The *Altitonantis* Charter

The last Worcester account of the priory's foundation can be found in the *Altitonantis* charter,[72] which suggests that Oswald forcibly expelled the secular clerks from Worcester cathedral in 963–964 in order to install a monastic community. The *Altitonantis* charter purports to be a grant by King Edgar to the monks of the newly established priory at Worcester. In it, Edgar gives a wide variety of rights to the monks who have replaced "the filth and lasciviousness of the clerks" (*clericorum neniis et spurcis lasciuiis*); in the future, he continues, those clerks shall have no rights there, "at least those who choose, to the peril of their holy orders and at the cost of their ecclesi-

---

[68] Dublin, Trinity College, MS. 503, fol. 72v. For an identification of this hand as John's see Weaver, *Analecta*, 5–7, and McIntyre, "Early-Twelfth-Century," 105.

[69] For example, the chronicle records Aelfere's attacks on the monasteries of Mercia after Edgar's death, and contains details not found in the Anglo-Saxon chronicle, including the fact that the monks were replaced by clerks and their wives. Unfortunately, the disappearance of the annals upon which the early section of the chronicle is based makes it impossible to determine definitively if this addition reflects the interests of the Worcester chronicler or his source.

[70] Florence of Worcester, *Chronicon*, 1: 57–59 (s.a. 1108); Weaver, *Analecta*, 20–22 (s.a. 1125) and 24–25 (s.a. 1127). The canons of the synod of 1108, taken from Eadmer's *Historia Novorum*, are added in the margin of Oxford, Bodleian Library MS. C. C. C. 157, p. 367; however, Thorpe prints them as part of the text.

[71] Oxford, Bodleian Library MS. C. C. C. 157, p. 337. It deals with the fate of a priest who, having slept with his wife the previous night nevertheless dared to celebrate mass the next day. The consecrated wine, we are told, turned pitch black, and tasted exceedingly bitter. Frightened by the event, the priest rode to the bishop's palace, confessed his sin, and swore to live a chaste life in the future.

[72] Listed in Sawyer, *Anglo-Saxon Charters*, no. 731.

astical benefices, to remain with their wives rather than serve God in a chaste and canonical manner."[73]

The dubious nature of this charter has been noted and discussed by several scholars; no one accepts it as authentic in its current form, although the extent to which it embodies material contained in a hypothetical authentic charter has been hotly debated.[74] The fact that this charter does not appear in Hemming's cartulary is, however, very suggestive, since Hemming's explicit assignment had been to gather and record charters for estates pertaining *ad victum monachorum*.[75] It seems most likely that in its current form the charter dates from c. 1125–1136; the earliest extant copy has "pseudo-antique" features, clearly designed to make it pass as a tenth century original, but the hand is datable to the reign of King Stephen.[76]

The circumstances under which this charter was put together are easy to discern. The *Altitonantis* charter confirms the monks' rights to several estates which were owned by the cathedral chapter before its conversion to monasticism. It also lists the manors belonging to the monks in Oswaldslaw and supports the monks' claims to a third of the profits from that triple hundred, as well as extensive jurisdictional rights. There is no evidence that the monks had historically possessed these rights. What *is* certain is that the relationship between the bishop and the monastic chapter had deteriorated rapidly during the episcopate of Simon (1125–1150), primarily as a result of disputes over their respective rights to the incomes from several of Worcester's estates. Ultimately, King Stephen confirmed the monks' rights—the same rights outlined in the *Altitonantis* charter—in c.1136–1139;[77] Simon granted the priory a general charter of confirmation in 1149 which recognized the monks' rights in Oswaldslaw.[78] It seems likely, then, that the *Altitonantis* charter was produced in order to induce Simon—and ultimately King Steven—to recognize the monks' claim to the disputed estates.

In this last picture of Worcester's early history, set in the times of the great monastic reformers, we can see the culmination of the evolution of the story of Worcester's foundation. The secular priests of

---

[73] Darlington, *Cartulary*, 4.

[74] Eric John argues for the charter's substantial authenticity in "An Alleged Charter". His conclusions have been challenged in detail by Darlington, *Cartulary*, xiii–xix.

[75] Hemming, *Chartularium*, 2:286.

[76] For this argument, see Darlington, *Cartulary*, xvi.

[77] Ibid., xvi.

[78] Ibid., xxii–xxiii; and no. 73.

Worcester are vilified much more extensively than in earlier accounts, accused by Edgar himself of living evil lives. The transformation of Worcester from a secular to a monastic institution is dramatic, as the clerks are expelled from the see, and their lands are given to the monks. Finally, the issue of clerical celibacy is brought for the first time into the story of the priory's foundation; the priests' licentiousness is contrasted with the monks' celibacy, and the sudden expulsion of the priests is justified in terms of their lack of chastity. Thus, the *Altitonantis* charter pulls together the various strands of the legend of the priory's foundation as told in the Worcester sources. It should be noted, moreover, that the story preserved in the records of the synod of 1092—that the secular priests converted and surrendered their property to the priory—would have served the specific purposes of Simon's monks just as well as *Altitonantis'* account of their expulsion. We can only conclude that the story of the priory's foundation preserved in the *Altitonantis* charter reflects the beliefs of the priory by the third decade of the 12th century.

Reviewing the various accounts of Worcester's foundation, a clear pattern emerges. The only version that can be dated unequivocally to Wulfstan's episcopate—the synod of 1092—implies a gradual and voluntary conversion of the secular community; there is no hint of any conflict between secular and regular clergy. Hemming's account, which could have been written during either Wulfstan's or Samson's rule, also suggests that change was gradual. However, the sources which date from the reigns of the Worcester's Anglo-Norman prelates—the *Vita Wulfstani*, the entry for 969 in the Worcester chronicle and its abbreviation, and Eadmer's *Life of Oswald*—tell a rather different story. In these sources, the secular priests are described in negative terms; they resist reform, and, in the chronicle's version, are consequently expelled. Finally, the *Altitonantis* charter represents the culmination of this trend, uniting hostility towards the secular clergy and the story of their expulsion with the issue of clerical celibacy.

William of Malmesbury and the Legend of Oswald's 'Holy Guile'

Outside the stream of Worcester tradition is William of Malmesbury's account of the priory's foundation in his *Vita Sancti Dunstani*, written between 1135–1143.[79] William based his narrative on Eadmer

---

[79] William of Malmesbury's account of Oswald's reform of Worcester cathedral is found in his *Vita Sancti Dunstani*, 303–305. For the date, see Gransden, *Historical Writing*, 168.

and adds nothing new to the story except a fateful turn of phrase; Oswald, he says, converted the secular priests through "holy guile" (*sancto ingenio*). These two words are troublesome: perhaps the story of Worcester's gradual transformation is only a "pious legend"[80] designed to extol Oswald's holiness. Such a conclusion, while understandable, is anachronistic. The evolving legend of the conversion of Worcester cathedral priory *does* incorporate a "pious legend," but that legend is *not* the story of Oswald's holy guile. The version of Worcester's transformation that is a "figment of pious twelfth-century imaginations"[81] is the story of Oswald's forcible ejection of the secular priests.

That expelling the secular priests from the cathedral would have been seen as holy by the monks of Worcester is supported by Coleman's account of a similar action on the part of Wulfstan in the *Vita Wulfstani*. According to Coleman, Wulfstan, who had himself resisted various assaults on his chastity, was a great champion of clerical celibacy, and ordered wedded priests to choose between their "carnal desires" and their churches. A few, "the better ones, who were ruled by reason" left their "illicit unions," and were allowed to retain their benefices.[82] We do not learn the fate of their wives. Those who chose to remain with their families were driven from their churches in disgrace (*cum iniuria*), and Coleman has no sympathy for them: some, he says, wandered about till they starved; others sought and finally found some other benefice. To avoid such a scandal in the future, Coleman concludes, Wulfstan refused to ordain anyone who would not swear to lead a celibate life.[83] For Coleman, and presumably for his brothers, the "scandal" of the episode lay not in the treatment of the priests, forced to choose between starvation and deserting the women and children dependent on them, but rather in the fact of their marriage in the first place.

If we take Coleman's account at face value, Wulfstan can be seen as an ardent supporter of Lanfranc's reforms. Indeed, he might be accused of excessive enthusiasm. During Wulfstan's pontificate, the decrees of the Council of Winchester of 1076 prohibited priests from taking wives; no action was to be taken, however, against parish clergy who were already married.[84] In forcing married priests to abandon

---

[80] See, for example, Eric John, "St. Oswald," 239, n. 2.

[81] Ibid.

[82] Darlington, *Vita*, 53.

[83] Ibid., 53–54.

[84] Canon 1, Council of Winchester, 1076, in *Councils and Synods, with Other Documents Relating to the English Church*, vol. 1: A.D. 871–1204, ed. D. Whitelock, M.

their wives, then, Wulfstan would have exceeded the reform measures set forth by Lanfranc himself, as several historians have pointed out.[85]

The ruthlessness with which Wulfstan imposed celibacy on the secular priests of his diocese appears, as his most recent biographer has noted, to be somewhat out of character.[86] It would seem, however, that what the *Vita* records is actually Coleman's fervor rather than the bishop's. One of Wulfstan's chaplains was a secular priest with the unusual name of Fritheric.[87] His name disappears after 1116; however, during Bishop Simon's reign, we find charters witnessed by a chaplain named John fitz-Fritheric.[88] The name is unusual enough to suggest that John was the son of Wulfstan's chaplain.[89] If this is in fact the case, Wulfstan apparently tolerated marriage among the secular clergy of his own household, even favoring one priest so encumbered. Such tolerance would more easily conform to Wulfstan's usual behavior, as described in the *Vita* and other contemporary sources, and is understandable in light of the fact that Wulfstan's father, Athelstan, was himself a priest.[90] On the other hand, Coleman's hostility

---

Brett, and C. N. L. Brooke, (Oxford, 1981), 619.

[85] See, for example, Darlington, *Vita*, xxxiv, Brooke, "Gregorian Reform," 11, and Mason, *St. Wulfstan*, 163. John Godfrey, *The Church in Anglo-Saxon England* (Cambridge, 1962), 491, n. 16, notes that Wulfstan's treatment of married clergy was much harsher than that of his early eleventh century namesake.

[86] Mason, *St. Wulfstan*, 163. Nevertheless, Mason assumes that both the *Vita*'s description of Wulfstan's attitude towards celibacy and its account of his treatment of the married clergy of his diocese are essentially correct. See *St. Wulfstan*, 38–41, 62–64, 163. For a similar assessment of Wulfstan's stand on clerical celibacy, see Anne Llewellyn Barstow, *Married Priests and the Reforming Papacy: The Eleventh-Century Debates*, vol. 12 of *Texts and Studies in Religion*, (New York, 1982), 87, 143.

[87] He witnessed several important charters, was present at the synod of 1092, and served the church of St. Helen's, a valuable and powerful church which exerted jurisdiction over 11 chapels in the area around the city. See Nigel Baker, "The Urban Churches of Worcester—a survey," in *Medieval Worcester: An Archaeological Framework*, ed. M. O. H. Carver, Transactions of the Worcestershire Archaeological Society, 3d series, vol. 7 (1980), 116. For Fritheric's career, see also McIntyre, "Early-Twelfth-Century," 161–63.

[88] John fitz-Fritheric witnessed several of Bishop Simon's charters; see Darlington, *Cartulary*, nos. 73, 144, 190. An original charter listing John fitz-Fritheric as witness can be found in PRO E 329/107 [1146–9]).

[89] For this suggestion, see McIntyre, "Early-Twelfth-Century," 161.

[90] Athelstan is described as "Athelstan, priest, the father of Bishop Wulfstan" in the obit list attached to Wulfstan's homiliary, printed on p. 30 of Atkins, "The Church of Worcester." It is not clear whether Athelstan was a priest at the time of his marriage; Wulfstan's mother and father both had late callings to the religious life, and Athelstan may have been ordained after this conversion, which occurred sometime before Wulfstan himself became a monk (Darlington, *Vita*, 7). Mason, however, argues that Athelstan was a priest at the time of his marriage (*St. Wulfstan*, 30–33).

towards the secular clergy is demonstrated throughout the *Vita*. Moreover, the *Vita Wulfstani* may have been written after harsher measures against married clergy had been promulgated by Anselm at the Council of Westminster in 1102, at which time married clergy *were* required to dismiss their wives.[91] If this is the case, Coleman's description was designed to bring Wulfstan's actions into line with current policy, thus enhancing his status. In any case, it is clear that Wulfstan's harsh treatment of the secular clergy, whether exaggerated or not, was thought by Coleman to be entirely appropriate behavior for a saint. Likewise, Oswald's toleration of the secular clergy as reflected in the earliest versions of the story of the priory's foundation must have seemed increasingly inappropriate to the Worcester monks who were struggling with both their new secular bishops and with the issues raised by the Gregorian reform movement. As the story was told and retold in the early twelfth century, the "pious legend" of Oswald's expulsion of the secular clergy gradually took form.

A number of important conclusions can be drawn from an analysis of the legends surrounding the foundation of Worcester cathedral priory. In the absence of primary sources from the period, the method by which Oswald transformed the secular chapter of Worcester cathedral into a monastic body cannot be ascertained with absolute certainty; having said this, however, there is little doubt that the description of this event found in the records of the synod of 1092— that Oswald gradually persuaded the cathedral clergy to convert to monasticism—is most credible. It is the earliest written account of the cathedral's conversion and clearly represents the received oral tradition at Worcester in the last decade of the eleventh century. It is supported by Hemming's description of the construction of the original St. Mary's during Oswald's pontificate, and there is nothing in the evidence that can be drawn from the witness lists of Oswald's charters and leases that would contradict it.

More important, however, than a clearer idea of what happened at Worcester during Oswald's pontificate is what an analysis of the sources tells us about the twelfth century monastic community. The legend of the foundation of Worcester cathedral priory changed dramatically in the period from 1092 to c.1140. The changes introduced into the narrative reflect, first of all, the growing hostility between the monks of Worcester and their new Anglo-Norman bishops. The transformation of the legend also coincides with the

---

[91] See Canon 5 of the Council of Westminster, 1102, in *Councils and Synods*, ed. Whitelock, Brett, and Brooke, 675.

controversy engendered by the Gregorian reform movement about the roles of secular priests and monks in society, and the debate over the value of their respective ways of life.

The history of the cathedral's conversion was more than just "history" to the monks of Worcester priory; it also served an important social function. The monks of the early twelfth century clearly looked to their past to legitimize their beliefs and reaffirm their sense of identity in a period of controversy. The continuing impact of oral tradition on written history in this period ensured that the past as they reconstructed it proved flexible enough to accomodate their changing needs. Thus, a study of the evolving legend of the foundation of Worcester cathedral priory serves several purposes: it provides a clearer picture of what *did* happen at Worcester in the tenth century; it elucidates the hopes and fears of the monks of Worcester cathedral priory in the early twelfth century by revealing what the monks wanted to *believe* had happened; and it demonstrates the persistence of "oral" ways of thought in a culture increasingly dominated by writing.

NANCY FREEMAN REGALADO

Speaking in Script: The Construction of Voice, Presence, and Perspective in Villon's *Testament*[1]

The poetry of François Villon, who wrote in Paris in the third quarter of the fifteenth century, lies at the far end of the shift from oral to written transmission of lyric poetry in the Middle Ages: past the efforts to achieve a written representation of oral performance in the thirteenth-century French chansonniers; past the separation of verbal poetry from music in the fourteenth century and the accompanying reshaping of lyric into the fixed-form genres of ballade and rondeau; past the artful books where Machaut, Froissart, and Christine de Pizan inscribed their lyrics for princely patrons.[2] Villon's poetry falls within the period where the last genre of the oral performance tradition—the theater—is fully incorporated into writing. New questions essential to our understanding of orality in the Middle

[1] I am grateful to Alice Deakins and Mariana Regalado for their helpful comments on linguistic aspects of this paper and to the American Council of Learned Societies and the National Endowment for the Humanities for fellowship support of my research on Villon's poetry.
[2] Nancy Freeman Regalado, "Gathering the Works: The Intergeneric Passage of the Medieval Lyric into Written Collections," forthcoming in *L'Esprit Créateur*, Special Number, ed. Donald Maddox and Sara Sturm-Maddox.

Ages arise out of this great tide of writing that engulfs works that had been composed, transmitted, and received by voice, memory, and oral re-creation. Writing eventually works profound changes upon oral syntactic and discursive practices,[3] upon the social and creative roles of performers and performance, and upon strongly codified forms such as the epic and lyric songs which had characterized literature within the discursive systems of orality. Sound yields increasingly to sight, to mimetic representations of orality and to the "virtual possibility of voicing" retained within the phonetic signs of our Western writing.[4] What, however, becomes of sound itself? What is the lyric status of sounds spoken and heard and of the quality of voice of an individual speaker within a poetry now conceived, transmitted, and preserved within writing? How can a poet speak in script?

Fifteenth-century French poets respond eagerly to this puzzle by exploring the re-creation and written representation of sound, speech, and speaker in their verse. The *grands rhétoriqueurs*, professional poets of the late medieval French and Burgundian courts, seek to exploit dimensions of the sounds displayed in their written texts. They experiment with rhyme, puns, and homonyms, with repetition, reversal, and rebus; they arrange their words orally and visually through alliteration, acrostics, and anagrams—often sacrificing meaning to written constructions of sound play. Sound, shown as phonetic signs and musical syllables, is inseparable from sight in poems such as Molinet's jolly "Recommendation à Jehan de Ranchicourt," whose first stanza rhymes on the tones of the scale (rech*ut*—conch*ut*—ador*é*—dor*é*—dem*y*—de *my*, etc.), recapitulated backwards and forwards in both the initial syllables and also in the last line of the second stanza, which rhymes on the syllables of the names of addressee and poet (Ran—chi—court—Mol—li—net) and ends with the diminutive of the poet's first name, "Jennet."[5]

---

[3] Suzanne Fleischman, "Philology, Linguistics, and the Discourse of the Medieval Text," *Speculum* 65 (1990): 19–37; Walter J. Ong, *Orality and Literacy: The Technologizing of the Word*, New Accents (London and New York: Methuen, 1982; repr., 1983).

[4] Michel Beaujour, "Phonograms and Delivery: The Poetics of Voice," *Notebooks in Cultural Analysis* 3 (1986): 270, and his "'Ils ne savent pas ce qu'ils font.' L'éthnopoétique et la méconnaissance des 'arts poétiques' des sociétés sans écriture," *L'Homme* 111–112, (June–December 1989): XXIX (3–4), 208–21. I am indebted to Michel Beaujour for his comments on a draft of this study and for pointing out how different the conventions of speech use within orality are from the device of represented everyday speech which he sees as "post-oral" and paradoxically linked to writing or limited to certain genres such as comedy and satire.

[5] Jean Molinet, *Les faictz et dictz*, ed. Noël Dupire, 3 vols. (Paris: Société des Anciens Textes Français, 1936–39), 2:804–805.

Mille gaurriers chanteront par b⟶ Mol
Mi, la, s'on pille, il y fait doulx et⟶ Mol

Requerons Dieu que le bon temps jo⟶ li
Reviengne brief et amaine anco⟶ li

Utile paix, se chanterons tout⟶ net!
Ut, ré, my, fa, sol, la, vive Jen⟶ net!

A thousand joyful fellows will sing in B-flat
If there's pillaging somewhere, here things are soft
   and easy
Let's pray God that the good times of pleasure
Come back soon and bring columbine
Profitable peace, so we all will sing well
Ut, re, mi, fa, sol, la, hooray for little Jean!

By means of such word play the *rhétoriqueurs* give complex rhymes and written representation of sound signs a preeminent place.[6] They do not, however, incorporate other dimensions of orality such as represented speech.

Speech is words spoken with all the paraverbal elements of intonation, pause, pace, and other qualities of voice, words sounded by a speaker present in a situation of utterance. When the verbal element of speech is represented or exploited in the context of orality, it is often profoundly stylized by highly codified formal structures, which are very unlike the casual organization of familiar talk, and by artifices of intonation, diction, and dialect.[7] Fifteenth-century writers show little interest, however, in re-creation or preservation of the archaic, stylized forms of oral poetry: they derhyme the old epics; they insert elegant ballades and rondeaux rather than rustic, old-fashioned *chansons de toile* and *caroles* into their larger poetic compositions.[8] But as writing increasingly encloses speech, many fifteenth-century authors take great delight in naturalistic representations of colloquial speech; they use represented speech to great effect in characterization. Stories such as the *Cent Nouvelles Nouvelles* are cast in lively direct and in direct discourse; ballades are written in dialogue, dialect, and thieves' slang. Theatrical dialogue plays with foreign accents, with

---

[6] François Rigolot, "1493—The Rhétoriqueurs," in *A New History of French Literature,* ed. Denis Hollier (Cambridge: Harvard Univ. Press, 1989), 127–33.

[7] Ong, 36, speaks of "heavy patterning and communal fixed formulas."

[8] Regalado, "Gathering."

popular songs, with the stylized patter of fools, quacks, and con men, as well as with the bumpy irregularities of domestic chatter and cursing.

It is Villon's poetry, however, that achieves one of the most sustained and believable representations of ordinary speech by an individual speaker in medieval French literature. Villon's *Testament* maintains the fiction of speech and speaker at every point while it accounts for the written record in the reader's hand, for it depicts a speaker dictating a will, an event that requires that a person speak simultaneously and coextensively with an act of writing. Thus fictionalized speaking and writing coincide throughout the poem. Moreover, together with the will-making, the *Testament* continuously represents the speaker's thoughts and comments about what he says in his will. The poem is thus filled with what Goffman calls changes in "footing," shifts of frame, tone, and stance that are "a persistent feature of natural talk."[9] Two examples will show how these shifts of topic and meaning are carried by a poetic language that constructs oral qualities of voice, presence, and perspective in writing and brings them into prominence in the *Testament*.

The first example, H. 137 (lines 1354–61) is one of a string of eight-line *huitains* or stanzas that carry the thematic burden of the ficticious will in the *Testament*. This *huitain* shows how Villon represents essential features of what Ong calls primary orality—sound, speech, and speaker. He does so by multiplying prosodic, lexical, syntactic, and even phonetic features typical of ordinary familiar speech,[10] by attributing that speech to a speaker, and by portraying that speaker in a vividly realistic setting.[11]

H.137	Item, a Thibault de la Garde ...	1354
	Thibault? je mens: il a nom Jehan,	
	Que lui donrai ge que ne perde?	
	— Assez j'ay perdu tout cest an,	
	Dieu y vueille pourvoir, amen! —	1358
	Le *Barillet*? Par m'ame, voire,	

---

[9] Erving Goffman, *Forms of Talk*, Univ. of Pennsylvania Publications in Conduct and Communication (Philadelphia: Univ. of Pennsylvania Press, 1981), 128.

[10] André Rigault, ed., *La grammaire du français parlé* (Paris: Hachette, 1971); Aurélien Sauvageot, *Analyse du français parlé* (Paris: Hachette, 1972).

[11] Paul Zumthor cites other "indices of orality"—musical notation, allusions to hearing, singing, saying and to genres such as "song" and "*dit*" (literally "spoken," a medieval generic term referring to non-musical, first-person verse compositions) in *La lettre et la voix: De la "littérature" médiévale*, Collection Poétique (Paris: Seuil, 1987), 37–46.

> Genevoys est plus ancïen
> Et plus beau nez a pour y boire.

H.137 *Item* to Thibault de la Garde ...   1354
     Thibault? I'm kidding, his name is Jean
     What should I give that I won't miss
     I've already lost enough this year
     May God make it up to me, amen   1358
     "The Wine Keg" of course that's it
     Though Genevois being older
     Has the brighter nose for drinking there.[12]

This stanza, like the whole of the *Testament*, is cast in first-person discourse, which characterizes the utterance of an individual speaker and the representation of speech. The speaker's presence in the poem is emphasized, moreover, by the reiterated pronoun "I"—"je mens"; "Que lui donrai ge que ne perde?"; "Assez j'ay perdu"—and the related possessive adjective in the expression "par m'ame" (literally, "upon my soul"). The fiction of the speaker's presence is given additional prominence by references to his situation or spatio-temporal context of utterance, defined here by a single mark of temporal deixis, "tout cest an." Deixis refers to those elements of language that code the speaker's presence and point of view in his speaking—"I, here, now"—and that define his universe of discourse; deixis is fundamental to the representation of familiar speech and to full characterization of the speaker in the *Testament*.[13] Embedded within represented speech, the historical proper names in Villon's poem are taken to be those of contemporaries peopling the speaker's world: "Thibault / Jehan de la Garde," is identified with Jean de la Garde, a rich spice merchant; "Genevoys" with Pierre Genevoys, prosecutor at the Châtelet, the criminal court of Paris; "Le *Barillet*," with a tavern near the Châtelet.[14] Even the Latin term *item* serves the ongoing fiction of presence by representing the speaker within a well-defined situation of

---

[12] Citations from Jean Rychner and Albert Henry, eds., *Le Testament Villon*, 2 vols., Textes Littéraire Français 207 and 208 (Genève: Droz, 1974) and from Galway Kinnell, trans., *The Poems of François Villon*, new ed. (Hanover and London: Univ. Press of New England, 1977).

[13] Nancy Freeman Regalado, *"En l'an de mon trentiesme aage"*: Date, Deixis and Moral Vision in Villon's *Testament*," in *Le nombre du temps. En hommage à Paul Zumthor*, ed. Emmanuèle Baugartner et al. (Paris: Champion, 1988), 237–46.

[14] Jean Dufournet, *Recherches sur "Le Testament" de François Villon*, 2nd ed., 2 vols. (Paris: SEDES, 1973), 2:453–59; Pierre Champion, *François Villon: Sa vie et son temps*, 2 vols., Bibliothèque du XVe siècle 20–21 (Paris: Champion, 1913), 1:75.

utterance that could be called "dictating my last Will and Testament."

In his poem, Villon enhances the realistic representation of presence of an individual speaker by incorporating many linguistic features of informal everyday talk. In H. 137, for example, he draws on features commonly used in conventional literary representations of informal speech in fifteenth-century genres such as comic dialogues and dramatic monologues: topics from the world of experience such as money, taverns, people; homely colloquial expressions such as "et plus beau nez a pour y boire" (cf. "a real nose for the bottle"); interjections that emphasize the speaker's opinion through numerous tagged-on phrases: "je mens; amen! Par m'ame, voire." Hesitations and reflexive self-corrections such as those in the first two lines (Thibault or Jehan?) are common in unplanned talk; they are also related to the rhetorical figure of *correctio*, a staple of medieval dramatic monologues where it is used with comic effect by characters such as the braggart soldier in *Le Franc Archier de Baignollet*[15]: "... nous apaisames / Noz couraiges et recullames / (Que dy je? nom pas reculer / — Chose dont on [ne] doybve parler —)" ("... we quelled our military ardor and retreated [What am I saying? not retreat—mustn't talk about that—]") (lines 94–97). In Villon's poetry as in the medieval farce, these topics, expressions, interjections, and hesitations create an effect of energetic, spontaneous talk.

Moreover, in H. 137 as throughout the *Testament*, Villon incorporates other features characteristic of real unplanned talk that are far less common in medieval representations of informal speech. These are ellipsis, fragmentation, asides, unexpected interruptions and digression[16]—all that makes the *Testament*'s flow unpredictable, ambiguous, and remarkably difficult to learn by heart. Thus in the second line of the stanza, the speaker corrects the name he stated in the first; in the third line he ruminates on how he will complete the legacy sentence begun in the first two: "Que lui donrai ge que ne perde?" In the fourth he comments on the word *perde* from the third line: "—Assez j'ay perdu tout cest an." Prayerful interjections concerning these losses are added in the fifth line : "Dieu y vueille pourvoir, amen!—" Finally the elliptical phrase "Le *Barillet*?" com-

---

[15] *Le Franc Archier de Baignollet*, ed. Lucie Polak, Textes Littéraires Français 129 (Genève: Droz, and Paris: Minard, 1966).

[16] Pierre Demarolle, "Réflexions préliminaires à une tentative de description de la syntaxe de Villon dans le *Testament*," in *Etudes de syntaxe du moyen français. Colloque organisé par le Centre d'Analyse Syntaxique de l'Université de Metz et par le Centre de Recherche pour un Trésor de la Langue Française (CNRS Nancy)*, ed. Robert Martin, Recherches linquistiques 4 (Paris: Klincksieck, 1978), 23–31; Rigault, 137–47.

pletes the sentence undertaken in the first, only to be followed by two and a half lines of afterthoughts or second thoughts: "Par m'ame, voire, / Genevoys est plus ancïen / Et plus beau nez a pour y boire." Instead of progressing forward, the syntactic line thus shifts step by step away from its initial topic, swoops back, then slips away again.

While we *moderni*—readers of Joyce and Beckett—are quite accustomed to such syntactic disruption and embedding, it is most unusual in medieval French literature. Even the bizarre associations of objects and actions found in the medieval French nonsense poems—the *fatrasie* and *resverie*—are laid out within complete and comprehensible syntactic structures. The obscurely allusive patter of the fifteenth-century dramatic *sottie* or fool's play maintains a smooth syntactic line even when it overflows into enumeration or when its verses are split up and batted back and forth between two characters.[17] Villon's fragmented discursive line enhances his representation of speech and of the speaker. By showing his speaker thinking aloud as he speaks—muttering comments, reactions, asides as he dictates his will—Villon effectively doubles the lines of speech. He thus floods the legal fiction with a powerful and convincing effect of talk about and around the will that dramatizes the speaker's presence, bringing him to the foreground.

These complex syntactic manipulations implant yet another element of orality into the poem, for they make readers physically experience sound and speech as they read by inscribing a need for sound to make sense of the silent written text. The manuscript versions and the first printed edition of the *Testament* (1489) were written virtually without punctuation except for capital letters, in accordance with the usual practice for French poems of the fifteenth century,[18]

---

[17] Jean-Claude Aubailly, *Le monologue, le dialogue et la sottie*, Bibliothèque du XVe siècle 41 (Paris: Champion, 1984), 392–405.

[18] Christiane Marchello-Nizia, "Ponctuation et 'unités de lecture' dans les manuscrits médiévaux ou: je ponctue, tu lis, il théorise," *Grammaires du texte médiéval, Langue Française* 40 (December 1978): 32–44; Jean Vezin, "La ponctuation aux XIIIe, XIVe et XVe siècles," in Henri-Jean Martin and Jean Vezin, *Mise en page et mise en texte du livre manuscrit* (n.p., Cercle de la Librairie-Promodis, 1990), 443–45, and M. B. Parkes, *Pause and Effect: An Introduction to the History of Punctuation in the West* (Aldershot: Scolar Press, 1992), 41–49. Villon emphasizes prosody rather than syntax in punctuating his autograph ballade in Paris, BN MS. Fr. 25458, pp. 163–64, for he places an emphatic period at each caesura to emphasize the paradoxical themes of his *Ballade of Contradictions*: "Je meurs de seuf . aupres de la fontaine" ("I die of thirst . beside the fountain"), ed. Jean Rychner and Albert Henry, *Le Lais Villon et les poèmes variés*, 2 vols. Textes Littéraires français 239–40 (Genève: Droz, 1977), 1:46–47; see Nancy Freeman Regalado, "*En ce saint livre*: La Mise en page et identité lyrique dans les poèmes autographes de Villon dans l'album de Blois" (BN Ms. fr. 25458), in *L'Hotellerie de pensée: Mélanges Daniel Poirion*, ed. Michel Zink,

as can be seen in a diplomatic transcription of H. 137 in Paris, BN MS. Fr. 20041, fol. 139:

> Item A thibault delagarde
> Thibault Ie men Il a nom Iehan
> Q[ue] lui donraige que ne perde
> Assez Iay perdu tout cest an
> Dieu y vueil pouruoir amen
> Le barillet p[ar] mame voire
> Genevoys est plus ancien
> Et plus beau nez a pour y boire[19]

Unpunctuated (except for capital letters) and devoid of subordinating conjunctions, the arrangement of these words in the manuscript compels readers to add oral, prosodic contours of pause and intonation (for themselves, if not out loud) in order to articulate syntactic connection and to make sense of these elliptical, loosely juxtaposed sentences, questions, and subordinated asides. When the poet Clément Marot re-edited Villon's *Testament* in 1533, he incorporated some of the newly established signs of punctuation that represent these prosodic elements visually, although in marginal notes he drew attention to the sounds of the words as well:

> Item a Thibault de la garde
> Thibault? Ie'ments, il a nom Iehan
> Que luy donray ie, que ne perde?
> (Assez ay perdu tout cest an   Le parisi
> Dieu le vueille pouruoir, Amen)   en dit par
> Le barrilet? par m'ame voyre   de, & non
> Geneuoys est plus ancien   perde.
> Et a plus grand nez pour y boire.[20]

Danielle Régnier-Bohler et al. (Paris: Presses de L'Univ. de Paris-Sorbonne, forthcoming).

[19] My transcription from Alfred Jeanroy and Eugénie Droz, eds., *Deux manuscrits de François Villon (Bibliothèque Nationale 1661 et 20041) reproduits en phototypie, avec une notice sur les manuscrits du poète*, Documents Artistiques du Quinzième Siècle 6 (Paris: Droz, 1932); Rika Van Deyck and Romana Zwaenepoel, eds., *François Villon Oeuvres d'après le manuscrit Coislin* [Paris BN MS. Fr. 20041], 2 vols., Textes et Traitement Automatique 2 (Saint-Aquilin-De-Pacy [Eure]: Mallier, 1974), 1:100–101.

[20] Marginal gloss: "The Parisian says *parde*, and not *perde*" (my translation). *Les Oeuvres de Françoys Villon de Paris, reueues & remises en leur entier par Clement Marot valet de chambre du Roy* (Paris: Galiot du Pré, 1533). I have here transcribed the text from the Marot's edition printed by François Juste in Lyon in 1537 (New York, Morgan Library PML 1077). See Regalado, "Gathering."

Such written punctuation as the comma and the question mark facilitated private, silent reading. Most important for Villon's poem was the parenthesis (which Paul Saenger has called the most original contribution of humanist scribes),[21] for it permitted inscription of *arrière-pensées*, thoughts behind thoughts. Villon's scrupulous editors Jean Rychner and Albert Henry have punctuated the poem very heavily, marking the end of almost every line, defining and setting off every syntactic break. While such punctuation marks explore, articulate, and resolve for the readers' eye all the prosodic movements the poet suggested by his words, they reduce our interest in sounding out the text for ourselves. A meaning is made visible, but the dynamic process of discovery of meaning through sound is short-circuited. In contrast with these punctuated versions, the fifteenth-century manuscript and early printed versions of the *Testament* lead readers to add effects of oral prosody. These added prosodic elements, moreover, are not optional, aesthetic ornaments of performance but prosodic acts readers must carry out to complete the meaning of the words on the page. They are required by the words themselves and must be actualized (by intonation or punctuation) no matter how the *Testament* is used, whether read aloud, memorized for performance, or perused by readers of a courtly anthology manuscript or a printed edition. The syntactic incompleteness or ambiguity of represented colloquial speech in Villon's poem thus re-creates a discursive situation of orality by requiring readers to sound the poem, to put an ear close to the words, to hear their pulse, to feel their breath, and to say them silently or aloud, to re-sound the marks on the page in order to comprehend them.

The reader's attention is repeatedly drawn to represented speech because the poet brings to the fore the contrast between the diction and prosody of familiar talk and the formal language of will-making. This dynamic opposition between represented ordinary speech and stylized discursive structures informs the overall composition of Villon's poem. The *Testament* is shaped as a compilation in which nineteen fixed-form ballades and rondeaux are set into a chain of muttering, ruminating, chatty *huitains*, as can be seen in the second example demonstrating Villon's construction of voice: the *Ballade en erre*, "Faulse beaulté" (*Ballade in R*, "False Beauty") which follows H. 92–93:

---

[21] "Silent Reading: Its Impact on Late Medieval Script and Society," *Viator* 13 (1982): 410.

H.92 Ce non obstant, pour m'acquicter   926
Envers Amours plus qu'envers elle
— Car oncques n'y peulz acquester
D'espoir une seule estincelle:
Je ne sçay s'a tous si rebelle   930
A esté, ce m'est grant esmoy,
Mais, par saincte Marie la belle,
Je n'y voy que rire pour moy —,

H.93 Ceste ballade luy envoye,   934
Qui se termine tout par erre.
Qui luy portera? Que je voye ...
Ce sera Pernet de la Barre,
Pourveu, s'il rencontre en son erre   938
Ma damoiselle au nez tortu,
Il luy dira sans plus enquerre:
"Orde paillarde, dont viens tu?"

BALLADE

Faulse beaulté qui tant me couste chier,   942
Rude en effet, ypocrite doulceur,
Amour dure plus que fer a macher,
Nommer que puis, de ma deffaçon seur,
Cherme felon, la mort d'un povre cueur, 946
Orgueil mussé qui gens met au mourir,
Yeulx sans pitié, ne veult droit de rigueur,
Sans empirer, ung povre secourir?

Mieulx m'eust valu avoir esté serchier   950
Ailleurs secours, ç'eust esté mon honneur.
Riens ne m'eust sceu hors de ce fait hacher:
Trocter m'en fault en fuyte et deshonneur.
Haro, haro, le grant et le mineur!   954
Et qu'esse cy? Mouray sans coup ferir
Ou pictié veult, selon ceste teneur,
Sans empirer, ung povre secourir?

Ung temps viendra qui fera dessechier,   958
Jaunyr, flectrir vostre espanye fleur.
Je m'en reisse, se tant peusse macher
Lors, mais nennil, ce seroit dont folleur:
Viel je seray, vous laide, sans couleur.   962
Or buvez fort, tant que ru peult courir;

Ne donnez pas a tous ceste douleur:
Sans empirer, ung povre secourir.

Prince amoureux, des amans le
    greigneur,   966
Vostre mal gré ne vouldroye encourir,
Mais tout franc cueur doit, par Nostre
    Seigneur,
Sans empirer, ung povre secourir.

H.92 Nevertheless to settle accounts   926
Not so much with her as with Love
For she never let me have
Even a spark of hope
And I never knew if she was as cold   930
With other men, this drove me crazy
But now by the fair Saint Mary
Nothing in it but a laugh for me,

H.93 I send her this ballade   934
With all the lines ending in R
Who'll deliver it? Let me think
Make it Perrenet of the Bar
Provided if he meets on the way   938
My young lady of the crooked nose
He'll say right off the bat
"Dirty tramp, where from this time?"

False beauty who makes me pay so dear 942
Rude in fact pretending to be tender
A love harder to chew than an iron bar
Now certain of my ruin I can name her
Cozening thief, death of a heart so poor 946
Or secret pride, man's executioner
Icy gaze, will not Justice with rigor
Save a poor man before he sinks under?

Much better if I'd looked for succor   950
At another's hands I'd have kept my honor
Remorse couldn't lure me from the affair
Turn tail I must in rout and dishonor
Haro, haro, both the greater and smaller 954
And what's this? Not a blow struck yet now
    surrender?

Or will Pity moved by my prayer
Save a poor man before he sinks under?

A time is coming that will wither   958
Tarnish and wilt your blossoming flower
I'll laugh if my mouth will open that far
But by then it would look queer
I'll be old, you ugly, sapped of color   962
So drink deep while yet flows the river
Don't lead everyone into this despair
Save a poor man before he sinks under.

Amorous prince and greatest lover   966
I don't wish to call down your disfavor
But every true heart must by the heavenly
          Father
Save a poor man before he sinks under.

Within many stanzas such as these, the prosodic effects of informal speech strain against the poetic order of meter, thereby bringing both speech and poetic structure into prominence. In these, as in many other passages in Villon, there are tensions between metrical shape and what may be called oral prosodic modeling whenever there is a break in the correspondence of meter and syntax.[22] The smoothest lines are those where grammatical and rhythmic pauses coincide in declarative sentences. Oral prosody most strongly models lines where syntax and rhythm do not match, resulting in enjambment and asymmetrical pauses, and lines where there are intonational shifts—often in mid-verse—because of exclamations, questions, asides, and interruptions.

Diction in fifteenth-century fixed-form lyrics tended to harmonize syntax and metrical structure.[23] In general the ballade "Faulse beaulté" maintains an even metrical line in which the syntactic groupings and prosodic pauses (//) correspond with great regularity to 4 + 6 or 6 + 4 divisions of the decasyllable as in lines 942–43:

          Faulse beaulté // qui tant me couste chier
          Rude en effet, // ypocrite doulceur

[22] David Crystal, "Intonation and Metrical Theory," *The English Tone of Voice* (London: E. Arnold, 1975), 105–24.

[23] Daniel Poirion, *Le poète et le prince. L'évolution du lyrisme courtois de Guillaume de Machaut à Charles d'Orléans*, Univ. de Grenoble Publications de la Faculté des Lettres et Sciences Humaines 35 (Paris: Presses Univ. Françaises, 1965), 447–49.

The enjambment at lines 950–51 of the second ballade stanza is smoothly absorbed by the four-syllable segment of line 951:

> Mieulx m'eust valu // avoir esté serchier
> Ailleurs secours, // ç'eust esté mon honneur.

Finally the repeated exclamations and questions in the last four lines of the second ballade stanza (lines 954–57) require heavy prosodic modeling through pauses, emphasis (**), and interrogative inflection (??):

> Haro, ** haro, ** // le grant et le mineur! **
> Et qu'esse cy? ?? // Mouray sans coup ferir ??
> Ou pictié veult, // selon ceste teneur,
> Sans empirer, // ung povre secourir? ??

The enjambment at lines 960–61 in the third ballade stanza, however, is very strongly marked, by a pause and an impatient interruption after the first syllable of line 961:

> Je m'en reisse, // se tant peusse macher
> Lors, // mais nennil, // ce seroit dont folleur:

Overall, however, there are only a half-dozen constructions in this twenty-eight-line ballade where oral intonation seems required to make sense of the unpunctuated written words.

In contrast with this fixed-form ballade, the syntax of H. 92–93 (like that of H. 137) forces numerous pitch markers, that is, interrogative, exclamatory, or subordinating tones modeling or complementing those required by the beginning and ending of phrases. These irregular prosodic breaks disturb the even flow of the rhythmic line: there are half a dozen such breaks in H. 93 and almost a dozen in H. 137. Line 934, for example, requires an intonation uptake to end the long parenthesis begun in line 928: "Ce non obstant, pour m'acquicter / Envers Amours plus qu'envers elle / [...] / Ceste ballade luy envoye." Line 934 also completes the legacy undertaken in H. 90, lines 910–12: "Item, m'amour, ma chiere rose, / Ne luy laisse ne cueur ne foye; / Elle aymeroit mieulx aultre chose" ("*Item* to my lover, my dear Rose / I leave neither heart nor liver / There's something she'd like even more"). This declaration itself is interrupted by a long digression on the speaker's erotic struggles (lines 913–25). New prosodic breaks in H.93, lines 936–37 are forced by a question—"Qui luy portera"—interrupted by a muttered aside—"Que je voye..."— followed by a subordinating conjunction interrupted by a second subordinate clause insertion—"Pourveu, // s'il rencontre en son erre." Prosodic articulation of the embedded clauses in line 938 is all the more necessary to mark suspension and resolve ambiguity since "pourveu" lacks its optional accompanying "que" ("provided that"). Finally, the last line of the *huitain* shifts to reported direct speech attributed to Pernet, who hurls an insulting epithet and a rude question: " 'Orde paillarde, dont viens tu?' " These are the prosodic patterns of familiar speech where unexpected pauses and interruptions, rising and falling tone contours agitate the even tenor of the octosyllables.

These contrasts construct yet another dimension of oral presence in the *Testament*, perhaps the most difficult to capture in script: the quality of the voice of the speaker. We hear his jeering, contentious tone when the speaker directs our attention to the harsh sounds of the three ballade rhymes, "Qui se termine tout par erre:" *-ier, -eur, -ir.* The snarling, growling R, *litera canina*, is anticipated by four repeats in the "b" rhyme of H. 93: "erre, Barre, erre, enquerre." The quality of the speaker's voice stands out also through contrasts in diction; the colloquial vulgarity of H. 93, with its low insulting talk about crooked noses and dirty tramps, jolts up against the elevated formality of the stylized invective of the ballade: "Faulse beaulté qui tant me couste chier, / Rude en effet, ypocrite doulceur." The clashing of familiar and elevated diction is intensified by the metrical contrast of octosyllables in the huitains and decasyllables in the ballade, whose formal shape is further marked by its repeated refrain and envoy. The dialogic effect of such discursive mingling strengthens Villon's characterization of his speaker's voice by making its tone complex and richly ironic.[24]

The speaker's voice dominates all the formal structures of the *Testament*: the legal will, the lyric ballades, and the metrical mold of the *huitains*. He is identified as exactly by the individual characteristics of his speech as by the acrostic letters stitched down the side of the ballade "Faulse beaulté" which spell FRANCOYS. Represented speech, voice, and presence emphasize at every point *his* opinion, *his* point of view, *his* experience of the world.[25] The very triviality of themes such as noses in H. 93 and 137, reinforced by patterns of

[24] Villon's characteristic mixing of styles invites consideration of the issues of "intonational quotation marks," heteroglossia, and dialogism developed by Mikhail Mikhailovich Bakhtin, "From the Prehistory of Novelistic Discourse," *The Dialogic Imagination*, ed. Michael Holquist, trans. Caryl Emerson and Michael Holquist, Slavic Series 1 (Austin: Univ. of Texas Press, 1981): 75–76.

[25] Regalado, "En l'an de mon trentiesme aage."

familiar speech, points to the world of experience, the unsorted, formless mass of events, impressions, and sensations of the here-and-now. Readers hear his digressive ruminations, his discussions with imaginary interlocutors, his bitter resentful tone which sets words into our mouths that are "harder to chew than an iron bar," (line 944) that would make us "laugh if [we] could but chew them" (line 960).

Villon thus opens a new path in medieval construction of subjectivity[26] by creating an art of lyric expression whose transparency does not flaunt in the reader's ear or eye the weight of its formal arrangement. It offers instead an art of believable, intensively individualized personal expression founded on the poetic qualities of orality: sound, speech, and the presence of the speaker.[27] Villon's convincing representation of informal speech effaces the lines from writing; that is, except in the ballades and rondeaux, it shifts awareness of formal poetic structure out of sight as it were, so that we believe we hear a voice speaking as we read the writing.

Represented colloquial speech in Villon's *Testament* thus becomes a poetic instrument of verbal perspective that enables the poet to portray a feeling, personal subject considering the world of experience from a unique point of view. Represented speech that articulates and highlights a speaker's perspective may well be compared with linear perspective, rediscovered in the fifteenth century and painted by Alberti, Leonardo, and Durer.[28] (3–4), For both verbal and linear perspective represent a world of space and time in relation to a beholder, a speaker. Villon thus restores within written poetry the unique qualities of orality: expressive and meaningful sound, an immediate, unique perspective defined by speech, and the unshakeable authority of poetic presence, speaking in script.

---

[26] See Michel Zink, *La subjectivité littéraire*. Collection Ecriture (Paris: Presses Univ. Françaises, 1985).

[27] Nancy Freeman Regalado, "*Effet de réel, effet du réel*: Representation and Reference in Villon's *Testament*," *Yale French Studies: Images of Power* 70 (1986): 63–77.

[28] Zumthor, 109. Although he compares the *rhétoriqueurs'* use of textual space to the laws of *perspectiva pingendi*, Rigolot, on page 131, speaks of spectacular visual display rather than of a speaker's point of view.

Index

CRTS

CDEÐIEVAL & RENAISSANCE TEXTS & STUÐIES
is the publishing program of the
Center for Medieval and Early Renaissance Studies
at the State University of New York at Binghamton.

CRTS emphasizes books that are needed —
texts, translations, and major research tools.

CRTS aims to publish the highest quality scholarship
in attractive and durable format at modest cost.

WITHDRAWN